THE BEFORE COLUMBUS FOUNDATION

POETRY ANTHOLOGY

Selections from the
American Book Awards
1980–1990

THE BEFORE COLUMBUS FOUNDATION POETRY ANTHOLOGY

Selections from the
American Book Awards
1980 • 1990

Edited by
J. J. PHILLIPS, ISHMAEL REED,
GUNDARS STRADS, and
SHAWN WONG

W·W· Norton & Company
New York • London

Copyright © 1992 by The Before Columbus Foundation
All rights reserved
Printed in the United States of America
First Edition
The text of this book is composed in 10.5/12.5 Avanta
with the display set in Bernhard Modern.
Composition and manufacturing by the Haddon Craftsmen, Inc.
Book design by Margaret M. Wagner.

*Since this page cannot legibly accommodate all the copyright notices, pages
427–29 constitute an extension of the copyright page.*

Library of Congress Cataloging-in-Publication Data
The Before Columbus Foundation poetry anthology: selections from the
American Book Awards, 1980–1990/edited by Ishmael Reed, J. J. Phillips,
and Gundars Strads.
    p.   cm.
Includes index.
    1. American poetry—20th century.   I. Reed, Ishmael, 1938–
II. Phillips, J. J., 1944–   .   III. Strads, Gundars.   IV. Before Columbus
Foundation.
PS615.B44   1992
811'.5408—dc20   91–22526

ISBN 0–393–03056–3 (Cloth)
ISBN 0–393–30833–2 (Paper)

W.W. Norton & Company, Inc., 500 Fifth Avenue, New York, N.Y. 10110
W.W. Norton & Company Ltd., 10 Coptic Street, London WC1A 1PU

1 2 3 4 5 6 7 8 9 0

This book is dedicated to

THE LANNAN FOUNDATION

and

THE EXPANSION ARTS AND LITERATURE
PROGRAMS OF THE
NATIONAL ENDOWMENT FOR THE ARTS
*for their generous support
and to our coeditor,*
ISHMAEL REED,
*founder of
the Before Columbus Foundation.*

*The editors of this anthology
would like to thank
the board of directors of the Before Columbus
Foundation*

ALTA
RUDOLFO ANAYA
MARIE ANDERSON
GEORGE BARLOW
JOHNNELLA BUTLER
BOB CALLAHAN
JEFF CHAN
LAWRENCE DI STASI
VICTOR HERNANDEZ CRUZ
ANDREW HOPE
YURI KAGEYAMA
DAVID MELTZER
SIMON ORTIZ
J. J. PHILLIPS
ISHMAEL REED
GUNDARS STRADS
JOYCE CAROL THOMAS
KATHRYN TRUEBLOOD
SHAWN WONG

Contents

Introduction

Language is a ford across the river of Time,
It leads us to the dwelling place of those who
are gone;
But he will not be able to come to this place
Who fears deep water.

Vladislav Illich-Svitych,
Proto-Nostratic epitaph
(in translation)

THIS collection of poetry—drawn from works which have been awarded the Before Columbus Foundation's American Book Awards—along with its companion volume of fiction represents a significant addition to the burgeoning body of American multicultural literature. Its eclecticism and breadth, while obviously not inclusive of every element making up our multicultural society, nonetheless encompasses much of America's marvelous cultural diversity and, for that reason alone, should prove an invaluable resource for students, general readers, and literary theorists alike.

The poets whose works are gathered here appear at first glance to be so disparate that to conceive of them brought together under one cover might seem to defy reason. Jayne Cortez and Charles Olson? Leslie Scalapino and Amiri Baraka? Josephine Miles and Allen Ginsberg? Askia M. Touré and Gary Snyder? However, as Ishmael Reed aptly puts it in his general introduction: "American literature is an ocean." And in that ocean many currents flow and many fish swim.

Whether or not one likes to acknowledge it, America always has been a multicultural society, and any literary canon which presents but a narrow band of the spectrum of American letters and claims to be representative is itself a fiction of the first water.

Though the concept of multiculturalism was generated from an ethnic matrix out of a need to redress the myth of a western European-derived American monoculture in which its true diversity has been whited out, there is much more to multiculturalism than ethnicity alone. In the general introduction Ishmael Reed recounts the collective evolution of the concept within the Before Columbus Foundation. Others who have seriously come to grips with the dynamics of multiculturalism have also realized that it cannot and should not be reduced—whether by woeful lack of vision or by consciously malign design—to a euphemistic and patronizing code-word for the oppositional Other, i.e., non-white, balkanized, quasi-tribal, hostile, (inferior) ethnic peoples and their cultures, with perhaps women, gays, and lesbians, and a few additional fringe groups, tossed in for good measure.

Ethnicity is of course an extremely important element, but in its fullest and most positive sense multiculturalism is all-embracing. To understand multiculturalism is to posit precisely the opposite of the negativizing, exclusionary paradigm advanced by those who cling with desperate tenacity to the myth of a western European-American monoculture which dreams itself superior to all others and only recognizes those others as objects of exploitation, plunder, fascination, loathing, and profound fear.

Roland Barthes remarked that "Culture is a fate to which we are condemned." Whatever he meant by that, I would offer the counter-thought that recognizing the essential multiculturalism of our society is an insight by which we may be liberated.

Just as American culture as a whole is formed by this marvelous diversity, so is each one of us constructed by it. The recognition that each of us partakes of and contributes to that polyculture is also what the idea of multiculturalism is about. Charles Olson, one of the seminal figures in the explosion of twentieth-century American poetry, was a leading member, along with Robert Duncan and Ed Dorn, of what has come to be known as the Black Mountain school of poetry. He influenced a number of other poets who are also included in this anthology, including Dorn, Amiri Baraka, and Susan Howe. Olson stood defiantly outside the traditional literary establishment; he prodded his students to open up the poetic line, as well as the poetic mind, to all of human experience and history, not with the eye of a pirate, but to gain existential insight into the here and now of the world and the self, for they are one—an eminently multicultural way of looking at the word and the world.

This kind of vision, whether directly influenced by Olson or not (and many others came to such insights through their own experiences), is very much evident in the poetry gathered here. The multicultural spirit embodied in this poetry encompasses the diversity of American experience—and beyond—in its various parts and as a whole. It is really a pan-cultural vision, for we are, after all, inhabitants of the global village. The poetry gathered here stands as a direct rebuttal to the paranoid, apocalyptic vision of the William Bennets, Allan Blooms, and Lynne Cheneys, whose jeremiads portray the idea of multiculturalism as spelling the corruption and death of American letters.

They are right, of course, if what they mean, and fear, is the death of European-American primacy—a loss of power, a loss of imagined purity and potency. But the handwriting is on the wall, for multiculturalism does, literally and figuratively, spell the death of American letters as a privileged domain inhabited only by white, predominantly male, writers. Indeed, in an effort to make manifest the limitedness of what passed as American culture, Georgetown University has recently retitled its English 112 course White Male Writers. It is high time the old, ossified literary canons were dismantled. It is the multicultural conviction that this elite hegemony must come to an end precisely so that American letters can flourish in *all* its fullness. To do this is not to discard members of the old canon as "dead white boys," as some would fiercely contend. There is plenty of room for Walt Whitman and Wing Tek Lum, T. S. Eliot and Ai, Ezra Pound and Jimmy Santiago Baca, and all the rest.

Whatever cultures we hail from and identify with, and however we define them, each of us is both a product and an element of this multicultural heritage, as are our artifacts, literature among them. Because the poets represented here are conscious of these dynamics as shaping their experiences and informing their writing, each in his or her own way challenges establishment assumptions about poetry—and language itself—in content and in form. Conventional notions of language and poetic form (in which, like everything else, the values of the monoculture are encoded) are questioned, deconstructed, and reconstructed here.

Some of these poets, most notably Susan Howe, Robert Kelley, and Leslie Scalapino, call into question traditional assumptions about poetic form, how a poem can be read—by the eye and by the voice—and what the mind makes of it. The radical formal departures of these poets present a challenge to linguistic convention, for they are rooted in the way each of them looks at the word, not simply as something that functions in a conventional syntactic continuum, but as something both particle and wave—an active, sometimes decomposable, mutable force in the field of the page, which can itself generate new syntaxes and startling explosions of meaning that conventional linguistic structures can never produce.

Some selections, such as the works by Juan Felipe Herrera and Cyn. Zarco, are prose poems, again raising fundamental questions about just how our sense of "proper" and "acceptable" form is shaped by a very limited set of criteria dictated by the dominant culture. A good many of the poets in this collection employ colloquial speech, the language of the street, jargon, and dialectal Englishes and make extensive use of foreign languages in a variety of ways. "My metaphor is a blues," says Quincy Troupe. Standard English holds no special privilege here—a pronouncement which will undoubtedly draw scorn from the protectors of the "purity" of our language. However, they should know that the very English they speak can be thought of as a Germano-Latin creole, with all the racist baggage of bastardy and mongrelization that the word "creole" conjures up, which is incompatible with the idea of the English language as we have been taught to think of it.

In the poem "Letters of the Book" Rose Drachler offers the reader, among other things, a radical way of looking at something we take for granted about our language: our alphabet. Writing in an English which is at the same time both contemporary and steeped in an ancient Judaic sensibility, she ruminates on the names for Hebrew letters. In doing so, Drachler addresses our own English writing system which, like the Hebrew, is derived (albeit in an often convoluted manner) from a proto-Semitic pictographic ancestor—*A, alpha, alp: ox head; B, beta, bayt: house;* and so forth. Thus she startles us into recognizing our own Semitic roots, right there on the page in the very shapes of our letters. She returns to us the old Semitic sounds of the names and the physicality of the elemental objects that our "abstract," "European" alphabet originally represented. Few of us realize that whenever we put pen to paper to write English we inscribe and reinscribe a Semitic legacy. Turn the capital "A" upside down and there is the head of the ox. That which we thought familiar suddenly becomes alien, and that which we thought alien is ours.

To the poets who draw their inspiration directly from the wellsprings of their ethnic heritage, poets like Sonia Sanchez, Tato Laviera, Elizabeth Woody, and Lorna Dee Cervantes, the matter of lost and suppressed language is crucial. The repression of language, often by violent means even today, is an extremely potent tool in effecting political oppression and cultural annihilation. Ancestral languages are suppressed and lost—the master's tongue imposed, dialects and creoles made objects of shame and derision. And when a culture's language is lost, the means of conveying the unique conceptual structures of that culture is obliterated as well, which is precisely why such linguistic exterminations occur. It is the work of these poets to find those lost and silenced voices and vocal rhythms, to let them be heard anew. In the work of poets like William Oandasan "the voice of an ancient age/dreaming of breath" is given voice.

Many women writers share this desire to speak the lost and suppressed languages and ways of looking at the world. For women's voices and women's speech have also been disarticulated and forcibly stilled. Poets like Lorna Dee Cervantes, Carolyn Lau, and Judy Grahn, in articulating their own speech as women, give voice to all those women in the past and present who have no voice, collectively or individually. In doing so they point to the bitter irony that one's native language is often termed the "mother tongue," yet throughout history, the mother's tongue has been silenced.

Susan Howe has observed that if one prefixes an "s" to "word" one gets "sword," neatly deconstructing that old bone of the high school debating team, "Which is mightier: the pen or the sword?" Would that so sweet a shift could turn swords into words and plowshares. But the world is never so simple and benign: when wars must be fought, far better that they be fought with words than swords. The writers in this anthology wield their word-swords, sometimes in pointedly political ways, in order to bear witness to injustice and to wage war against those who perpetuate it. Jayne Cortez voices boldly a call to battle in "For the Poets":

> I need tongues like coiling pythons   ah
> spearheads gushing from the gulf of Guinea   ah.

For gay and lesbian poets to speak forthrightly about their sexuality is still extremely threatening to a large, vocal, politically powerful segment of society, which does not hesitate to wield its power to silence them. When Jewish-American poet Hilton Obenzinger writes poetry sympathetic to the plight of the Palestinians he places his health and safety in jeopardy right here in the land of the free and home of the brave, as surely as if he were a citizen of Gaza or the West Bank with a stone in his hand. Julia Vinograd's intensely mystical and intimate dialogues between Jerusalem and God cannot but be read in light of the sad and disturbing contemporary events in that part of the world.

The creative power of language is infinite. The poetry in this anthology stands as a testament to that power and to the ferment of voices that is American literature.

—J. J. Phillips
Berkeley, California
March 1991

The Ocean of American Literature

ISHMAEL REED

IN 1976, I applied for and received a modest grant from the Coordinating Council of Literary Magazines to begin a distribution outlet for "third world" magazines. The names of the magazines we distributed reflected the multicultural audience we were attempting to reach: *Roots, Ravens Bones Journal, Revista Chicano-Requena, Truck, Telephone, Tree, Black Scholar, Unmuzzled Ox, New World Journal, Carp, Sun Tracks, Tejidos, Obsidian, Puerto Del Sol, HooDoo, De Colores,* and *Tin Tan.*

The grant required that I have a partner, and so I chose poet Victor Hernandez Cruz, whom I'd met in New York in 1966. I was working in the Poetry in the Schools program then, and I remember going to Benjamin Franklin High School and announcing, during my reading there, that one of the best American poets was enrolled in the school. When I mentioned Victor's name, the students and teachers gasped. Victor Cruz, who has since that time gained a reputation as an international bilingual poet, was failing Spanish. He was eighteen at the time. By the early eighties, *Life* magazine would run a story in which Victor was featured as one of eleven of America's most distinguished poets.

The next member to join the distribution group—which I named Before Columbus, in order to acknowledge the existence of an American literature before the arrival of the Europeans—was Shawn Wong. Shawn had been introduced to me by playwright Frank Chin, whose work had appeared in a Doubleday anthology I edited entitled *Nineteen Necromancers from Now.* Shawn had also been one of the editors of the Asian-American issue of *Yardbird Reader,* which Al Young and I used

to edit. He was also an editor of *Califia,* an anthology of mul-
ticultural writing that Al Young and I published.

We then added Rudolfo Anaya, who was beginning to build
an international reputation with his novel *Bless Me Ultima.*
Rudolfo had been my colleague on the board of the Coordinat-
ing Council of Literary Magazines and was one of those who
was instrumental in changing the composition of the board
from mostly white male to multicultural, not by demonizing
white males but through dialogue.

With Shawn, Victor, Rudolfo, and me, Before Columbus
included members of the main colored ethnic groups. Still,
though our administrator, Mary Taylor, was of European an-
cestry, no one else from this important element was included
on the board of Before Columbus, a group that defined mul-
ticulturalism inclusively. (When Mary left the organization,
Gundars Strads took over her duties, and he has managed the
foundation since then.) In 1977, then, we invited an Irish-
American writer and publisher, Bob Callahan, to join.

A few of the colored nationalists in the distribution group
objected to our decision to add European-American ethnics.
One could understand their concerns. Many whites are edu-
cated to believe that it is their mission to lead and civilize those
whom the educational system, whether consciously or not,
treats as their inferiors. The Omniscient Boomers, whom we
are so familiar with in California, pretend to know more about
the cultures of other ethnic groups than the members of those
groups, yet they fail to identify with their own ethnicity. They
classify themselves simply as "white."

And the Omniscient Boomer is only the latest incarnation
of the type that in American history has done so much to divide
members of different ethnic groups. Before Omniscient Boom-
ers, there were the sixties Liberals who believed that their role
in the civil rights movement was to lead. The abolitionists of
the nineteenth century made the same error. They didn't per-
mit the black antislavery lecturers in their employment to ex-
press independent judgment, and when their employees
balked, as Frederick Douglass did, they were dismissed as being
ungrateful. Such patronizing attitudes on the part of whites

have made multiculturalism difficult to achieve and, unfortu-
nately, such attitudes persist.

And so when some of the third world nationalists had
reservations about the admission of European-Americans into
Before Columbus, they had a bitter history upon which to
base those reservations. Not only do whites continue to
stereotype the cultures of members of ethnic groups (includ-
ing those of Irish- and Italian-American ethnics), but their
judgments are usually based upon ignorance, since they've
only read those tokens that have been presented to the public
by the mass media. The American literary establishment
seeks to set literary trends by retaining house hitpersons
whose job seems to be to reward those who push an assimila-
tionist patriotic literature—the literature of the main-
stream—and chastise those whose literature might make the
target audience of mostly white consumers uncomfortable.
Haki Madabuti calls this "white nationalism," the tendency
of some whites to give credit to other whites for supremacy
in art forms that were created by members of colored ethnic
groups. For Boomer-type cultural commentators on National
Public Radio, for example, white musicians have "evolved"
the blues or given sophistication to rock and roll lyrics. Some
whites also have a tendency to divide and conquer when ap-
proaching the cultures of others, by, for example, congratulat-
ing different groups for not being like blacks. A Chicano edu-
cator was recently praised on National Public Radio for not
making demands upon the curriculum as "radical" as those of
black educators.

We were lucky enough to enlist European-American writers
whose intellects were restless enough to be willing to spend as
much time on their cultures as we Hispanic, Native American,
and African-American writers have spent studying European
culture. They were not running away from their own cultures
into some homogeneous wasteland of whiteness, but were thor-
oughly steeped in Italian-, Irish-, and Jewish-American cul-
tures. Instead of practicing cultural imperialism upon us, they
brought their own contributions to a cultural potluck. Not only
have they learned from us, but we have learned about Irish-

American, Italian-American, and Jewish-American cultures from them.

During a recent appearance in Washington, D.C., I was asked by an Italian-American student for the names of books that would help her understand the Italian-American tradition. Because of my contact with European-American ethnics in Before Columbus, I was able to provide some key titles. Through such experiences, we have found that the cultures of colored ethnics are not the only ones ignored by a school system devoted to luring students into the "mainstream," a code word for Eurocentrism. The Italian-American, Irish-American, and Jewish-American cultures have also been lost.

The multicultural contacts within Before Columbus have added a dimension to our own creative work. It was because of my discussions with our Latvian-American executive director, Gundars Strads, that I was able to include an Eastern European perspective in my novel *The Terrible Twos* (1982), which accurately predicted the ethnic uprisings that occurred behind the Iron Curtain in the late eighties and which was able to pinpoint the year when a Soviet-American détente would happen—1987, the year of Reykjavík. Our European-American board members do not dismiss colored ethnic cultures as "arcane" or "exotic"; nor do they rely upon subsidized "third world" scouts to tell them what the natives are up to—the practice of some of our leading "intellectual journals," journals that embarrass themselves before the international community of scholars by accepting what amounts to often faulty and self-serving intelligence. Bob Callahan, Gundars Strads, Lawrence DiStasi, David Meltzer, and Kathryn Trueblood have gone beyond mere study of Asian-American, Native American, African-American, and Hispanic cultures. Alta, founder of Shameless Hussy Press, was the first to publish Ntozake Shange's *For Colored Girls Who Have Considered Suicide When the Rainbow Was Enuf*, and Bob Callahan was responsible for reprinting the works of Zora Neale Hurston well before the Hurston boom.

Clearly, by the end of the seventies, the Before Columbus Foundation's definition of multiculturalism was inclusive. We meant Italian-Americans and Irish-Americans, as well as Asian-

Americans, African-Americans, and Native Americans. We meant masculinists as well as feminists. In 1979, we enriched the provincial New York scene by sponsoring a huge reading of African-American, Asian-American, Hispanic, and Euro-American writers at Columbia University, which was recorded on Folkways Records. Joe Knipscheer gave Before Columbus credit for inspiring Amsterdam's One World Poetry Festival of which he was codirector.

Also at the end of the seventies, we inaugurated the American Book Awards. They started humbly. I remember lugging the books by the winners to the West Side Community Center in 1978. About twenty people attended. Tisa Chang's Pan Asian Repertory Group provided a skit. The next year the awards were sponsored by the New York Shakespeare Festival. Among the presenters were Donald Barthelme, Toni Morrison, Stanley Crouch, and Ed Bullins, and the audience was enlightened and entertained by Hugh Masakela, Bill Cook, and Howard "Sandman" Sims. Since that time, the awards have been held in cities throughout the country. Except for the Oakland P.E.N./Josephine Miles awards, the judges for the other major awards are white males of similar tastes and backgrounds with, perhaps, a token "minority" guest judge who sits with the other panelists from time to time. A minority member who occasionally receives one of those awards doesn't know whether he or she is being recognized for talent or for race, or whether the award is based upon the mimicking of the literary establishment's political line at any given time. In the 1960s, the line was left-wing. During the late seventies and eighties, when feminists wielded some power, black, Asian, and Latino male bashing was in. And as the decade of the nineties begins, there seems to be a preference for those who push blame-the-victim neoconservatism, or the notion that black talent is rare. This comforts the tastemakers in their essentially white settler mentality, afraid of being overrun by the "Other," as it is now fashionably called.

This is why I believe that the first recognition of the Before Columbus Foundation came from abroad. Those who decide the winners of the American Book Awards are drawn from backgrounds as diverse as our literatures. For this reason, we are often ahead of the other awards in recognizing literary talent. Jessica Hagedorn, for example, received an award from the American Book Awards in 1983. She wasn't recognized by the National Book Award until 1991. And since our judges and nominees are drawn from various ethnic groups, it is possible for more than one member of a particular ethnic group to win an award during a given year instead of every thirty years, like some of the other awards. In 1991, the National Book Award recognized one black writer. The 1990 American Book Awards recognized nine.

Those who oppose the multicultural curriculum say that such a curriculum would diffuse our common culture, by which they mean that the natives would stray from the true and correct European catechism. Oddly enough, many European intellectuals reject this notion. I have visited European universities, some of which were founded over seven hundred years ago, and have never found the sort of scornful criticism of multiculturalism that one finds written by American intellectuals for mass media publications. Indeed, on European campuses there seems to be an enormous interest in American culture, African-American, Hispanic, and Asian-American literatures included. I asked a European scholar the reason why, and he said it's because Europeans see the United States as a civilization, not merely a dominant mother culture with an array of little subcultures tagging along. Criticism of multiculturalism also reveals the lack of analysis that often underlies pronouncements issued by members of the humanities community, where offering proof for ideas doesn't seem necessary, despite the humanities' attempt to use the language of science.

The Before Columbus Foundation has discovered, through experimentation, that common ground does exist among the different cultures of the United States. Monocultural intellectuals and op-ed writers should have been present during the Before Columbus Institute, which was held at the University of California at Berkeley during the mid-eighties. Through team teaching, artists, scholars, and writers from different backgrounds were able to discover, by focusing upon themes found in their various literatures, that no group has a corner on universality. Such commonality was expressed by board member

Lawrence DiStasi, who, after watching Frank Chin's portrait of a Chinese-American family in *The Year of the Dragon* (1974), said that this family could have been an Italian-American family. We have plans under way to transform the Before Columbus Institute into an accredited college where scholars, artists, and students from throughout the United States and the world may assemble to discuss and study our common heritage, the heritage of the world.

Before Columbus does not believe that literature is like a laboratory frog, to be dissected so that its parts may be coldly examined. We believe that literature has a higher purpose. Margaret Atwood said of the late Northrop Frye, "He did not lock literature into an ivory tower; instead, he emphasized its centrality to the development of a civilized and humane society." We hope that Before Columbus has in its small way contributed to the development of such a society. We also hope that the reader of this anthology will discover that American literature in the last decade of this century is more than a mainstream.

American literature is an ocean.

THE BEFORE COLUMBUS FOUNDATION POETRY ANTHOLOGY

Selections from the
American Book Awards
1980–1990

Ai

THE poet Ai brings a bold and distinctive voice to contemporary American poetry. Born in 1947, her childhood was spent in various parts of the west and southwest, including Tucson, Los Angeles, and San Francisco. Ai received a Bachelor of Arts degree in Japanese language and literature from the University of Arizona and has a Masters of Fine Arts in Creative Writing from the University of California at Irvine. She has been the recipient of fellowships from the Guggenheim Foundation, the Radcliffe Institute, and the Massachusetts Arts and Humanities Foundation, as well as grants from the National Endowment for the Arts and other literary organizations.

A true child of America's multiethnic and multicultural drift, Ai's father was Japanese and her mother part black, Choctaw, and Irish. Just as she refuses to compromise her particular vision by writing from some preordained "women's" point of view (a fact which draws criticism from some), she refuses to be placed into any ethnic pigeonhole.

Since the publication of her first book, *Cruelty* in 1973, on through *Killing Floor* (1979) and *Sin* (1986), Ai has steadily developed in her métier as a poet writing dramatic monologues. In each poem she assumes the persona of a historical or fictional character located in a particular place and time. Speaking in an interview in *Ironwood* magazine, she says of this process:

> Before I write anything down . . . I've got to have my character. I've got to know what kind of person he or she is. What are they doing? What would they wear? What colors do they like? Everything. What I'm doing, really, is painting—I've got to picture

them before I can write. . . . I have to *be* that person. (Volume 12, 1978)

The poetic identities she assumes are wide-ranging: historical personages known and unknown from Yukio Mishima to J. Robert Oppenheimer, John Kennedy, Salome, Marilyn Monroe, Pizarro, her deceased cousin. Sometimes she renders her characters, like the photojournalist who watches a Buddhist nun immolate herself and the teen-age parricide, in a more distanced manner.

Nevertheless, Ai's poetry relentlessly goes for the jugular. As if speaking directly to the reader who holds one of Ai's books in hand, one of the characters in *Killing Floor* matter-of-factly states "It's time to cross the border / and cut your throat with two knives." Critics have commented on the knife-like quality of Ai's writing; and her poems do slash sharply—through history, across contemporary cultural divisions, and deep into the consciousness of the reader—to lay bare the profound disorder that lies just beneath the surface of things.

The worlds her characters inhabit are at once real and surreal, sacred and profane. Much of her poetry explicitly focuses on violence and death, often coupled with sexual themes in a way that calls to mind the writings of Georges Bataille on the relations between eros, death, and the sacred. Ai employs these themes to examine the structure of the human condition at its extremities—at those desperate points where things, physical and psychological, come apart at their seams and the world breaks down.

In "The Testament of J. Robert Oppenheimer" from *Sin*, the eponymous physicist, speaking as if to sum up how all Ai's characters function in her poetic universe, declares

> We strip away the tattered fabric
> of the universe
> to the juicy, dark meat,
> the nothing beyond time.
> We tear ourselves down atom by atom,
> till electron and positron,
> we become our own transcendent annihilation.

That paradoxical last phrase, "transcendent annihilation," is the crux of Ai's poetic vision, not simply with regard to the resolution of each poem or the particular situation each character is placed in, but as a teleological conundrum of the human condition with which each of us must grapple.

—J. J. Phillips

Salome

I scissor the stem of the red carnation
and set it in a bowl of water.
It floats the way your head would,
if I cut if off.
But what if I tore you apart
for those afternoons
when I was fifteen
and so like a bird of paradise
slaughtered for its feathers.
Even my name suggested wings,
wicker cages, flight.
Come, sit on my lap, you said.
I felt as if I had flown there;
I was weightless.
You were forty and married.
That she was my mother never mattered.
She was a door that opened onto me.
The three of us blended into a kind of somnolence
and musk, the musk of Sundays. Sweat and sweetness.
That dried plum and licorice taste
always back of my tongue
and your tongue against my teeth,
then touching mine. How many times?—
I counted, but could never remember.
And when I thought we'd go on forever,
that nothing could stop us
as we fell endlessly from consciousness,

orders came: War in the north.
Your sword, the gold epaulets,
the uniform so brightly colored,
so unlike war, I thought.
And your horse; how you rode out the gate.
No, how that horse danced beneath you
toward the sound of cannon fire.
I could hear it, so many leagues away.
I could see you fall, your face scarlet,
the horse dancing on without you.
And at the same moment,
Mother sighed and turned clumsily in the hammock,
the Madeira in the thin-stemmed glass
spilled into the grass,
and I felt myself hardening to a brandy-colored wood,
my skin, a thousand strings drawn so taut
that when I walked to the house
I could hear music
tumbling like a waterfall of China silk
behind me.
I took your letter from my bodice.
Salome, I heard your voice,
little bird, fly. But I did not.
I untied the lilac ribbon at my breasts
and lay down on your bed.
After a while, I heard Mother's footsteps,
watched her walk to the window.
I closed my eyes
and when I opened them
the shadow of a sword passed through my throat
and Mother, dressed like a grenadier,
bent and kissed me on the lips.

The Mother's Tale

Once when I was young, Juanito,
there was a ballroom in Lima
where Hernán, your father,
danced with another woman
and I cut him across the cheek
with a pocketknife.
Oh, the pitch of the music sometimes,
the smoke and rustle of crinoline.
But what things to remember now
on your wedding day.
I pour a kettle of hot water
into the wooden tub where you are sitting.
I was young, free.
But Juanito, how free is a woman?—
born with Eve's sin between her legs,
and inside her,
Lucifer sits on a throne of abalone shells,
his staff with the head of John the Baptist
skewered on it.
And in judgment, son, in judgment he says
that women will bear the fruit of the tree
we wished so much to eat
and that fruit will devour us
generation by generation,

so my son,
you must beat Rosita often.
She must know the weight of a man's hand,
the bruises that are like the wounds of Christ.
Her blood that is black at the heart
must flow until it is as red and pure as His.
And she must be pregnant always
if not with child
then with the knowledge
that she is alive because of you.

That you can take her life
more easily than she creates it,
that suffering is her inheritance from you
and through you, from Christ,
who walked on his mother's body
to be the King of Heaven.

Miguel Algarin

MIGUEL ALGARIN (b. 1941) is a man of passion and commitment. He is a man of the world, one who is comfortable in many cultures. He appreciates life and people, and he exults in the power of language. To read the poems of this Puertoriqueno from New York is to read poetry that touches your heart. Here is a man who feels and writes about the daily throb of life around him. He was also one of the principal writers continuing the Nuyorican movement into the 1970s.

The poets and writers of Puerto Rican heritage living on the mainland created a literary movement which expressed their identity. Heirs to a rich Caribbean history, the Puerto Rican writers living in New York claimed the streets of the city as their reality. The Caribbean literary sensibility, its music, and the various contributions of the islands' ethnic groups, mixed with the reality of the American mainland, are reflected in Miguel's poetry.

His poetry is full of music, street talk, New York City sounds and the intense Puerto Rican Spanish he loves. Miguel is a careful observer of the daily life and hustle of the street. He knows intimately the people and the feelings he describes in his poetry and reveals the Nuyorican Manhattan experience to the world. Life in New York is complex, and Miguel appreciates that complexity as both his poetry and his life reveal. Miguel loves and nurtures the rainbow spectrum of the arts, music and dance, he admires the genius and individuality of each person he meets, and he reflects that love in his poetry.

He knows intimately what's going on in dance, theater, and music in the city. Visit him and the evening might be spent at the Poets Cafe or in a reading of poetry at Amiri Baraka's. The following afternoon might find him at Lincoln Center enjoying a new program by a modern dance group. He recognizes and appreciates the flow of creativity in his community, and in order to bring various literary and musical talents to his barrio, he established the Poets Cafe. Over the years Miguel has been a center around which revolve guest artists from all over the world.

Miguel is also a Shakespearean scholar who teaches at Rutgers University. He knows the bard of Avon's work as well as he knows the *siglo de oro* of Spain, the Latin American writers of the twentieth century, and the contemporary literature of this country. He reflects, in his love of art and life, the very Renaissance he knows so well. A complex man with many tastes, he grasps reality in all its chaotic and fragmented forms and gives it meaning in his poetry.

In one poem he will lead the reader into the joy of sensuality and the body electric; in the next he will lead us to reflect on the power of the media over our lives. His poetry insists that we analyze both our own political situations and the political landscapes of Latin America. We're all bound together, he says, and so we have to be committed.

Miguel is intensely aware of the needs of people. He exorts us to identify and resist limitations, to become what we are capable of becoming. That range of possibility is illuminated by poetry; it is the space poetry can create; it is the space each one of us can create as we seek to know ourselves.

There is a liberating power in Miguel's poetry. His poems reveal his view of reality to us, but the most consistent theme in Miguel's poetry is love, because it is love which holds the power of liberation.

—Rudolfo Anaya

Relish

I'm frightened by so much heat,
sweating so much desire, sliding,
greased by tenderness,
enduring the sensual whirlpool
of your lips moistened by mutual saliva,
your hands caressing
my juices, transforming them into flesh,
made of blood and sperm,
the only actual possibility
for desire become the gelatin
of you and me
writhing in the sea.

At the Electronic Frontier

I search the chemistry of specific emotions,
a combination of earth and air
that evokes the vital detail,
the phrase that heats the frying pan,
the look that smiles,
offering signals that localize,
where I am, and clarify what I see.
I'm child of the Electronic Frontier.

I learn off the radio waves
of 98.7 Kiss F.M. salsa/disco jams,
that come from a Sony,
bought even though I need a coat,
even though I'm behind on my payments
for the Trinitron Remote Control Color T.V.
that I picked up at Crazy Eddie's last month.
I'm child of the Columbia Space Shuttle,
and I need to know all the electronic gimmicks
invented yesterday
that are already primitive cousins
to those developed today
from eight to five P.M. in Japan.

And in the U.S.A.

(State of emergency in New Brunswick, N.J.)

If something is not done
Criminal Justice will collapse,
or worse, there will be riots in jails
just like those in Essex, Union and Bergen Counties.
Prisons overflow, they can't hold,
there's no space, the courts dismiss everything,
only extreme cases are retained,
though it's still difficult to hold on to
people who react with brutal crimes.
The hitch is in the rapid dismissals,
can't keep up with those handcuffed,
the courts are jammed,
the list of fugitives grows.
If beds aren't found,
the jails'll explode,
set on fire by inmates
who yield to violent passions.

But with a difference

Change arrives,
a new medicinal rhythm pulverizes pain,
I search the flow of a song
that surges for you, for me,
sweet melody that screams:
what's for me?
with change there's difference,
showing steps not taken,
offering kisses that begin to fill,
lips that start to nourish,
tongue that washes,
hands that relieve,
arms that embrace change without fear.

My proposal is that...

I want to live with you,
enjoy first, then procreate
children for the new century,
leaving clues and roots,
a nettling that repels,
and receives what was,
converting it into what is,
I want to unite bodies,
sowing space
for two tying a knot.

Jimmy Santiago Baca

JIMMY SANTIAGO BACA'S poetry goes beyond the canon of Chicano literature to present a realistic, yet mythical American experience that must be told if the public is to comprehend forces that have shaped Latino culture over the last five hundred years. Baca's mestizo vision, set forth in *Martín & Meditations on the South Valley,* is the story of one character, but it is also the drama of many forgotten lives caught in the passionate landscapes of the desert, an environment that encompasses both a tragic and a triumphant blending of cultures. Through Martín and his journey, Baca takes us beyond the adobe houses, hot barrios, and empty roads of New Mexico to Martín's South Valley, the archetypal home for all of us who have lived or encountered such lives. Baca's achievement in this tale lies in his skillful use of narrative poetry, as well as his control of voice and time, a control that also dominates his other books, *Immigrants in Our Own Land* and *The Black Mesa Poems. Martín & Meditations on the South Valley,* as does all of Baca's work, records the renewal of a distinct way of being.

Having been abandoned as a child, Martín wants to live a life of giving that includes a closeness with the earth and an inner search for salvation. These needs form the basis for his story. But as an autobiographical storyteller, Baca knows the mestizo outcast will confront hurdles to the fulfillment of these desires, hurdles thrown up by an American society that isolates those who do not fit in. Poverty and street smarts are crucial ingredients in Martín's world; still he searches for family values in the strong, familial ties of Chicano-Catholic culture, a culture peopled by the grandparents, *vatos,* and *curanderas* we have known in our own lives and that we recognize in Baca's poem. What Martín learns from them and passes on to us is the driving force of Baca's poetry. It is a reaction to American history, how it dictates where we are born, who we are, and what sacrifices we must make before reaching our own South Valley.

These forces take Baca beyond the expected concerns and themes of most Chicano poets, challenging him as a writer, living and creating in the desolation of the desert. Baca's mestizo is an American whose struggle will work as a catalyst for any tribe of Chicanos, Indios, or Mejicanos making their own attempts at diverting personal and social history away from its usual hopelessness.

In the second section of *Martín & Meditations on the South Valley,* Baca builds momentum toward finding resolution and reaffirmation in the ashes of Martín's journey. In part XXVIII, Martín proclaims:

> I gave birth to a house.
> It came, cried from my hands,
> sweated from my body,
> ached from my gut and back.
> I was stripped down to the essential
> force in my life—create a better world, a better me,
> out of love. I became a child of the house,
> and it showed me
> the freedom of a new beginning.

After his life as an orphan, becoming "a child of the house" is Martín's ultimate goal. Out of the ashes of a previous home burned down, Martín arises triumphant. This is Baca's ultimate gift: He creates his own house in the desert culture of all mestizos and does it in a way which validates that culture. Baca's house is the house of the outcast, but it is also the house of any close family, shaped out of many barrios, torn down or still standing. To reach this home, every Martín must cross the desert, and Baca must confront what lies beyond the next small town.

Although Baca's body of work really needs to be read in its entirety if the reader is to find the road home, even this small portion can offer a way in to the myths of restless mestizo-time being recorded by a number of Chicano-Indio writers. They know these myths celebrate the richness of poor, humble beginnings, confront love and betrayal, face the mysteries of religious superstitions, and most of all, bring the mestizo to the forefront of contemporary writing, defining through these South Valley journeys what mestizo-time is. Works like Baca's celebrate the movement away from the social restrictions placed on the mestizo and give this poetry the power to become a poetry for all people who want to examine our country's real history. Baca knows that carving a road from wilderness makes for a long journey: His poetry is marked by the passing of time, years spent creating new landscapes out of old, the constant setting forth from town to town. But with each desert barrio his Martín enters, Baca will find that what he has overcome is etched in the adobe of a new house in which all of us can find a place.

—Ray Gonzalez

XIV

El Pablo was a bad dude.
Presidente of the River Rats
(700 strong), from '67 to '73.
Hands so fast
he could catch two flies buzzing
in air, and still light his cigarette.
From a flat foot standing position
he jumped to kick the top of a door jamb
twice with each foot.
Pants and shirt creased and cuffed,
sharp pointy shoes polished to black glass,
El Pachucon was cool to the bone, brutha.
His initials were etched
on Junior High School desks,
Castaneda's Meat Market walls,
downtown railway bridge,
on the red bricks at the Civic Auditorium,
Uptown & Downtown,
El Pachucon left his mark.
Back to the wall, legs crossed, hands pocketed,
combing his greased-back ducktail
when a Hyna walked by. Cool to the huesos.
Now he's a janitor at Pajarito
Elementary School—

> still hangs out
> by the cafeteria, cool to the bone,
> el vato,

                     still wears his sunglasses,
                     still proud,
he leads a new gang of neighborhood parents
to the Los Padilla Community Center
to fight against polluted ground water,
against Developers who want to urbanize
his rural running grounds.
Standing in the back of the crowd
last Friday, I saw Pablo stand up
and yell at the Civic Leaders from City Hall,
                    "Listen cuates, you pick your weapons.
                    We'll fight you on any ground you pick."

XVII

I love the wind
when it blows through my barrio.
It hisses its snake love
down calles de polvo,
and cracks egg-shell skins
of abandoned homes.
Stray dogs find shelter
along the river,
where great cottonwoods rattle
like old covered wagons,
stuck in stagnant waterholes.
Days when the wind blows
full of sand and grit,
men and women make decisions
that change their whole lives.
Windy days in the barrio
give birth to divorce papers
and squalling separation. The wind tells us
what others refuse to tell us,
informing men and women of a secret,
that they move away to hide from.

XXIII

Pancho, the barrio idiot.
Rumor is that una bruja from Bernalillo
le embrujo. Unshaven, chattering
and nodding to airy friends
that follow him,
he roams the barrio all day.
I see him at least twice a day—
walking on the ditch behind my house,
hours later walking across the bridge.

Harmless, la gente leave him alone
in his own fantasies,
to share his bread with invisible companions,
to speak back to voices
that brim over from his childhood memories.

I have seen him
on all fours in Raul's field
with the sheep. Or last Christmas
in the tree meowing like a cat.
You always fill my heart Pancho
with delight.

Amiri Baraka
(LeRoi Jones)

By 1964, when we met for the first time at the Negro Writers Conference at Asilomar in California, Everett "LeRoi" Jones was already a culture hero. Because I didn't have the fee for registration, lodging, and meals, I had crashed the conference, and even worked up the nerve to go knocking at his door.

"Uh, Mr. Jones?" I said, when he opened up.

"Why are you standing in the doorway," he asked, "talking all this 'Mr. Jones' crap? Just come on in."

Then as now, the nickname he went by was Roi, which he still urges me to call him.

Already well known and virtually revered in ultrahip literary circles, Roi had become by then a Greenwich Village luminary. Along with New York's Ted Joans and San Francisco's Bob Kaufman, he was among a handful of mid-century African American poets whose early reputations are identified with the Beat Generation. We're talking here of course about a literary movement shaped, loosely speaking, by Whitmanesque confessionalism, the modernist iconoclasm of Ezra Pound, T.S. Eliot and William Carlos Williams, as well as by abstract expressionist painting, Eastern mysticism, drug culture, and jazz.

Having followed closely Roi's career up to that time, enjoying his poetry, jazz criticism, and social commentary, which appeared in narrowly circulated books and magazines, I was a fan. The books he'd already published were *Preface to a Twenty Volume Suicide Note, Blues People: Negro Music in White America, The Moderns: An Anthology of New Writing in America,* and *The Dead Lecturer.* The subterranean journals and ephemeral publications he published in or edited included *Kulchur, Yugen* (coedited with Hettie Cohen), *The Floating Bear* (a literary newsletter coedited with Diane DiPrima), *Big*

Table, Hearse, Jazz Review, Metronome, White Dove Review, and Grove Press's influential *Evergreen Review.*

Cranky, vulnerable, and forever urbane, LeRoi Jones's early poems and poetic prose appealed to me for their bebop openness to new sounds and ideas. I sensed in his stuff an openness to contemporary life itself, to pop culture especially and the cadence of vernacular speech. As much as I cherished writing by Paul Laurence Dunbar, Langston Hughes, Richard Wright, Chester Himes, Ann Petry, Ralph Ellison, and James Baldwin, they often seemed to be singing the same old songs—those spirituals and blues America demands of her darker stepbrethren. John A. Williams once called it the "Bleed for Me, Baby" syndrome. Literarily, back in the 1920s the waggish uptown novelist Wallace Thurman had tagged it the "Tell-Me-How-Tough-It-Is-to-Be-a-Nigger" book.

"Niggerati Manor" was Thurman's fictionalized gathering place for the Harlem Renaissance bohemians depicted in his disturbing 1932 novel, *Infants of the Spring.* The bohemia LeRoi Jones inhabited in the 1950s was way downtown in Greenwich Village. Before the turn of the century the Village had been a black community, but now it was a largely white neighborhood. Looking back, it's easy to see how Roi's cool, antibourgeois, high-modernist poems showed all the embryonic earmarks of black cultural nationalism. But that was only one of several political philosophies this energetic artist would sequaciously espouse and then oppose. The seeds of Amiri Baraka— the passionate political militant—were sown in Roi's earlier work; they only required the globally warmed social climate and acid rain of the later sixties to take root firmly and flower. "There is something/in me so cruel, so/silent." So begins Roi's poem, "The New Sheriff," a stalwart anthology piece and, for me, an early personal favorite. "It hesitates to sit on the grass/ with the young white/virgins."

Like Clay, the fastidiously assimilated, clean-cut anti-hero of *Dutchman,* his celebrated 1964 play that drew worldwide attention, Roi himself was, as early writings reveal, his own toughest critic. This was so much the case, I thought, that I once took the title, *Preface to a Twenty Volume Suicide Note,* at face value; I saw it as being prophetic. The man who's been called the black Baudelaire was clearly as touchy, as ambivalent about his own self-image as he was about the integrationist mentality of the black bourgeoisie.

Less than a year and a half after we met, Roi came back to California, this time as a visiting professor at San Francisco State College, where he directed student productions of his plays, including *The Slave, Slave Ship, The Baptism,* and *The Toilet.* Playwright Ed Bullins and actor Danny Glover were among those students whose talents Jones tapped and encouraged. He had by then co-founded the Black Arts Repertory Theatre/School in Harlem, and, in Newark, Spirit House and the Spirit House Movers and Players. He had also helped found two Islamicized organizations: United Brothers and the Black Community Defense and Development.

When *In Our Terribleness (Some Elements and Meaning in Black Style)* appeared in 1970, I figured (not counting anthologies he'd edited and broadsides he'd published) that this was, indeed, Roi's twentieth book. This means I gave some casual thought to the possibility that, at any moment, the man now known as Imamu Amiri Baraka might take his own life. I wondered about it, though. Was suicide simply a metaphor in that early title piece of Roi's, or what? The more I thought about it, the more I recognized the massive symbology that characterized Baraka's dizzying succession of ideological systems, each of them as complex as Dante's.

By 1970, Baraka had eased out of the briarpatch of black cultural nationalism and into a kind of Maoist cabbage-patch socialism. Or was it Mau Mauist patch-quilt socialism? After that, I began to piece together a pattern. Each time we met up, whether on the west or east coast, Roi was working, as it were, out of a different philosophical bag. By turns he co-created with Ron Karenga the political religion known as Kawaida; he headed the Congress of African Peoples, which he turned into the Revolutionary Communist League; he moved with the speed of an early Charlie Parker solo from bourgeois bohemianism to Marxism-Leninism to Maoism to populist socialism.

The man who wrote a book blasting the very avant-garde music he once championed—almost to the point of being its co-creator—made up his mind in the early 1980s that "Black working-class music" (the likes of James Brown, the O'Jays, and Kool and the Gang) was the only valid music. By his reckoning, post-Coltrane jazz and its experimentally expressive off-shoots were just another form of "bourgeois navel-watching." (Recently, though, Roi has signed a contract with a major New York publisher to write a book about composer/arranger Quincy Jones.)

"You know what?" he said to me in 1986 at Bennington College. I was there conducting a fiction-writing workshop, and Roi was on campus to celebrate Parents' Night with his high-school-age son, who was enrolled in a summer program for the college bound.

"I've been trying to get into these soap operas."

"How do you mean, Roi?"

"Well, pals of mine from the Village and the Lower East Side are writing scripts for these TV soaps and making a fortune. I've been submitting scripts of mine to the networks, but they have a hard time with stuff by Black writers, don't they?"

Three years later, at poet Sam Abrams's home in Rochester, Roi and I found ourselves booked together for several wintry days of talks and readings in upstate New York. Roi, now diabetic, had just been discharged from a Newark hospital, barely in time to make the gig. His wife Amini had assiduously written out for him a diet and meal schedule, which he studied dejectedly every couple of hours.

One night, while the rest of us sat around the TV, enjoying the ice cream Sam's wife Barbara was dishing out, Roi, frustrated that he couldn't have any, squinted at footage of the doings in riot-menaced Miami, where a Cuban-American police officer was going on trial for having shot and killed a young African American. The city had become culturally polarized. Deeply concerned, Roi excused himself to go upstairs, where he and his son were bunking.

Early the next morning Roi handed me a proclamation he'd typed. Dated "4 Feb 1989" and titled "Black and Latino Unity Statement," it read in part:

We are a group of concerned Black and Latino citizens, intellectuals, activists, politicians, academicians. . . . We are not enemies, in fact, or at heart. We are peoples who have been portrayed by the media as antagonists, but we are not! We, the intended victims of this age old "divide and conquer" power scenario, understand that this division is being orchestrated and projected to distract us from our common historical and cultural bonds and political goals!!

"What do you think?" he asked.

"I think it's important," I said.

"Can I put your name on it? Claude Brown and Rudolfo Anaya have already agreed."

"I don't see why not," I said.

And there you have one version of Newark-born (7 October 1934) Everett LeRoi Imamu Amiri Baraka Jones: Howard graduate (religion, English literature, and German philosophy), U.S. Air Force weatherman and gunner, poet, playwright, director, screenwriter, essayist, novelist, short story writer, editor, publisher, organizer, teacher, philosopher, political theorist, and activist.

Above all, in all stages of his private and public unfolding, Roi has counted on the freshness of poetic utterance—whether modernist or streetwise—to see him through his many missions, his every social stance. As critic George F. Butterick once commented: "[Baraka's] poetry, in its various developments, is an encouragement that liberation only *begins* with oneself."

—Al Young

At the National Black Assembly

"EEK

    a nigger

communist," the lady democrat
nigrita squeeked, eek
an "avowed"
nigger
communist, & almost swooned
except you cd hear static chattering
from her gold necklace chairman
Strauss dialing trying to get through
her papers spilled
& the autographed picture
of Teddy K. & George W.
hugging each other in
the steam bath
fell out.

You see she
say I can't not be
you see
with you niggers
with no nappy head commie
America's been good
to me. The democrats, God
bless'em, have allllllllways

done good
by us
by colored folks
you see she say I studied
commies, them chinese maoists
specially (She scooped her papers
up & thought deliciously
about the time her man
Scoop J & she licked on the same ice
cream
cone
right down to the hairs!
Specially them
Maoists, I studied

                 They tacktix
She say. They tacktix
is to take over
the microhone &
be against the democrats)

                  sweeping out
                    wrist radio tittering
                Straus waltzes &
                Proposed ripoffs
                Straight from Watergate

Going to the airport
interviewed by WLIE
She smiled powering her
conversation
   & caught a plane
      to
         petit bourgeois
             negro
               heaven

Dope

uuuuuuuuuu
uuuuuuuuuu
uuuuuuuuuu uuu ray light morning fire lynch yet
          uuuuuuu, yester-pain in dreams
          comes again. race-pain, people our people
              our people
          everywhere . . . yeh . . . uuuuu, yeh
          uuuuu. yeh
          our people
          yes people
          every people
          most people
          uuuuuu, yeh uuuuu, most people
          in pain
          yester-pain, and pain today
          (Screams) ooowow!   ooowow! It must
              be the devil
          (jumps up like a claw stuck him) oooo
              wow! oooowow! (screams)

          It must be the devil
          It must be the devil
          it must be the devil
          (shakes like evangelical sanctify
          shakes tambourine like evangelical sanctify
              in heat)

          ooowow! ooowow! yeh, devil, yeh, devil
              ooowow!

          Must be the devil must be the devil
          (waves plate like collection) mus is mus
              is mus is
          mus is be the devil, cain be rockefeller
              (eyes roll

up batting, and jumping all the way around
    to face the
other direction) caint be him, no lawd
aint be dupont, no lawd, cain be, no lawd,
    no way
noway, naw saw, no way jose—cain be
    them rich folks
theys good to us theys good to us theys
    good to us theys
good to us theys good to us, i know, the
    massa tolt me
so, i seed it on channel 7, i seed it on
    channel 9 i seed
it on channel 4 and 2 and 5. Rich folks
    good to us
poor folks aint shit, hallelujah, hallelujah,
    ooowow! oowow!
must be the devil, going to heaven after i
    die, after we die
everything gonna be different, after we
    die we ain't gon be
hungry, ain gon be pain, ain gon be sufferin
    wont go thru this
again, after we die, after we die owooo!
    owowoooo!
after we die, its all gonna be good, have all
the money we
need after we die, have all the food we
need after we die
have a nice house like the rich folks, after
we die, after we die, after we
die, we can live like rev ike, after we die,
hallelujah, hallelujah, must be
the devil, it ain capitalism, it aint capital-
ism, it aint capitalism,
naw it aint that, jimmy carter wdnt lie,
"lifes unfair" but it aint capitalism
must be the devil, owow! it ain the police,
jimmy carter wdnt lie, you

know rosalynn wdnt not lillian, his
drunken racist brother aint no reflection
on jimmy, must be the devil got in im, i tell
you, the devil killed malcolm
and dr king too, even killed both kenne-
dies, and pablo neruda and overthrew
allende's govt. killed lumumba, and is
negotiating with step and fetchit,
sleep n eat and birmingham, over there in
"Rhodesia", goin' under the name
ian smith, must be the devil, caint be vor-
ster, caint be apartheid, caint
be imperialism, jimmy carter wdnt lie,
didn't you hear him say in his state
of the union message, i swear on rosalynn's
face-lifted catatonia, i wdnt lie
nixon lied, haldeman lied, dean lied,
hoover lied hoover sucked (dicks) too
but jimmy dont, jimmy wdnt jimmy aint ly-
ing, must be the devil, put yr
money on the plate, must be the devil, in
heaven we'all all be straight.
cain be rockfeller, he gave amos pootbootie
a scholarship to Behavior
Modification Univ, and Genevieve
Almoswhite works for his foundation
Must be niggers! Cain be Mellon, he gave
Winky Suckass, a fellowship in
his bank put him in charge of closing out
mortgages in the lowlife
Pittsburgh Hill nigger section, caint be him.
        (Goes on babbling, and wailing, jerk-
ing in pathocrazy grin stupor)
Yessuh, yessuh, yessuh, yessuh, yessuh,
yessuh, yessuh, yessuh, yessuh, yessuh,
put yr money in the plate, dont be late,
dont have to wait, you gonna be in
heaven after you die, you gon get all you
need once you gone, yessuh, i heard

it on the *jeffersons,* i heard it on the *rook-
ies,* I swallowed it
whole on *roots:* wasn't it nice slavery was
so cool and
all you had to do was wear derbies and
vests and train chickens and buy your
way free if you had a mind to, must be the
devil, wasnt no *white* folks,
lazy niggers chained theyselves and threw
they own black asses in the bottom
of the boats, [(well now that you mention it
King Assblackuwasi helped throw yr ass
in the bottom of the boat, yo mamma, wife,
and you never seed em no more)] must
a been the devil, gimme your money put
your money in this plate, heaven be here
soon,
just got to die, just got to stop living, close
yr eyes stop
breathin and bammm-O heaven be here,
you have all a what you need, Bam-O
all a sudden, heaven be here, you have all
you need, that assembly line
you work on will dissolve in thin air
owowoo! owowoo! Just gotta die
just gotta die, this ol world aint nuthin,
must be the devil got you
thinkin so, it cain be rockefeller, it cain be
morgan, it caint be capitalism
it caint be national oppression owow! No
Way! Now go back to work and cool
it, go back to work and lay back, just a little
while longer till you pass
its all gonna be alright once you gone.
gimme that last bitta silver you got
stashed there sister, gimme that dust now
brother man, itll be ok on the
other side, yo soul be clean be washed pure
white, yes, yes, yes, owow.

now go back to work, go to sleep, yes, go
to sleep, go back to work, yes
owow, owow, uuuuuuuuuu,
    uuuuuuuuuuu,
uuuuuuuuuuu, yes, uuuuuuu, yes.
uuuuuuuuuu.
a men

Mei-mei Berssenbrugge

MEI-MEI BERSSENBRUGGE was born in Peking, China, of Chinese and Dutch parents. (1947–   ) She was raised in Cambridge and Framingham, Massachusetts. She is the author of five books of poetry—*Fish Souls* (1971), *Summits Move with the Tide* (1974), *Random Possession* (1979), *The Heat Bird* (1983), and *Empathy* (1989)—and a play, *One, Two Cups.*

I first met Mei-mei at an odd little conference in 1973 held at the Stevens Point campus of the University of Wisconsin. Organized by the poet Ed Burrows, the two-week long conference had no audience, no real agenda, not even a real goal, yet it was to be a remarkable moment in the lives of those writers present. I like to think that all of us shared a common spiritual sense of place and that each of us began to set roots down in the literary landscape out of our shared experience, shared knowledge, even shared heart. The writers present were for the most part just beginning their careers or at the most had one book published. The names are remarkable, considering it was 1973—Leslie Silko, Frank Chin, Lawson Inada, Gary Soto, Ricardo Sanchez, Simon Ortiz, Sandra Maria Esteves, Joseph Bruchac, Mbembe (Milton Smith), Phil George, and Mei-mei Berssenbrugge, among others.

When reading work by these writers today (with now several dozen books among us) I like to think that our work is somehow always informed by that experience, that something in the words keeps time with the pulse of the memory. For awhile all of us sent letters as quickly and as often as if they were supplies. Later, the books we wrote bridged the distance between then and now, and the words sought out the connection to the memory, sought to redefine memory. From Mei-mei's *Summits Move with the Tide:*

I want to already know what the old know
like an infant straining
to master a more complex move
I want to see my death
remembering my birth my first love
my second without ever
healing to any death
When gods separated man from woman
for being too perfect
they doubly separated us
I want to be the man and the woman
and the child and the elder

In her *The Heat Bird* the present is somehow elusive as it
fades or remains distant even as we attempt to embrace it, even
as it includes us, no matter how stark the contrast, how clearly
painted the detail of the vision, or how geometrically direct we
point ourselves toward the words:

The only quiet place was in the well where they
kept the melons. There she could hear most distinctly
people's cries in China. Even at twilight up there
you might see a white dog out of the corner of your eye
trying to hide as you drive past, then see it trotting
down the road, growing smaller in your mirror in blue
air the same color as the shadow of water dripping from
a faucet in your tub. The tub is the white dog. The
shadow is a thinking line for half an inch before
breaking up, like a blade of grass across a spout at
the water hole, where all their saris are the same
color at dusk. I too easily give up the meaning of a
picture.

Perhaps the lesson learned between the first poems pub-
lished in a limited edition chapbook entitled *Fish Souls* and
the poems from her latest book, *Empathy,* is the difference
between what is immediate and sensory ("the stars quaver in
your flesh/weigh lord on your waters/fine delicate nettles/in
the tissues of your heart/my belly fears for you") and what is
illusory, suspended, unbordered, even distrustful:

She may suppress or otherwise lose all memory of a dimension,
    and how it felt.
Then she would refer to it as if it were happening to
    someone else.
She would wish his wish was to penetrate her behavior by
    means of referring to what she is feeling,
in order to reach the same place her reference to
    herself occupies, that is, before
she would express the feeling. It is how a particular color
    would be the knowledge
that would come of the light of the color . . .

    In the end we're left with the quality and measure of our
belief. I reread Mei-mei's poetry sometimes before starting my
own writing because I trust her distrust of words and images.
The distrust comes through her need to redefine each feeling
and each image in order to find the belief at the heart of each
line.

                    —*Shawn Wong*

From

THE HEAT BIRD (1983)

The Eurasian at the party would not speak to her. Little lights
inside paper sacks cast willow flames on the snow
the little lights that line paths
of the courtyard. You have to assume each is the same, so
the maze recedes and is not a vertical map of varying sacks
on a blank wall, since it is dark, oh
Mei-mei, you've walked in that garden before. I'm sick of
these dry gardens. Everyone tells me I should get angry at him
The nun's voice quavered behind a screen. There was a shadow
voice to hers of another one singing quietly and
a little off. I prefer to think it was the light back
How can he dream of tying me to his bed, in a blizzard
with snow to my thigh? He tells me I am flirting
with the void. I am not Chinese. I invite him to step
out to the garden for plum blossoms. They would be
very beautiful, now. Their petals would
blanket the snow like snow on sand
but it is morning

Fresh wind blows the other way at dawn, so
I'm free to wonder at the kind of charge such a mass
of death might put on the air, which is sometimes clear
with yellow finches and butterflies. That poor heap
is all sleeping meat by design with little affect
I decide in a supermarket, whose sole mystère is
an evocative creak in a wheel. Not unlike a dead stinkbug
on the path, but unlike a little snake I pass over
All night I pictured its bones for a small box of mine
Today I remembered, on my last night you wanted to

linger after the concert, drinking with other couples,
like a delicate dragonfly

She did a pretty good job at elucidating something
she didn't understand and had no interest in
out of duty. She has evoked a yen for dance. Any
beat with wind through it. In an apricot tree
were many large birds, and an eagle that takes off
as if tumbling down before catching its lift. I thought
it was flight that rumpled the collar down like a broken neck
but then as it climbed, it resembled a man in eagle dress
whose feathers ruffle back because of firm feet
stamping the ground in wind. The other birds discreetly
passed their minutes with old drummers of stamina
but eagles entered swept ground oblivious to other drummers
making streams of rhythm in their repetitions
until pretty soon some of the other ladies' white feet
moved to them, too, bound thickly around the ankles
so their little claws look especially small

Peter Blue Cloud

Peter Blue Cloud (b. 1933) is a Mohawk writer from the Kahnawake Mohawk community on the southern side of the St. Lawrence River just across from Montreal. A former steelworker and an editor (more than once) of the activist Native newspaper, *Akwesasne Notes*, Blue Cloud's life and his writing continually span the gaps between different realities and between different parts of the American continent. His works present, sometimes subtly and sometimes with the directness of a war club, the clash between a spiritually-based Native American heritage and the timebound unreality of contemporary culture, between old ways which value sharing and family and new European mores which turn money and property into religion.

Trickster heroes abound in the rich folk traditions of the Mohawk people—Rabbit, Fox, and Turtle are among the animals which have cycles of Trickster stories linked to them. But Peter Blue Cloud chose none of those animals native to his own eastern woodlands. Instead, influenced by his years of residence in the foothills of the Sierra Nevadas of California—and by the traditions of the Native people of the far west—he found himself spinning new stories about Coyote.

Coyote is alive in the eyes of Peter Blue Cloud. The elemental force of the North American trickster can be found in Peter Blue Cloud's often whimsical and always double-edged poetic tales of those times he has called "back then, tomorrow," the times when the sounds of an elderberry flute mix with the rhythms of early creation. His work is about laughter, song, and creation, and it says (to me, at least) that in many ways laughter, song, and creation are one. Gary Snyder is quite right when he said, speaking of modern writers who have introduced Coyote into their work, that "the oldest, funniest Coyote Man is in the long poems of Peter Blue Cloud."

Blue Cloud's choices, to tell of Coyote and to tell "new" old stories, are interesting ones. The last few decades have seen many non-Indian writers dabbling in various ways in Native American mythology, "retelling" traditional Native stories in verse. As Gary Snyder notes in his essay "The Incredible Survival of Coyote," there is a problem "when modern white men start changing the old texts, making versions, editing. . . ." By striking out in a different direction, Peter Blue Cloud avoided several traps—the trap of being seen as a "sell-out," an Indian who writes or tells his people's traditions for his own personal gain; the trap of simply going over old terrain and doing nothing really creative; the trap of seeming to be caught in a mythical past with no relation to the present day. The Coyote of *Back Then Tomorrow* is omnivorous, able to eat "an Angus bull, four heifers, a broke-to-saddle mustang, and a 1930 Ford pick-up." He is a Coyote as likely to be found wandering city streets, "stopping to read scraps of paper," or "close-eyed and back-side to a university wall" as "stealing first fire." He is funny and serious, wonderfully creative and also dark and dangerous. His work is that of both the old and the new mythic time, a time which is circular, back then tomorrow.

It is important to note that the figure of Coyote has now become almost inextricably mixed with contemporary Native American art, both writing and painting. Coyote is found not only in the writings of Peter Blue Cloud, but in the works of many other American Indian artists whose oral traditions bear no mention of that four-legged trickster, whose range—like that of the real-life coyote—has spread to encompass an entire continent. In the face of almost five hundred years of European attempts to wipe out both Coyote and American Indian culture, neither shows any sign of disappearing. And no Native writer has done a better job than Peter Blue Cloud in celebrating that trickster spirit of survival.

—Joseph Bruchac III

Coyote Makes the First People

COYOTE stopped to drink at a big lake and saw his reflection. "Now there's a really good-looking coyote," he said, leaning farther over.

And of course he fell in. And of course you will think this is a take-off on an old theme.

But what happened was, he drank up the whole lake to keep from drowning. And because he didn't really like the taste of certain fish, he spat them out. And because he felt sorry when he saw them flopping around, he sang a song to give them legs.

"Maybe they'll become the first people," Coyote mused aloud.

"Oh, no you don't," said the headman of that tribe of fish, "if it's all the same with you, could you just put us back where we were? And could you please take away these stupid legs?"

So Coyote regurgitated the lake and put everything back the way it was.

Again he saw his reflection and said, "Okay, you're pretty good-looking, but are you smart? I've been trying to make the first people for a long time now, but nothing wants to be people. So, what do I do, huh, can you tell me?"

His reflection studied him for a long time, then it squatted and dropped a big turd.

"Okay," said Coyote, "I guess that's as good an answer as any."

Then he himself squatted, and began to fashion the first people.

Coyote Man and the Young Lady

This young girl was good-looking and worked hard
and had her young man all picked out,
she never looked at that Coyote Man who was
always saying, "hello there, young lady!"

"hello yourself," her Closer Aunt told Coyote Man,
"your thing always red and sticking out there in front
maybe you think it's a digging stick for only
using to get all those tender young plants."

Coyote Man, he stooped over and studied the ground
in front of Closer Aunt, "well, would you look
at those!" and of course Closer Aunt stooped
and Coyote Man ran behind and stuck it all the way,

and in and out Coyote Man was really going
and even up and over once or twice and in and out,
and Closer Aunt said, "yes," she stooped farther over,
"yes, I can see those much better now, yes."

and of course the Closer Aunt was making all this
time pass, so that young girl could be grinding
all that acorn and talking through the knothole
to her lover, making all those plans that they do,

about how the lover would come there later on
and they'd fuck through this same knothole,
but all the same Coyote Man so busy, but
sends his ears as birds to listen to the lovers,

then puts a big branch up into Closer Aunt and
hangs a big rock on her back and, "don't you move
until you feel my burning inside of you,
then you must run about yelling, it's done, it's done!"

and Coyote Man runs around the house to catch
the young lover, a man known for his love of gambling,
and by then Coyote Man is kneeling there throwing
his eyes out over the ground and saying, "I won! I won!"

"what, what, how can you win, and how do you play?"
the young lover asked Coyote Man, and he
only said, "huh! you young people don't even know
the good old games we used to play for days,

and days it sometimes lasted, and O, what winnings,
and all the young girls admire a man who wins,
and all you have to do is cast your eyes along
the ground and wait for them to click together,

and sometimes they click many times, and all these
win counters, though you must be very patient,
and the longer you wait the more clicks you hear,"
so the young lover let Coyote Man take out his eyeballs.

and the young girl was all nervous and kept looking
and looking at the knothole until she finally
saw the big red thing stick through, and she
put herself on it, and at the same time pretended

to be reaching way up to get something, and
up and down, up and down she was going real steady,
and feeling pretty damn good, too, was Coyote Man,
even when the sun had set and getting to be colder

outside where he was standing against the house,
but quickly got too cold and so he reached for wood
to build a small fire as his teeth began to
chatter, and he didn't even know that the wood

was the same one that was in Closer Aunt, and
when the fire reached her tailbone she began
yelling, "it's done, it's done!" and the young lover
heard Coyote Man's teeth clicking many times,

began yelling, "I won, I won!" and the young girl
hearing all this and feeling pretty good going up and
down, she cried, "me too, me too, it's done, I won!" but
  Coyote Man, he was already far away.

Coyote running, running Coyote, sniffing the cyanide death
trap of the game keeper's cunning; forever it seems, running,
the snap and pop and frozen, teeth grinning death. Coyote
hide thrown over barbed wire fence, the vulture on post is
judge and jury; stiff and dirty hide, how do you plead? Where's
the evidence, the witnesses, and what's the charge? Hmmm,
yes, I see: devoured an Angus bull, four heifers, a broke-to-
saddle mustang, and a 1930 Ford pickup. How do you plead?
Hell, how'd I get this bullshit job? I'm a vulture, I didn't kill
him, I only ate his eyes and picked his bones.

Coyote trotting, vague shadow, trotting Coyote, nudging
our gentle sleep; forever it seems touching the fringes of dream-
ing. Coyote stealing first fire, a moon bark between sage and
sand, obsidian claws clicking the count of unrecorded graves.
Coyote, his shadow upon muted lives, medicine song bark and
herbs he spreads to all directions. Coyote, your burden basket
of upturned sky as you trot upon star paws.

Coyote walking, walking Coyote, the city's streets are strewn
with tattered lives, hollowed heart echoes resound painfully
emptied. Coyote walking, sniffing in occasional boredom, here
a lamppost, there a hydrant, someone's leg, a quick jet of piss.
Ignoring city dogs too peopled in their lust. Stopping to read
scraps of paper, candy wrappers, banana skins, sticks, foil, ciga-
rette butts; finding more truth in this miscellaneous mosaic
than in any sacred tabloids cut to accommodate a shriveled
mind.

Coyote resting close-eyed and backside to a university wall.
Scholastic dreams hold little interference, a scrap of paper with
embossed seal to fashion into tiny boats and set afloat. Legs
twitch in sleep that would the mountains trot again.

Lorna Dee Cervantes

CRITIC Marta Ester Sanchez, in her book *Contemporary Chicana Poetry: A Critical Approach to an Emerging Literature* (1985) explains race and gender in Lorna Dee Cervantes' volume of poetry, *Emplumada* (1981):

> What is unsaid in Cervantes' poetic world is the desire to harmonize a social voice as a Chicana with her voice as a poet who has concerns other than social ones. Cervantes, therefore, does not integrate community and poetry, history and utopia, when she speaks from a position of race. Rather, she integrates them when she speaks from a position of gender. It is easier for her to envision harmony between men and women than to envision harmony among different racial groups.

The narrator in "Beneath the Shadow of the Freeway" makes a plea to her mother about her man that she couldn't possibly make or believe if she were to make the same plea with respect to interracial harmony:

"But Mama, if you're good to them
they'll be good to you back."

Indeed, Cervantes' notes the difference in "Poem for the Young White Man . . .":

These bullets bury deeper than logic
Racism is not intellectual.
I can not reason these scars away.

Outside my door
there is a real enemy
who hates me.

The two voices are as distinct as the difference between what is possible and what is not possible in Cervantes' perilous journey and exploration of race and gender.

—*Shawn Wong*

From
EMPLUMADA (1981)

Meeting Mescalito
at Oak Hill Cemetery

Sixteen years old and crooked
with drug, time warped blissfully
as I sat alone on Oak Hill.

The cemetery stones were neither erect
nor stonelike, but looked soft and harmless;
thousands of them rippling the meadows
like overgrown daisies.

I picked apricots from the trees below
where the great peacocks roosted and nagged
loose the feathers from their tails.
I knelt to a lizard with my hands
on the earth, lifted him and held him
in my palm—Mescalito
was a true god.

Coming home that evening
nothing had changed. I covered Mama on the sofa
with a quilt I sewed myself, locked my bedroom
door against the stepfather, and gathered
the feathers I'd found that morning, each
green eye in a heaven of blue, a fistfull
of understanding;

and late that night I tasted
the last of the sweet fruit, sucked the rich pit
and thought nothing of death.

Beneath the Shadow
of the Freeway

1

Across the street—the freeway,
blind worm, wrapping the valley up
from Los Altos to Sal Si Puedes.
I watched it from my porch
unwinding. Every day at dusk
as Grandma watered geraniums
the shadow of the freeway lengthened.

2

We were a woman family:
Grandma, our innocent Queen;
Mama, the Swift Knight, Fearless Warrior.
Mama wanted to be Princess instead.
I know that. Even now she dreams of taffeta
and foot-high tiaras.

Myself: I could never decide.
So I turned to books, those staunch, upright men.
I became Scribe: Translator of Foreign Mail,
interpreting letters from the government, notices
of dissolved marriages and Welfare stipulations.
I paid the bills, did light man-work, fixed faucets,

insured everything
against all leaks.

3

Before rain I notice seagulls.
They walk in flocks,
cautious across lawns: splayed toes,
indecisive beaks. Grandma says
seagulls mean storm.

In California in the summer,
mockingbirds sing all night.
Grandma says they are singing for their nesting wives.
"They don't leave their families
borrachando."

She likes the ways of birds,
respects how they show themselves
for toast and a whistle.

She believes in myths and birds.
She trusts only what she builds
with her own hands.

4

She built her house,
cocky, disheveled carpentry,
after living twenty-five years
with a man who tried to kill her.

Grandma, from the hills of Santa Barbara,
I would open my eyes to see her stir mush
in the morning, her hair in loose braids,
tucked close around her head
with a yellow scarf.

Mama said, "It's her own fault,
getting screwed by a man for that long.
Sure as shit wasn't hard."
soft she was soft

5

in the night I would hear it
glass bottles shattering the street
words cracked into shrill screams
inside my throat   a cold fear
as it entered the house in hard
unsteady steps   stopping at my door
my name   bathrobe   slippers
outside a 3 A.M. mist heavy
as a breath full of whiskey
stop it   go home   come inside
mama if he comes here again
I'll call the police

inside
a gray kitten   a touchstone
purring beneath the quilts
grandma stitched
from his suits
the patchwork singing
of mockingbirds

6

"You're too soft . . . always were.
You'll get nothing but shit.
Baby, don't count on nobody."
—a mother's wisdom.
Soft. I haven't changed,
maybe grown more silent, cynical
on the outside.

"O Mama, with what's inside of me
I could wash that all away. I could."

"But Mama, if you're good to them
they'll be good to you back."

Back. The freeway is across the street.
It's summer now. Every night I sleep with a gentle man
to the hymn of mockingbirds,

and in time, I plant geraniums.
I tie up my hair into loose braids,
and trust only what I have built
with my own hands.

For Edward Long

> *"There are some who are not of this world.*
> *Take what you need. Covet.*
> *The child is one. They will comfort her soon."*
>
> —*E. L. (In a letter to my mother from the*
> *Atascadero State Hospital. Fall, 1965)*

Pardner, you called me
that first morning my grandmother
found you, drunk, homeless, and you stayed
long enough to give me my voice.

You taught me to read all those windsongs
in the verses of Stevenson.
You'd pay me a quarter to sing on your lap
beneath the dust storm of your scruffy chin.
In those still nights your wine breath
sweetened the air for me.

You were father, grandfather, the man
who dug ditches for the county
and knew a code so secret
they locked it away.

Pardner, Doctor, crazy
mathematician and sometimes
wizard to the child I still am,
I still believe you.
I still gaze at the fall winds
you once taught me to describe.
I still shadow you. I know
wherever you are
you'll be reading poems
and this is how
I'll find you.

For Virginia Chavez

It was never in the planning,
in the life we thought
we'd live together, two fast
women living cheek to cheek,
still tasting the dog's
breath of boys in our testy
new awakening.
We were never the way
they had it planned.
Their wordless tongues we stole
and tasted the power
that comes of that.
We were never what they wanted
but we were bold. We could take
something of life and not
give it back. We could utter

the rules, mark the lines
and cross them ourselves—we two
women using our fists, we thought,
our wits, our tunnels. They were such
dumb hunks of warm fish
swimming inside us,
but this was love,
we knew, love, and that was all
we were ever offered.

You were always alone
so *another lonely life*
wouldn't matter.
In the still house
your mother left you,
when the men were gone
and the television droned
into test patterns, with our cups
of your mother's whiskey
balanced between the brown thighs
creeping out of our shorts, I read
you the poems of Lord Byron, Donne,
the Brownings: all about love,
explaining the words
before realizing that you knew
all that the kicks in your belly
had to teach you. You were proud
of the woman blooming out of your
fourteen lonely years, but you cried
when you read that poem I wrote you,
something about our "waning moons"
and the child in me
I let die that summer.

In the years that separate,
in the tongues that divide
and conquer, in the love
that was a language
in itself, you never spoke,

never regret. Even
that last morning
I saw you with blood
in your eyes, blood
on your mouth, the blood
pushing out of you
in purple blossoms.

He did this.
When I woke, the kids
were gone. They told me
I'd never get them back.

With our arms holding
each other's waists, we walked
the waking streets
back to your empty flat,
ignoring the horns and catcalls
behind us, ignoring what
the years had brought between us:
my diploma and the bare bulb
that always lit your bookless room.

Poem for the Young White Man Who Asked Me How I, an Intelligent, Well-Read Person Could Believe in the War between Races

In my land there are no distinctions.
The barbed wire politics of oppression
have been torn down long ago. The only reminder
of past battles, lost or won, is a slight
rutting in the fertile fields.

In my land
people write poems about love,
full of nothing but contented childlike syllables.
Everyone reads Russian short stories and weeps.
There are no boundaries.
There is no hunger, no
complicated famine or greed.

I am not a revolutionary.
I don't even like political poems.
Do you think I can believe in a war between races?
I can deny it. I can forget about it
when I'm safe,
living on my own continent of harmony
and home, but I am not
there.

I believe in revolution
because everywhere the crosses are burning,
sharp-shooting goose-steppers round every corner,
there are snipers in the schools . . .
(I know you don't believe this.
You think this is nothing
but faddish exaggeration. But they
are not shooting at you.)

I'm marked by the color of my skin.
The bullets are discrete and designed to kill slowly.
They are aiming at my children.
These are facts.
Let me show you my wounds: my stumbling mind, my
"excuse me" tongue, and this
nagging preoccupation
with the feeling of not being good enough.

These bullets bury deeper than logic.
Racism is not intellectual.
I can not reason these scars away.

Outside my door
there is a real enemy
who hates me.

I am a poet
who yearns to dance on rooftops,
to whisper delicate lines about joy
and the blessings of human understanding.
I try. I go to my land, my tower of words and
bolt the door, but the typewriter doesn't fade out
the sounds of blasting and muffled outrage.
My own days bring me slaps on the face.
Every day I am deluged with reminders
that this is not
my land
and this is my land.

I do not believe in the war between races.

but in this country
there is war.

Jayne Cortez

NOT too long ago, as I was daydreaming on the bus I take from
school to home, I heard a black teenager yell to his friend a
couple of seats back: "Listen to that sound, bro." He was mov-
ing to a stanza printed in the ad space called Poetry Fare, a new
feature on East Bay buses. I love Poetry Fare (it so succintly
embodies the idea that poetry is democratic), and I've watched
with delight the curious expressions of folk who can't believe
what they're seeing, a poem on the bus. But I'd never heard
such blatant appreciation from one of my riding companions. I
followed his flat top bopping head to these lines:

> (for Leon Damas)
> if you see a medley of slow moving currents
> spinning into a hum of furious tornados
> at midnight
> Tell everybody
> The Red Pepper Poet
> moving like the eye of a hurricane is going home.
> Jayne Cortez

I was not surprised at the effect "The Red Pepper Poet" was
having on somebody who did not look as if he read poetry for
poetry's sake. It was the sound—Jayne Cortez's sound—had
pulled him in. "Who's this Jayne Cortez?" my bopper asked.
"Gotta be black—who else could sound like that!"

Cortez's sound is not just sound, in the Western sense; it is
not the dirty noise from your refrigerator; rather it is sound
flowing through meaning-spirit-fire that challenges us sleep-
walkers, a sound that might be too fire-spitting for some, yet
often resonates as "real," "honest" to those others confronted

by the discordant clashings barely camouflaged by TV's squeaky-clean America.

> My friend
> they don't care
> if you're an individualist
> a leftist   a rightist
> a shithead   or a snake
>
> They will try to exploit you
> absorb you   confine you
> disconnect you   isolate you
> or kill you
>
> *(from "There It Is")*

I wonder how my flat-topped friend would react if Poetry Fare had printed that.

I first heard Jayne Cortez read in the early 1970s from her just published volume, *Pisstained Stairs and the Monkey Man's Wares* (1969). Her sound was such a cacophony of swirling, haming, chanting that I had to have her books. I've found that her poetry, which she generally publishes herself (no big capitalist publishing company for her), is not always available even in "intellectual" bookstores unless you clamor for it. Still, in the last two decades Cortez has put out many volumes, always studded with evocative artwork by Mel Edwards: in 1971 *Festivals and Funerals,* in 1973 *Scarifications,* in 1977 *Mouth on Paper,* in 1982 *Firespitter.* And in 1984 a volume of selected poems, *Coagulations,* was published by the small but roaring press Thunder's Mouth. This volume is especially significant for an understanding of Cortez's poetic vibrancy, not only because her selection of poems underlines the character and coherence of her particular vision, but also because only a few Afro-American women—Gwendolyn Brooks, Audre Lorde, June Jordan come to mind—have had the opportunity to publish a selected.

As important as her printed volumes is the fact that Cortez records her poetry. These recordings are avant-garde jazz performances in which her poetry is one of many instruments. Like Billie Holiday, whose voice sometimes is a horn, Cortez *plays* her poetry. "Celebrations and Solitudes" (1975), "Unsubmissive Blues" (1981), "There It Is" (1982), "Everywhere Drums" (on CD and tape; 1990) are dazzling examples of how poetry can be jazz. They amplify our awareness of this brilliant contribution of Afro-American culture to poetic form, a contribution that is often ignored by those who teach poetry.

Cortez's recordings of her poetry also inform us about her concept of what poetry can be—that poetry can *do* something significant in the world and should be available to those who usually have the least access to it. Clearly she wants to reach those who do not usually *read* poetry bound between two covers. Her recordings are a sure sign of her commitment to an audience that is usually characterized as uninterested in poetry and as lacking the sensitivity to appreciate it.

Cortez's use of confrontational imagery in many of her poems also leaves no doubt that she insists on interacting with that audience. Her poetry awakens us to what we may not know but what we need to know; it rouses us to see that which we know but do not want to know; it alerts us to the "marquees of false nipples" in our cities, "the enemies polishing their penises between / oil wells at the Pentagon," "the stockpiling of frozen trees / in the deep freeze of the earth." Yet for Cortez, that awakening is not enough: she also celebrates those who resist the horrors. Her poem "Rape" is a good example of her poetic process. First, in clear, authoritative language she *names* rape:

> What was Inez supposed to do for
> the man who declared war on her body
> the man who carved a combat zone between
> her breasts

Cortez pushes on, celebrating the rightness of Inez's response:

> She stood with a rifle in her hand
> doing what a defense department will do in
> times of war

It is this rhythmic process, the naming of the horror, the singing resistance to it, which I feel is central to Cortez's poetic vision, a vision emanating from the possibility of change throughout the world, the core of hope in action.

> Soweto i tell you Soweto
> when i see you standing up like this
> i think about all the forces in the world
> confronted by the terrifying rhythms of young
> students
> by their sacrifices
> and the revelation that it won't be long now
> before everything
> in the world changes.

In the African tradition, sound is a powerful means of defining space; like a mother it generates feeling and thought. Sound itself changes the vibrations of body-spirit-mind, and Cortez's poetry continues that tradition. Like a lion-maned priestess her working words and chants, lyrical swirling, playing sounds themselves, create a movement that moves us to move, in ourselves, and in the world:

> i need spirits ah i need ankles ah i need
> hurricanes ah
> to make a delta praise for the poets ah

Yes indeed. We need our griots and Jayne Cortez is such a one. Ah Firespitter, Celebrator. Ah!

—*Barbara Christian*

For the Poets

(Christopher Okigbo & Henry Dumas)

I need kai kai   ah
a glass of akpetesie   ah
from torn arm of Bessie Smith   ah

I need the smell of Nsukka   ah
the body sweat of a durbar   ah
five tap dancers   ah
and those fleshy blues kingdoms from deep south   ah
to belly-roll forward praise for Christopher Okigbo   ah

I need a canefield of superstitious women   a
fumes and feathers from port of Lobito   a
skull of a white mercenary   a
ashes from a texas lynching   a
the midnight snakes of Damballah   a
liquid from the eyeballs of a leopard   a
sweet oil from the ears of an elder   a
to make a delta praise for the poets   a

On this day approaching me like a mystic number   oh?
in this time slot on death row   oh
in this flesh picking sahelian zone   oh
in this dynamite dust and dragon blood and liver cut   oh

I need cockroaches   ah
congo square   ah

a can of skokian   ah
from flaming mouth of a howling wolf   ah

I need the smell of Harlem   ah
spirits from the birthplace of Basuto   ah
mysteries from an Arkansas pyramid   ah
shark teeth   ah
buffalo   ah
guerillas in the rainy season   ah
to boogie forward ju ju praise for Henry Dumas   ah

In this day of one hundred surging zanzibars   oh?
in this day of bongo clubs moon cafes and paradise lounges   oh
in this day's pounded torso of burgundy mush   oh
in this steel cube in this domino   in this dry period   oh

I need tongues like coiling pythons   ah
spearheads gushing from gulf of Guinea   ah
the broken ankles of a B. J. Vorster   ah
to light up this red velvet jungle   ah
I need pink spots from the lips of trumpet players   ah
the abdominal scars of seven head hunters   ah
a gunslit for electric watermelon seeds   ah
to flash a delta praise for the poets   ah

Because they'll try and shoot us
like they shot Henry Dumas   huh
because we massacre each other
and Christopher Okigbo is dead   uh-huh
because i can't make the best of it   uh-hun
because i'm not a bystander   uh-hun
because mugging is not my profession   uh-unh

I need one more piss-ass night to make a hurricane   a
i need one more hate mouth racist
sucking the other end of another gas pipe to make flames   a
i need one more good funky blood pact
to shake forward a delta praise for the poets   a

On this day of living dead Dumas
on this day of living dead Okigbo

I need kai kai ah   i need durbars   ah i need torn arms   ah
i need canefields   ah   i need feathers   ah   i need skulls   ah
i need ashes   ah   i need snakes   ah   i need eyeballs   ah
i need cockroaches ah i need sharkteeth ah i need buffalo ah
i need spirits   ah   i need ankles   ah   i need hurricanes   ah
i need gas pipes   ah   i need blood pacts   ah   i need   ah
to make a delta praise for the poets   ah

Mercenaries & Minstrels

A mercenary like Rolf Steiner
will split open your head with a bottle of I.W. Harper
in a liquor store in boston
he will shoot through every cell in your body
and blow you up for kicks on pay day
he'll cut off your legs
fire-up your thighs
and twist your balls
into an american eagle and swastika emblem
for this bi-centennial

So don't tell me to be cooperative
and let the SS colonel knock me off
don't tell me that this plantation is changing
and so i should be cool and let the paratroopers fuck me
don't tell me that i'm just a plain ordinary citizen
because the mercenaries of the world don't give a shit

They have teeth like firing squads
naked women like red devils with rancid breaths
thoughts like infested rivers of dismembered bodies
jokes like invasions into angola

faces like ten german shepherd dog tongues
look Steiner is washing his mouth with the blood
of five more africans
his combat boots go berserk up ass holes
there's no controlling this bereted pimp
when the smell of dark flesh enters his brain
he goes crazy
gasoline spurts from his navel
rockets launch from his eye lids
he's a butcher a killer
with a sweet tooth especially for niggers

Ogun's Friend

I saw your eyes like bumps of flint
i saw your shoes like high-top boulders
i saw your hands like faces of fire
i saw your fingers like axes of Shango
i saw your body like a rocker of steel

Yo
i heard a hum down there
i heard a rumble down there
i heard a ghost down there
i heard a thunderbolt expell down there
i heard a anvil in the night go hummmmmmmmm
down there

Hey whose metals are shouting so loud
they must be the tapper that Ogun knows

whose are those beads so hot and black
they must be brass for Ogun to fill

who's that worker with corrugated gums
it must be the worker that Ogun chose

who's that one with feet like flames
it must be the welder that's Ogun's friend

Yo
i smell a chicken in here
i smell some charcoal in here
i smell a goat in here
i smell some wax in here
i smell a dog in here
i smell some clay and some oil and some blood in here

Hey i see your chains like links of teeth
crow-bars
i see your coils like female pouches
barbwire
i see your grills like braided snakes
fish-net
i see your ladder like a totem of pliers
crocodiles
i see your pipes like razors on tusks
wine bottles
i see your scissors and your keys on the table in there
uh-huhn

Yo
you got pant legs made into hats
you got diamond plates made into walls
you got straightening combs made into steps
you got hammer-heads made into skulls
you got flat-rings made into ears

Pant legs diamond plates
straightening combs hammer-heads
flat-rings
yo

I feel your flux
i feel your sander

i feel your drill bit
i feel your grinder
i feel your drill press
i feel your hack saw
i feel your brick ax

Yo
i saw your windows like sheets of steel
i heard a gong down there
i saw some navels like bushes of wire
i heard a bird down there

Hey
you got lizard tongues made into tongs
i feel your bald spot
you got snakeskins covered in bronze
i feel your chin marks
lizard tongues bald spots
snakeskins chin marks

Yo
i smell some fish in here
i see a rail down there
i smell some toes in here
i see a horn down there
i smell some funk in here
i see a knife down there
i smell some ratheads in here
i see a person down there

Whose that one so brown and fine
Ogun's friend
whose that one in green on green
Ogun's friend
whose that one who eats so fast
Ogun's friend
whose that one with toothpaste lips
Ogun's friend

whose that one who spits on tools
Ogun's friend
Yo Ogun's friend

In the Morning

Disguised in my mouth as a swampland
nailed to my teeth like a rising sun
you come out in the middle of fish-scales
you bleed into gourds wrapped with red ants
you syncopate the air with lungs like screams from yazoo
like X rated tongues
and nickel plated fingers of a raw ghost man
you touch brown nipples into knives
and somewhere stripped like a whirlwind
stripped for the shrine room
you sing to me through the side face of a black rooster

In the morning in the morning in the morning
all over my door like a rooster
in the morning in the morning in the morning

And studded in my kidneys like perforated hiccups
inflamed in my ribs like three hoops of thunder through a screw
a star-bent-bolt of quivering colons
you breathe into veiled rays and scented ice holes
you fire the space like a flair of embalmed pigeons
and palpitate with the worms and venom and wailing flanks
and somewhere inside this fever
inside my patinaed pubic and camouflaged slit
stooped forward on fangs
in rear of your face
you shake to me in the full crown of a black rooster

In the morning in the morning in the morning

Masquerading in my horn like a river
eclipsed to these infantries of dentures of diving spears
you enter broken mirrors through fragmented pipe spit
you pull into a shadow ring of magic jelly
you wear the sacrifical blood of nightfall
you lift the ceiling with my tropical slush dance
you slide and tremble with the reputation of an earthquake

and when i kick through walls
to shine like silver
when i shine like brass through crust in a compound
when i shine shine shine
you wail to me in the drum call of a black rooster

In the morning in the morning in the morning
gonna kill me a rooster
in the morning
early in the morning
way down in the morning
before the sun passes by
in the morning in the morning in the morning

In the morning
when the deep sea goes through a dogs bite
and you spit on tip of your long knife

In the morning in the morning
when peroxide falls on a bed of broken glass
and the sun rises like a polyester ball of menses
in the morning
gonna firedance in the petro
in the morning
turn loose the blues in the funky jungle
in the morning
I said when you see the morning coming like
a two-headed twister
let it blow let it blow
in the morning in the morning
all swollen up like an ocean in the morning

early in the morning
before the cream dries in the bushes
in the morning
when you hear the rooster cry
cry rooster cry
in the morning in the morning in my evilness of this morning

I said
disguised in my mouth as a swampland
nailed to my teeth like a rising sun
you come out in the middle of fish-scales
you bleed into gourds wrapped with red ants
you syncopate the air with lungs like screams from yazoo
like X rated tongues
and nickel plated fingers of a raw ghost man
you touch brown nipples into knives
and somewhere stripped like a whirlwind
stripped for the shrine room
you sing to me through the side face of a black rooster

In the morning in the morning in the morning

Edward Dorn

IN 1980, when Ed Dorn (1929-) received the first of his two American Book Awards (in 1989 he received a Lifetime Achievement Award), he said, "Coming from the south, I assumed the only thing before Columbus was Cincinnati." Dorn is a poet, short story writer, critic, novelist, essayist, translator, and editor of some fifty books. Andy Hope, Tlingit writer, notes, "Ed and his longtime collaborator in translation, Gordon Brotherston, have produced a number of fine source texts on the literature of the Americas, particularly *Image of the New World.* His commitment to the development of the small press has been unswerving. Witness his publishers through the years: Four Seasons, Wingbow, Turtle Island, Black Sparrow and Frontier." In many respects, Ed Dorn's writing career may be a metaphor for the Before Columbus Foundation itself.

He was a student at Black Mountain College in North Carolina, a school noteworthy for its association with writers such as Charles Olson, Robert Creely, Allen Ginsberg, Denise Levertov, William Carlos Williams, and Gary Synder. Dorn has said of the experience, "I think I'm rightly associated with the Black Mountain 'school,' not because of the way I write, but because I was there."

"Being there," of course, takes on fabulous definitions in the work of Ed Dorn. His four-volume epic poem, *Slinger* (1968), is rooted in what Marjorie Perloff described in the *New Republic* (April 24, 1976) as "one of the most ambitious and interesting long poems of our time, a truly original cowboy-and-indian saga, rendered in the most ingenious mix of scientific jargon, Structuralist terminology, junkie slang, Elizabethan sonneteering, Western dialect, and tough talk about kicking 'a gorilla in the balls.' Indeed, the real hero of *Slinger* is neither Gunslinger nor the curious 'I' but language itself, the language of our time, refracted, distorted, heightened, but always recognizable as the jumble of speech we hear around us and see in print."

Peter Ackroyd, in the *Spectator* wrote that Dorn is "the only plausible political poet in America . . . [which] has nothing whatever to do with the extent of the poet's political knowledge, his *savoir faire*, or even the 'side' he takes; it has to do with the quality of his response to public situations, not whether that response is 'right' or 'wrong' " Ultimately, his poems define sense of place.

—Shawn Wong

From

THE COLLECTED POEMS
1956–1974 (1975)

Eugene Delacroix Says

dated Valmont 10–16
october 1849
the common people
will always be
the majority

they make a mistake
in thinking
that great estates
are useless

But furthermore he says
It is the poor
who benefit most by them

And the profits gained do not
impoverish the rich who
let, them,
take advantage of the little
to be sure
windfalls
which they find on their estates.

Now let us begin again this morning.
The poor.
And the middle class
or anyone might

fence off their approaches
necessity is a naturally
more separable thing
                    than poverty.
In this case the poor were
allowed to gather fuel
on the estates, given them that right
by the republican, fear that word,
government.

Much as today the man bent between the tracks
in Appalachia east kentucky
his malnourished and unemployed fingers
articulating very small pieces of coal indeed
and his children grimly beautiful
because their eyes have been made large
as witnesses
as the lean roll of years and owners
stripped the hills of their former
mountain glamour.
                    Bent in the dim light
of that specific cabin space they had,
those unlucky children, a meal
of various cereal dumped on the market
to make room for vaster crops next year
a thing they couldn't have understood
or that charity is quite often
a device to prevent spoilage,

                            nor were they
ever allowed to consider that the merely farinaceous
will not support the life
of a carnivore. But this is just
the bestiality of the major euphemism
of our day, supplementation.
Retrained they may become garage mechanics
and press the temptation
of match cover education
between their fingers

the rest of their days here in the western hemisphere.
Now, if a fire has to be made
and a supper has to be got, that's not
here nor there, here,
but back of Recife they *wonder* a lot of the time
in Kentucky they do not
in all of Hazard county they do not.
And it is an inevitability that one day
those ugly eyes prolix with beefsteak will be
snatched out, and south america
will have been all along much to their amazement
a specific location not to have been misused
and kentucky will have been a noun
that smouldered like a burning mine
and, I have to add, I hope those satraps
do not wake in time.

Song: Venceremos

(For Latin America)
(For préman sotomayor)

And there will be fresh children once more
in planalto and matto grosso
green mansions for their houses
along the orinoco
      take away the oil
      it is not to anoint their heads
      take away the cannon
      and the saber from the paunch belly
      overlaid with crossed colors
      those quaint waddling men
      are the leaden dead toys
                only their
    own

children
caress

while the great eyed children
far away in the mountains, out of Quito
pass thru the crisp evening streets
of earth towns, where they caress
the earth, a substance of *majority*
including the lead of established
forces,
who can do nothing
but give us the measures of pain
which now define us

Take away the boats from the bananas
they are there for the double purpose
to quell insurrection first
and next to make of an equatorial food
a clanging and numerical register in chicago
this is not an industrial comment,
it is not Sandburg's chicago
not how ugly a city you did make
but whitman's fine generosity I want
a specific measure of respect returned for the hand
and the back that bears away the stalk
as a boy, in illinois
peeled away, in amazement, the yellow, brown lined case
thicker place

when the arced phenomenon
was first put in his hand
a suggestion and a food, combustion!
keep your fingers from the coffee bush.

Nor,
on the meseta Basáltica, or back in town
in Paso de Indios
can the people be permitted
the luxurious image of Peron

Love Songs

1

It is deep going from here
from the old world to the new
from Europa home
the brilliant scrolls of the waves
                    wave
the runic secret of homeward
when Diego de Landa
the glyphic books destroyed
there were old towns
            in our hemisphere sadness
now as then

no sense in old towns chontal
                    got to have
newtowns of the soul

2

Inside the late nights of last week
under the cover of our selves
you went to sleep in my arms
and last night too

you were in some alarm
of your dream
                    some tableau
an assembling of signs
from your troubled day glows
and trembles, your limbs
divine with sleep
gather and extend their flesh
along mine

and this I surround, all this
I had my arms around

   3

My speech is tinged
my tongue has taken
a foreigner into it
Can you understand
my uncertainties grow
and underbrush and thicket
of furious sensibility
between us and wholly
unlike the marvelously burning
bush which lies at the entrance
to your gated thighs

My dear love, when I unsheathe
a word of the wrong temper
it is to test that steel
across the plain between us

Home on the Range, February, 1962

Flutes, and the harp on the plain
Is a distance, of pain, and waving reeds
The scale of far off trees, notes not of course
Upon a real harp but chords in the thick clouds
And the wind reaching its arms toward west yellowstone.
Moving to the east, the grass was high once, and before
White wagons moved
                    the hawk, proctor of the hills still is

Oh god did the chunky westerner think to remake this in his
    own image
Oh god did the pioneer society sanctify the responsible citizen
To do that
                face like a plot of ground
Was it iron locomotives and shovels, hand tools
And barbed wire motives for each man's
Fenced off little promised land

                            or the mind of bent

Or of carson, oh earp
These sherpas of responsible destruction
Posses led by a promising girl wielding a baton upon the street
A Sacagawea wearing a baseball cap, eating a Clark bar.
And flutes and the harp are on the plain
Bring the last leading edge of stillness
Brought no water, brought dead roots
Like an allotment of tool handles to their premises—
    and they cry
In pain over daily income—a hundred years of planned greed
Loving the welfare state of new barns and bean drills
Hot passion for the freedom of the dentist!
Their plots were america's first subdivisions called homesteads

Lean american-gothic quarter sections gaunt look
Managing to send their empty headed son who is a ninny
to nebraska to do it, all over again, to the ground, a prairie
Dog hole,
And always they smirk at starvation
And consider it dirty . . . a joke their daughters learn
From their new husbands.

Prolegomenon

Goddesse, excellently bright,
thou that mak'st a day of night.
You tell us men are numberless
and that Great and Mother
were once synonymous.

We are bleached in Sound
as it burns by what we desire
and we give our inwardness
in some degree to all things
but to fire we give everything.

We are drawn beneath your fieryness
which comes down to us
on the wing of Eleusian image,
and although it is truely a small heat
our cold instruments do affirm it.
So saith Denis, the polymath.

We survey the Colorado plateau.
There are no degrees of reality
in this handsome and singular mass,
or in the extravagant geometry
of its cliffs and pinnacles.

This is all water carved
the body thrust into the hydrosphere
and where the green mesas give way
to the vulcan floor, not far
from Farmington and other interferences
with the perfect night
and the glittering trail
of the silent Vía Láctea
there is a civil scar
so cosmetic, one can't see it.

A superimposition, drawn up
like the ultimate property
of the ego, an invisible claim
to a scratchy indultum
from which smoke pours forth.

But now, over the endless sagey brush
the moon makes her silvery bid
and in the cool dry air of the night
the winde wankels across the cattle grid.

Rose Drachler

ROSE DRACHLER may have always been a poet, but she began a visible practice during the mid-seventies when she was in her sixth decade (born in 1911). What I know of her life is piecemeal—we corresponded for five years before her death in 1981, and I acted as both editor and publisher of her first two books, *Burrowing In, Digging Out* (Tree Books, 1974) and *The Choice* (Tree Books, 1977). When I asked her for an autobiographical statement, she replied:

> I am truly a non-person. I have been mistaken for the janitor's wife, a nurse for dogs, an aunt, a good witch, a poet, a distinguished (dead) actress, a mother. I suffer from the spiteful machinations of my grand piano. I am compelled to continue a needlepoint rug the size of a ballroom by the lust of the eye of the needle for friction with wool. Strangers tell me the most intimate story of their lives and drunken Ukranians propose marriage to me on the subway on Friday afternoons. I am old and ugly. I was born old but interested. Water loves me. I have been married to it for more than half a century. I know the language of fish and birds. Also squirrels and toads. I am a convert to Orthodox Jewry, also I have tried riding a broomstick. I had a vision of the double Shekinah on Amsterdam Avenue and 110th Street. I have taught cooking and sewing to beautiful Cantonese girls and the affectionate daughters of Mafiosi. I am married to an irascible but loving artist. A nay-sayer. My parents drove each other crazy. Me too. Which turned me to books and poetry and I thank them for it.

She lived in Brooklyn with her husband Jacob, an artist, and had as strong a sense of the appearances and disappearances of the seasons as if she had lived in a backyard in Wisconsin. Yet she was complexly urban, intensely interested in the worlds of art and literature so abundantly diverse in Manhattan, matrix of a thousand careers. Her affiliation with diasporic themes mixed with the everyday, reflecting Jewish-American experiences specific to the presence and participation in urban culture. She was a feminist without a theory other than the praxis of poetry. She became a role model to young women poets during the seventies; her work also engaged the attention and respect of Jerome Rothenberg, Jackson MacLow, Armand Schwerner. In 1976 she took a workshop with John Ashbery— "to look at the face of a poet and people who are trying to be poets once in a while. . . . I think Ashbery could be an antidote to my Russo-Yiddish streak of sentimental fiddlemusic. But I find myself more similar to my own self all the time. What to do?"

Through her poems (and less concealed in her letters) moved a marvelous activity I call "serious play," essential to the creative process. Her "biographical" statement is a good example of her fusing (and refusing) everyday occurrence into a disordering clarity. She had the ability to discern (and fracture through her lens), the exact aspect of a moment suitable to the economy of her poem. A lively play of irony, self-criticism, and direct wisdom weave through her work, as well as an edge of melancholy inevitably toppled by her affirmative will and passion.

"I had a friend who had a small black dog with a pugnose. Someone walked by her porch and said, 'My goodness that is an ugly little dog.' To which she replied, 'To me he looks the way a dog should look. He is my dog. All other dogs look wrong to me inasmuch as they differ from him.' So it is with our children and with our poems too. It is hard to believe that other people do not see in them what we see" (from a letter, August 26, 1976).

—*David Meltzer*

From
THE CHOICE (1977)

Smaragd the Emerald

The emerald, smaragd, protector of women
Binder of bowels, preventer of fits
Treasured by Cleopatra and Alexander
Worked intaglio by the ancient Greeks
                        (Although in most languages
                        the S before a consonant
                        is used for a word of contempt
                        as smear, snot, spit
                        sbilenco—bowlegged
                        smerdare—befoul)
Smaragdos the blue-green color
Crystals hexagonal, prisms breaking
On the basal plane imperfectly
At right angles to the geometric plane
Soft, not much harder than quartz
A low specific gravity, the cut stone
Not much brilliance or fire

The oriental emerald, green corundum
Lithia emerald miscalled hiddenite
Uralian emerald, demantoid
Brazilian emerald, green tourmaline
Evening emerald rightly a peridot
Pyro emerald, fluorspar
Mother of emerald, green quartz

From Muzo, Egypt, Etbai
Jebel Sikait, Jebel Zabara
Near the Red Sea east of Assuan
Bogota, Columbia, Peru, Coscuez, Smondoco
Found in the Urals
On the shores of the Takovaya River
In Habachtal of the Salzburg Alps
In Eidvold, Norway

Found in mica schist in talc schist
In nests of calcite in black bituminous
Limestone containing ammonites
Of lower cretaceous age
Associated with quartz, dolomites, pyrites
Found in mica schist with aquamarines
Alexandrite phenacite and beryl

Taken internally
Smaragd, the emerald is good for the eyesight
Worn on the person it is a help
Against epilepsy a cure for dysentery
Assists women in childbirth
Keeps away evil spirits
Preserves chastity

Zippora Returns to Moses at Rephidim

By the wells
Alone and running
You found my dark skin a comfort
A home of maternal wetness

Now I bow, since I must
To your unseen Lover

My son is well named a stranger
For me

If there are others
You may cut them
Before they have learned to suck
Using bronze not stone
Oh bitter husband to me

Distracted lover
I shall sleep in your tent alone

My father has brought me back
He will stay to teach you
To govern your inconstant people
Constant only in revolt

It was his craft brought you this far
His and the hand of your Bridegroom

No more shall I be troubled
By the smiles of my six glutted sisters

Send your Nubian concubine to me
We shall both be darkly forsaken

While you fast
And adore in the wind
Your jealous
Bridegroom of blood

The Letters of the Book

Aleph the cow with wide horns
Her milk in the night sky
Walks slowly on clouds
Aleph to the tenth power
She leads with symbolic logic
To the throne of milky pearl
Aleph the sky-cow with lovely eyes
Wide-horned giver she gives mankind
Her sign of is-ness. The cow

Bayz the house snug
Under the heat of the sun
Out of the rain and the snow
We curl up in a corner
Under the roof of Bayz
Out of the daily sorrow
Bayz the comforter
Inhabited by humanity
Cat-like and childlike
Inside of his Bayz

Ghimel the camel
Carries man into the book
The leaves and waves
Of the forest the sea of the book
Boat of the desert the camel
Long traveler drinking the task
Ghimel drinks the dry road of daily observance
It slakes the thirst for communion

Daled the door like a wall
No hinges no handle
Daled the mysterious opener
Into a place with a road

The six hundred and thirteen small roads
Of derekh eretz

I have swallowed Vav the hook
It had something tasty and nourishing on it
A promise of plenty and friendship
With someone more than myself
I've got Vav the hook in my gut
I shift to rearrange the discomfort
Like a sharp minnow inside
When he draws up the line
Attached to the hook
When he rips the Vav out
There will be strange air around me
Burning my gills

Yod the hand
And Koff the palm
Rested gently
On Raish the head
Of Abraham our father
Who crossed over
Burning the idols
Behind him in Ur
He looked upward
At stars sun and moon
Then looked further
For a pat on the head
From Yod and Koff
The unseen hand and palm

In the crook
Of the Lammed leaning forward
I put my neck when I pray
My shepherd makes me meek
He makes my knees bend
He guides me I follow
With the loop of the Lammed

On my throat
I go

Mem is the water
Sweetly obeying
The red-raging water
Which parted
Mem came together
And drowned the pursuers
Stubborn refusers of freedom
The enslavers Mem drowned them
Mem was the water
Brackish tormenting
Sweetened with leaves
By our Moses
The waters of trust
Which he struck from the rock
Mem mayim water

The jelly-glowing eye full of love
Sees past the eye the Ayin
Like a dog it perceives the hidden
It turns and stares at its master
It pleads with him to come home
The longing for certainty
Fills him too full
Return, my master, he says
Your eye to my eye
Ayin

Peh the mouth speaking hastily
Praying easily fast without reverence
Full of gossip causing estrangement
Let my soul be as dust to Peh
The loud quarreler the prattler
The carrier of tales to and fro
The beguiler the mouth Peh better still

Shin is the tooth
It chews on the word
(With the dot on the left
It is Sin)
So much sharper than Shin the tooth
Is learning in the study
Together by dimlight
Chuckling together at the tooth
The horn that was known to gore
The tooth for a tooth in our story
The sharp-toothed father
Of our fathers
Who was wont to gore in the past

Conversation with Rilke about Dragons

Sicknesses
That are superficially and foolishly handled
Withdraw
After a pause
They break out again more fearfully
They are unlived, spurned
Lost life of which one may die

Perhaps if we knew
We would then endure our sorrows
With greater confidence than our joys
For they are moments when
Something new has entered into us
Something unknown

                When I was so sad
                Those times when I seemed to attract

Misfortune
It was because I had built this destiny up
Myself
By my past, my special character
So peculiarly suited to misfortune

Our feelings grow mute
In shy perplexity
Everything in us withdraws
A stillness comes
And the new which no one knows
Stands in the midst of it
And is silent
                My future stood before me
                Waiting for me to move up into it
                Silent

Letter Written in the Year of the Carrying Away to Babylon

My Kinsman Hanamel,

The deed is buried by the Horse Gate
On the side of Jerusalem looking inward
Toward the place of gifts and sacrifices

Tell your children born away from home
To write the place on their hearts
Let them set their teeth into the carrying away
Let them bite the hurt places hard

Remember where the deed is
Remember where the field is

Let them be mild and untroublesome there
So they may not be diminished
In times of evil let them be silent and discreet
So they may save a remnant to return

My near kinsman Hanamel, my uncle Shallum's son
I was commanded to buy your field
The voice was familiar and so was the time
I pay you these seventeen shekels of silver
Weighed and witnessed by reliable men

So that after the Chaldeans have gone
After their fruit has withered from above
After their root has dried from below
Those of ours that remain may return

> In dreams my faith is not painful
> Someone burns my mouth with coal
> And it does not hurt me to believe
> It does not hurt to speak dreamspeech

> Beastseed and manseed increase in your
> well watered field

> Jeremiah, your uncle's son

Robert Duncan

Robert Duncan (1919–1988) was a singular American modernist whose rich and complex work unfolds on its own terms and in a deeply informed vocabulary of presences and correspondences. His is a unique body of work one approaches with a sense of commitment and challenge—starting with *Heavenly City, Earthly City* (1947) and concluding with the second volume of *Ground Work* (1988).

Born in Oakland, California, Duncan has been identified with (and participated in) San Francisco literary movements from the Berkeley Renaissance (in association with Jack Spicer, Robin Blaser, Mary Fabilli, and William Everson), to the beat movement (at first in an oppositional way), to the L-A-N-G-U-A-G-E poets (again, as a critical voice). He was a conscientious objector during World War II and an active voice of resistance; a participant in the Black Mountain College school of postwar arts (with Charles Olson, Robert Creeley, John Cage, Buckminster Fuller, Robert Rauchenberg, and Josef Alberts); an early and culturally courageous spokesperson for the legitimation of gay rights; and an active voice during the anti-war movement of the sixties.

His work incorporates modernist discourses in linguistics and deconstruction with earlier Romantic positions and arguments. This notable synthesis of seemingly dissimilar categories of being and seeing gives Duncan's work a texture unequaled by his peers. A poet of wide aesthetic and philosophic interests, he took, as it were, a vow of silence for a decade, circulating samizdat-like copies of his work to a select group of peers he considered capable and willing to engage with his work. Duncan served as a core-faculty member at New College of California during the first few years of its unique M.A. program in poetics, an inspiring presence whose energetic discourse transformed classroom lectures into quests of the spirit:

> The poet is such a child in us. And in the poem, the instrument of music that he makes from men's speech, has such a hunger to live, to be true, as mathematics has. Numbers and words were both things of a spell. To dream true, to figure true, to come true. Here poetry is the life of the language and must be incarnate in a body of words, condensed to have strength, phrases that are sinews, lines that may be tense or relaxed as the mind moves. Charles Olson in his essays toward a physiology of consciousness has made us aware that not only heart and brain and the sensory skin but all the internal organs, the totality of the body is involved in the act of a poem, so that the organization of words, an invisible body, bears the imprint of the physical man, the finest imprint that we feel in our own bodies as a tonic consonance and dissonance, a being-in-tune, a search for the as yet missing scale. . . . Our engagement with knowing, with craft and lore, our demand for truth is not to reach a conclusion but to keep our exposure to what we do not know, to confront our wish and our need beyond habit and capability, beyond what we can take for granted, at the borderline, the light finger-tip or thought-tip where. . . .

> —*David Meltzer*

From

*GROUND WORK: BEFORE
THE WAR (1988)*

Near Circe's House

Not far from Circe's house I met a man,
derelict, swept by the winds, to whom I was
I knew an apparition of some plan
half-forming in his mind he and I were
as if driven to by assembling Fates,
and, "Where are you going?" I askt,
"You are so alone my own life
which was eternal and self-contained
opens up vast breaches of promise in the
thought of you you know nothing of."

Behind me as I speak to you I hear
all your men, your shipmates,
fallen where they are into evil ways, ensnared,
closed round in Circe's circles,
grunting, rooting, snuffling, fucking
at the gates. And in your eyes
I seek to open a gate that I would enter
momentarily. I am trying to tell you
—Take my heart from me
and it will beat for you, wildly.

I am trying to tell you
Hermes I would be for you as I
have been for others to protect
in falling in love, take heart from me,
for from the very loom where She

weaves and undoes each night your odyssey
I bring this herb, black at the root
and milky white where it blooms. See,

from the very ground here where we stand
I pull the magic plant that was meant
to help you enter and pass through
Her darkening intent. It is the heart
I spoke of fed this stem in me,
torn out of its own darkness,
this herb calld *Moly* by the gods.

Rites of Passage: I

These are
the passages of thought
from the light air
into the heavy flesh
until from the burning
all the slumb'ring dark
matter comes alight,
the foot that has
its reason in bright ratios
it would measure

hardens and beats
the trembling earth,
reaches out of measure
into the hoof that
tramples
pleasure and pain compounded
into a further brightness.

Dark Satyr,
your blood is like a
light behind an

almond bough, now
something is taking
place in me
all nature awaits
behind the trembling
tapestry of leaves
and buds, of
hidden, about-to-be-
awakened birds.

The damp submissive grass
now stirs from sleep,
now turns in every
green blade grown
alert
with listening.

What is Spring
that everywhere bursts upon my world
with such a chorus of first voices
and to my flaring nostrils brings
rank odors of the root of things
but this—the year's like expectancy?

And half a century grows fresh in me.
A hearing stiffens, strains at the leash of a wild dancing.
As if answering an as-yet-unspoken need,
upon the brow of a silence behind my words
the pensive horns of a new yearning thrust.
The force of a rime impending runs abroad
forebodings at the edge we are in ourselves,

edge now of arriving hooves we
        almost hear, the prancing
advances in our feet,

edge now of the rush that attends
        your coming, where we are not,
an edge of home in me, of Pan.

Rites of Passage: II

Something is taking place.
Horns thrust upward from the brow.
Hooves beat impatient where feet once were.
My son, youth grows alarming in your face.
Your innocent regard is cruelly charming to me now.
You bristle where my fond hand would stir
to strike your cheek. I do not dare.

Irregular meters beat between your heart and mine.
Snuffling the air you take the heat and scan
the lines you take in going as if I were or were not there
and overtake me.
　　　　And where it seems but yesterday I spilled the wine;
you too grow beastly to become a man.

Peace, peace. I've had enough. What can I say
when song's demanded? —I've had my fill of song?
My longing to sing grows full. Time's emptied me.

And where my youth was, now the Sun in you grows hot,
　　　your day
is young, my place you take triumphantly. All along
it's been for you, for this lowering of your horns in challenge,
　　　She
had her will of me and will not

let my struggling spirit in itself be free.

Allen Ginsberg

"But Cody said, 'Further, further' "

—Jack Kerouac, Visions of Cody

THE beginning of a career often contains within itself the seeds of future development.

The amazing career of Allen Ginsberg begins, not with his birth on June 3, 1926, in Newark, New Jersey (his father, Louis, a poet, his mother, Naomi, the subject of one of her son's most famous poems, "Kaddish"), but at the privileged moment in 1956 of the publication by City Lights Books of *Howl and Other Poems* in pocket book format. The book was immediately recognized by some to be an American classic. By others, however, it was thought scandalously pornographic, and the publisher, Lawrence Ferlinghetti, was arrested on the grounds that he had "willfully and lewdly printed and sold obscene and indecent material." The publicity surrounding the trial and Ferlinghetti's subsequent acquittal are part of the literary history of San Francisco and of that enormously influential group of writers (including Ferlinghetti, Jack Kerouac, Bob Kaufman, Michael McClure, Gregory Corso, and others, as well as Ginsberg) called, in Kerouac's phrase, "the beat generation." The word "beat" had many meanings for these writers, but one of the most important was the sense of transcending defeat (transcending being *beat*en) by breaking through, often by means of drugs, to ecstasy (*beat*itude).

Ginsberg had in fact read the opening section of his poem, prior to its publication, at the Six gallery in San Francisco in 1955. The reading caused a sensation and, as his biographer, Barry Miles, puts it, "catalyzed the Bay Area literary community." In the audience was Ginsberg's friend and mentor (four years his senior) Jack Kerouac, who chanted "Go!" at the end of each line, as if encouraging a jazz soloist. At the time of that recital, another of Ginsberg's mentors, Ezra Pound, was incarcerated in St. Elizabeth's Hospital, an insane asylum in Washington, D.C., and had narrowly escaped being tried for high treason. Carl Solomon, to whom the poem is dedicated, was in Rockland State Mental Institution. And Ginsberg refers to his mother, Naomi, in the poem as "my mother in the insane asylum." Not surprisingly, the poem is alive with the fear and fascination of madness, a fear which is finally alleviated, not by the clinical help which had in fact been offered to Ginsberg, but by nothing less than poetry itself. Despite the rush and intensity of its language, "Howl" presents itself not as the ravings of a madman (though the madman may be a blood brother to the poet) but as a *poem*, the product of an inspired, sophisticated, and highly judgmental poet: "I have seen the *best minds* of my generation. . . ."

The poem's title was, in legend, suggested by Kerouac, though this has been questioned by Barry Miles. It is in any case not a howl of defeat but, as Kerouac's "Go!" suggests, something equivalent to the jazz term, "wail." "I depended on the word 'who,' " wrote Ginsberg, "to keep the beat, a base to keep measure, return to and take off from again onto another streak of invention." For both Ginsberg and Kerouac, the jazz musician (later, for Ginsberg, the rock musician as well) was the primary analogue of the alienated, marginalized, and yet enormously potent poet. (Their friend, the doomed Neal Cassady, was in a way the Elvis Presley of the movement: the pure embodiment of, in Norman Mailer's phrase, "the white Negro.")

Ginsberg's title, "Howl," also suggests the unmistakably oral thrust of the poem—its status as something in the mouth, not on the page—and this too connects it to the jazz musician. In the era of New Criticism and the seven types of ambiguity, Ginsberg insisted on the poet as *performer,* and it was as a performer that he was to gain considerable success and notoriety. (In the early days his performances often included nudity.) At this moment of his career Ginsberg was inventing, among other things, performance poetry—though he was of course aware of poets like Antonin Artaud, to whom the phrase might apply as well. In addition, his poem was flagrantly and ecstatically both homosexual and Jewish. The former was attested to by the number of bowdlerized printings of the poem, the latter, as Richard Eberhart noted at the time of its initial appearance, by its Biblical rhythms, its Old Testament tone—and by the fact that it was addressed to a man significantly named Solomon. In a letter to Jack Kerouac quoted by Miles, Ginsberg writes that the Bible depicts the "culmination of peaceful holy land in wise Solomon's time, the building of the Temple and after that, Spenglerian degeneration, . . . whoring and queerness and worship of Moloch"—the central villain of "Howl." It is as if, at this moment, the entire history of the Jews merges with that of "the best minds of [Ginsberg's] generation."

One is tempted to parody Ginsberg's famous remark, "First thought, best thought," by saying, "First book, best book." But that would be quite inaccurate. Nevertheless, the elements named with extraordinary vividness in *Howl and Other Poems* remain with the poet throughout his career. In working out the various ramifications of his identity, Ginsberg gave enormous impetus to, among other things, the Gay movement, the McLuhanesque concern with media, confessional poetry, the various interests of the sixties and of the counter culture— Ginsberg's anti-war activity was of enormous importance and issued in such powerful poems as "Wichita Vortex Sutra"— even, through his concern with Buddhism, the spirituality of the "New Age." But the burden of all his poetry has consistently been, not the "rebellion" of which "Howl" was accused in the fifties, but *continual, ecstatic revelation,* and this burden remains in evidence today. What is revealed, as he has insisted over and over again, are *the contents of his mind and of "these States,"* contents which the poet *assumes* are revealable provided only (as Kerouac argued) that one write spontaneously and honestly out of the direct experience available.

Ginsberg creates not a multiplicity of "I"s (as T. S. Eliot does in *The Waste Land*) but an "I" that is constantly in motion, exploring, continually returning to a base but continually opening to the world as well. His poetry's dangerous persuasiveness—and, ultimately, its *fiction*—is rooted in the promise that, in a world shot through with repression it will tell you the truth. Ginsberg's moral imperative remains undiminished even as the poet enters his middle sixties. In his most recent book,

White Shroud, he writes (sounding a bit like Ralph Waldo Emerson): *"Sincerity / is the key / to Bliss in this / Eternity."* It is this quality of "sincerity" which keeps his poetry dangerous. What is a "sincere" man likely to say or do? As he wrote to Neal Cassady over forty years ago: "I will break your mind and soul open and I warn you that now."

—Jack Foley

From

THE COLLECTED POEMS
1947–1980 (1984)

Father Guru

Father Guru   unforlorn
Heart beat Guru whom I scorn
Empty Guru Never Born
Sitting Guru every morn
Friendly Guru chewing corn
Angry Guru Faking Porn
Guru Guru Freely torn
Garment Guru neatly worn
Guru Head short hair shorn
Absent Guru Eyes I mourn
Guru of Duncan Guru of Dorn
Ginsberg Guru like a thorn
Goofy Guru Lion Horn
Lonely Guru Unicorn
O Guru whose slave I'm sworn
Save me Guru Om Ah Hūm

Austin, February 14, 1978

A Supermarket in California

What thoughts I have of you tonight, Walt Whitman, for I
walked down the sidestreets under the trees with a headache
self-conscious looking at the full moon.

In my hungry fatigue, and shopping for images, I went into the neon fruit supermarket, dreaming of your enumerations!

What peaches and what penumbras! Whole families shopping at night! Aisles full of husbands! Wives in the avocados, babies in the tomatoes!—and you, García Lorca, what were you doing down by the watermelons?

I saw you, Walt Whitman, childless, lonely old grubber, poking among the meats in the refrigerator and eyeing the grocery boys.

I heard you asking questions of each: Who killed the pork chops? What price bananas? Are you my Angel?

I wandered in and out of the brilliant stacks of cans following you, and followed in my imagination by the store detective.

We strode down the open corridors together in our solitary fancy tasting artichokes, possessing every frozen delicacy, and never passing the cashier.

Where are we going, Walt Whitman? The doors close in an hour. Which way does your beard point tonight?

(I touch your book and dream of our odyssey in the supermarket and feel absurd.)

Will we walk all night through solitary streets? The trees add shade to shade, lights out in the houses, we'll both be lonely.

Will we stroll dreaming of the lost America of love past blue automobiles in driveways, home to our silent cottage?

Ah, dear father, graybeard, lonely old courage-teacher, what America did you have when Charon quit poling his ferry and you got out on a smoking bank and stood watching the boat disappear on the black waters of Lethe?

Berkeley, 1955

Song

The weight of the world
        is love.
Under the burden
        of solitude,
under the burden
        of dissatisfaction

        the weight,
the weight we carry
        is love.

Who can deny?
        In dreams
it touches
        the body,
in thought
        constructs
a miracle,
        in imagination
anguishes
        till born
in human—

looks out of the heart
        burning with purity—
for the burden of life
        is love,

but we carry the weight
        wearily,
and so must rest
in the arms of love
        at last,
must rest in the arms
        of love.

No rest
      without love,
no sleep
      without dreams

Sunflower Sutra

I walked on the banks of the tincan banana dock and sat down
     under the huge shade of a Southern Pacific locomotive to
     look at the sunset over the box house hills and cry.
Jack Kerouac sat beside me on a busted rusty iron pole,
     companion, we thought the same thoughts of the soul,
     bleak and blue and sad-eyed, surrounded by the gnarled
     steel roots of trees of machinery.
The oily water on the river mirrored the red sky, sun sank on
     top of final Frisco peaks, no fish in that stream, no hermit
     in those mounts, just ourselves rheumy-eyed and hung-over
     like old bums on the riverbank, tired and wily.
Look at the Sunflower, he said, there was a dead gray shadow
     against the sky, big as a man, sitting dry on top of a pile of
     ancient sawdust—
—I rushed up enchanted—it was my first sunflower,
     memories of Blake—my visions—Harlem
and Hells of the Eastern rivers, bridges clanking Joes Greasy
     Sandwiches, dead baby carriages, black treadless tires
     forgotten and unretreaded, the poem of the riverbank,
     condoms & pots, steel knives, nothing stainless, only the
     dank muck and the razor-sharp artifacts passing into the
     past—
and the gray Sunflower poised against the sunset, crackly bleak
     and dusty with the smut and smog and smoke of olden
     locomotives in its eye—
corolla of bleary spikes pushed down and broken like a
     battered crown, seeds fallen out of its face,
     soon-to-be-toothless mouth of sunny air, sunrays
     obliterated on its hairy head like a dried wire spiderweb,

leaves stuck out like arms out of the stem, gestures from the
    sawdust root, broke pieces of plaster fallen out of the black
    twigs, a dead fly in its ear,
Unholy battered old thing you were, my sunflower O my soul,
    I loved you then!
The grime was no man's grime but death and human
    locomotives,
all that dress of dust, that veil of darkened railroad skin, that
    smog of cheek, that eyelid of black mis'ry, that sooty hand
    or phallus or protuberance of artificial worse-than-dirt
    —industrial—modern—all that civilization spotting your
    crazy golden crown—
and those blear thoughts of death and dusty loveless eyes and
    ends and withered roots below, in the home-pile of sand
    and sawdust, rubber dollar bills, skin of machinery, the guts
    and innards of the weeping coughing car, the empty lonely
    tincans with their rusty tongues alack, what more could I
    name, the smoked ashes of some cock cigar, the cunts of
    wheelbarrows and the milky breasts of cars, wornout asses
    out of chairs & sphincters of dynamos—all these
entangled in your mummied roots—and you there standing
    before me in the sunset, all your glory in your form!
A perfect beauty of a sunflower! a perfect excellent lovely
    sunflower existence! a sweet natural eye to the new hip
    moon, woke up alive and excited grasping in the sunset
    shadow sunrise golden monthly breeze!
How many flies buzzed round you innocent of your grime,
    while you cursed the heavens of the railroad and your
    flower soul?
Poor dead flower? when did you forget you were a flower?
    when did you look at your skin and decide you were an
    impotent dirty old locomotive? the ghost of a locomotive?
    the specter and shade of a once powerful mad American
    locomotive?
You were never no locomotive, Sunflower, you were a
    sunflower!
And you Locomotive, you are a locomotive, forget me not!
So I grabbed up the skeleton thick sunflower and stuck it at
    my side like a scepter,

and deliver my sermon to my soul, and Jack's soul too, and
 anyone who'll listen,
—We're not our skin of grime, we're not our dread bleak
 dusty imageless locomotive, we're all golden sunflowers
 inside, blessed by our own seed & hairy naked
 accomplishment-bodies growing into mad black formal
 sunflowers in the sunset, spied on by our eyes under the
 shadow of the mad locomotive riverbank sunset Frisco hilly
 tincan evening sitdown vision.

Berkeley, 1955

Judy Grahn

*"Judy Grahn is a poet at the heart and center of
her time and world, and ours."*

—*Ursula LeGuin*

JUDY GRAHN'S (b. 1940) work has given voice to what was
previously voiceless. Her body of work is extensive, including
seven books of poetry, *The Common Woman Poems, She
Who: A Graphic Book of Poems, Edward the Dyke and Other
Poems, A Woman Is Talking to Death, The Work of a Com-
mon Woman, The Queen of Wands,* and *The Queen of
Swords;* two books of nonfiction, *The Highest Apple* and *An-
other Mother Tongue;* a novel, *Mundane's World;* and two
volumes of a short story collection she edited, *True to Life
Adventure Stories.* These books form a remarkable body of
work by a gifted writer who has taken the risk of naming what
had been nameless for so long and of giving voice to a reality
that was previously hidden from mainstream literature.

Grahn's writing is part of the movement she helped create.
As an activist Grahn has been instrumental in organizing for
gay and lesbian rights and women's rights. She founded one of
the first women's presses, helping to make women's words
available to a growing audience. Her involvement in the early
movement gave rise to the Lesbian Mother's Union, A
Woman's Place bookstore (in Oakland, California), prisoners'
rights groups, welfare rights groups, and anti-rape campaigns.
Grahn's writing comes from a base of understanding formed in
the women's community.

The heart of Grahn's voice is poetic. Her nonfiction is per-
ceptive, revelatory, and brilliant. Her first novel is a remarkable
woman-centered mythic work about female rites of passage.
Grahn's writing, an integral part of the movement she was so
instrumental in founding, is grounded in the reality of women's
lives. I still remember first reading *A Woman Is Talking to
Death,* the moment, the place, the feelings the work elicited

from me. It tapped a deep rage and then released me into hope and action. Grahn's poetry is part of the "House of Women" she speaks of in *The Highest Apple.*

> The decision an artist makes, to speak for women and to speak as a woman . . . is probably the most powerful decision she will make. For in making it, she chooses autonomy, she chooses to stand somewhere in particular, to speak out to her society. Her work, in locating itself so specifically, socially and historically takes on a power it cannot have if she chooses, instead, to speak anonymously, 'universally,' (Judy Grahn, *The Highest Apple,* Spinsters Ink, 1985)

—Margarita Donnelly

From

THE QUEEN OF WANDS (1982)

They say she is veiled

They say she is veiled
and a mystery. That is
one way of looking.
Another
is that she is where
she always has been,
exactly in place,
and it is we,
we who are mystified,
we who are veiled
and without faces.

But I mean any kind of thief

When I went
looking for the Foe
I called him "he"
the one in the fast
car and the outside lane,
the getaway man
who came and took
and went, a stranger

but I mean any kind of thief—
of souls, pride, the heart,
of land, space, air and work.
I mean the thief of truth
of meaning

the one who goes
by what is said
and not by what is done
that one
that kind of liar
the fantasizer

smoker of bad wishes;
the cold one who, shivering
steals your thunder and your fire
then calls you poor,
calls you "Queen of Wants"

and wants.

When I went looking
for the Foe I thought of
boots and leather, barbed
wire fences, aggressive
legal stances and the
colonizer
who takes the heart
out of your sky, diverts
the light from your eye
into his own

but I mean any
kind of Foe, her, the
sap-sucking cannibalizer,
idea-eater, and the one,
the ones who make war
with rents and wages

the masked mate,
who makes war with love
and personal rages
the raper who takes
your sense of self
and wholeness,
flame of trust
and leaves you trembling,
crusted with his fear.

the daisy bringer
who calls you Queen for a Day
and takes your year

the friend who cries on your shoulder
and never sees your grief
who looks in your mirror
and calls you low
and calls you less
than who you are
I mean the Foe
that one
I mean any kind of thief.

Old Helen

Discarded in old town, bunched,
wearing indigo-blue
worsted leg veins,
you were a beauty once,
Helen, weren't you—
before the ships came.

You were a beauty once
before the ships came

to your (oh oh) rescue,
bearing gifts or promises or chains,
field labor or the mills,
warping you with pain,
debts or deadly chemicals,
spinning your beauty down
to an empty spool in old town.

You were a beauty once
Helen, a singer and a weaver,
spinner and a storyteller too,
of greatest fame,
before the ships came.

Now your face shows
what you have had to know
about the use of beauty,
youth, flying fingers too
(where they fly to).
You know the first name of the booty
they got, and as you lug
your burdens down the street
with no one to help you,
you remember what they mean by "rescue."

You were a beauty once
Helen and you will be.
Your expressions prophesize.
The anger migrates through your veins
like great flocks of flesh-devouring
birds, wheeling and diving, gathering the drives
to unknit the terrible pattern of our lives.

9. Spider:

And still it is a loom, simply,
still just a frame, a spindle,
heddle bars lifting
so a shuttle can be thrown across
the space created
and the new line
tapped down into place;

still there is a hot and womblike bucket
somewhere boiling up the stuff of thread
in cauldrons, and some expert fingers
dancing . . .

Still it is the one true cord,
the umbilical line
unwinding into meaning,
transformation,
web of thought and caring and connection.

Just as, Helen you dreamed and weaved it
eons past, just as your seamy fingers
manufactured so much human culture,
all that encloses, sparks
and clothes the nakedness of flesh and
mind and spirit,
Helen, you always were the factory.
Helen you always were the factory.
Helen you always were the factory.
Helen you always were producer.
Helen you always were
who ever is
the weaving tree
and Mother of the people.

Juan Felipe Herrera

POETRY is the flowers which grow out of experience; after turmoil comes contemplation: mother of pearl boats on the Pacific. It is peaceful thought that rhythmically dances with and explains, reacts to, reality. Music is a biological treatment upon the nerves totally destroying us. Poetry enters through reason and makes us disappear; the heavens could be similar, but everyone uses different transportation.

With Juan Felipe Herrera we could say that his mind is at his ankles, in his belly, or somehow ahead of you in the room you are about to enter. In the person and in the poetry the entity knows no limitations—his light zooms down on México City, San Diego, the Mission District of San Francisco, Cactus; it swings from Cactus into the imagery of the 1950s. We get views of small California towns and preurban characters who saw the construction trucks enroute towards the city carrying the materials to build skyscrapers.

The mark of a great poem is the administration of balance, between action and meditation, the earthly and the celestial, the imaginative life flirting with the practical. Within Juan Felipe's poetry we find this quality present organically: it is there without the need of strenuous thought to mold it.

Think of the crossroads he is suspended in: linguistically, Spanish and English. Through the Spanish he is connected to the great poetic pulse of Spain and Latin America, to the singers of *Boleros* and cultivators of *El Cuento*. His mind is constantly translating back and forth between two world languages, and we are all the more enriched by his method of synthesis. The Spanish of the Americas unifies diversities. It has been infused with indigenous and African vocabularies. As such, it is the language of evolution; it secretly contains old

Arabian tales and ancient native mythological flashbacks—
Herrera is drippling all this through the tongue of Milton and
Shakespeare. But his English is not English. He might not be
able to go to Margaret Thatcher's house with his hispanectical
hybrid verses. But neither would Thatcher be able to visit his
adobe, making the vacuum for her much greater 'cause there's
a mean chili at Juan Felipe's place that could stretch your
tongue beyond the confines of your cheek.

His poetry expands without missing the minute; he takes
local issues into the stars; he listens to the suggestion made by
the neighboring folklore and takes it beyond the horizon. I was
going to say "minuet" instead of "minute" because it is also a
dance or organized flurries—look at that "or" quickly followed
by another "or" to go on to "ganized"—he breaks the language
down in that manner occasionally exploding into sculpture.

He is a learned poet mixing reality to the explosions of lan-
guage sound. He is interested in both the shape and meaning of
his deliveries: he filters all global cultures through his classical
seashell. History and politics weave through the poetry in non-
dogmatic forms. Study how he could mix the qualities of an
essay into a lyric. He sets the issue of politics versus art for us
into perspective; he is looking for a liberation that is much
more than just physical rupture, and he unhinges our minds
from colonialisms and imperialisms whether personal or gov-
ernmental with the intonations of his words. He knows that the
space of nature will blast through all the polemicals—he seems
to know what people mean even when they themselves don't
know what they are saying.

Juan Felipe Herrera is as close as we come to a total expres-
sion mechanism. His senses are not just multicultural; they are
coming at us through a variety of artistic forms. He is a writer,
poet, musician, and actor; he could make you the rail carrying a
train shaped blues guitar. He lives on the wires connecting all
forms, and readers of this book are only getting a glimpse of
what he is doing—you must imagine the gestures, the panto-
mime, the street talker, the singer. His inventive somersaults
are always packed with a parade of information that helps us
live the now. When he writes about events that have occurred
they seem to be following him, because he knows the symbols

and is not fooled by anything, not stuck on trivial facts; his poetry reveals to us and leaves us naked in front of the mirror and our face is never in that mirror because it is a game that the gods are playing.

—Victor Hernández Cruz

From

FACEGAMES (1987)

Story & King Blvd:
Teen-age Totems

SKIRT fenders on a two-tone Plymouth like the one my uncle
Ferni drove to Mexico City back in '57. At night the street
looks like Xmas. Angelina ran away from the shelter. Her foster
mother wants to keep her, but she lost her license. She got
caught with cocaine, the kids said. Angie's boyfriend used to
bring it over. Now, this is heresay, ok? He got stabbed last
week. He said he was going to support her. I used to want to be
a singer. Her grandfather did things to her for years. She just
met her brother who's 19 years old. They told me he was my
uncle. I hate social workers, why don't they leave me alone. You
have to turn yourself in to the shelter, Angie. Maybe when I
have my baby, my mom will be happy. I know she will. And
we'll talk and she'll take care of me. I hate her. She misses you.
She hits my sister all the time. She says its ok to go out, but,
when I come home she calls me a slut. The counselor is looking
for your file. But, I am going to have my baby, anytime, now.
What are you going to name him, her? It's going to be a boy.
Anthony, or maybe, Carlos. She manipulates you, she knows
the system. She can't have her way. She's still under age. 14.
Tell her I have a satellite home for her. As of now, I have a
warrant on her. I used to want to be a singer. Who's that girl at
the bus stop. It's midnight.

Revolution Skyscraper

*"Let me count the stars inside you
and breathe the air in your mouth."*

—*Margarita Luna Robles*

LOOK at me! I am a tux dressed crew-cut Chicano lifting an invisible curtain with my eyebrows. I walk & shuffle down this asphalt album where humans are paisley notes stretching by the neon lit fast food chicken special signs. Warm breeze on a Sunday nite. Listen to me. The Japanese are busy finishing with the Obon festival on Jackson street selling tickets for the two thousand dollar raffle. The guy calling me to buy 5 for three dollars reminds me of an old sergeant. But, deep inside he's a No-No boy. He'll never forget Manzanar, Tule Lake, the Loyalty oath in front of the Mad Salivator Recruit dog monster called America back in '42. I can see the tattoo—NISEI RE-VENGE—through the finely pressed khaki shirt, man! Strolling. That's what I call it. The sky is a blue-black newspaper cut out with a Marine bayonet screaming "Ban Gay Sex" in a Supreme Court accent. God's moon quivers epileptic with secret sperm. They don't want nobody cruising or dancing on the street in spicy angles. Only Soldier positions are legal in Freetown. Maxim #5: Destroy every human cell that spells Love. Everything is on a fancy ferris wheel of blood, disguise and artificial crank. Basketball idols and football heros crackle on a pyre at the center of Main Street, and the music from a lonely and heart-torn Corvette of teen resentments spills. All the bedroom windows are breaking into a confetti of hot laughter. Heterosex-Megaton Man is wearing his favorite polka-dot tie and is on a tap dance marathon with the Soviets. I think of Little Manuel in second grade. Logan Heights Varrio. 1957. I see Ms. Simmons slamming him in the cloak room. Manuel is frozen. Looking into a red liquid mirror on the oak grain floor. You ain't nothing but a hound dog. *Elvis and Chevys Forever* is written on every classroom wall. The horrible cloak room shrinks and disappears into a yellow knot with the face of Csilla Molnar; a seventeen year old blonde beauty queen that committed suicide today because she couldn't handle all the attention that the public was giving her. Csilla and the public and in-between, the Mad Salivator Recruit Dog counts the dollars in his pin-stripe jacket. Csilla, your hair is olive oil pouring from the Hyatt Regency, slowly, covering all the escape ladders with feverish glass. Pink fingernail polish floods the dining rooms. Olive tar webs stream down the Manikin panty house empire legs twitching in the Department store. Csilla, Miss Hungary 1986, can you hear me? My uncle Beto Quintana taught us all about rage in a Mexican way. I never thought I would tell you this. In the 20's we migrated North with thousands carrying splinters and old vases. My mother, Lucha, my aunt, Lela, my grandmother, Juanita: three in black silent mourning of a life past crucified with brick beds and long walks through *La Colonia Roma* looking for food and Destiny. Later, somehow, in El Paso, my uncle put together a comedy show—El Barco de La Illusión—where he showed *Tin-Tan* how to crack a joke and where *El Charro Avitia* made his first debut. Then, one day he came here, made tortillas on a tortilla machine, Mexican candy in dark kettles and spun Mexican oldies for Radio KOFY. We followed. His hands were made of anise and basil. He took us to the wharf where the illegal boats docked. And he opened up the crate of smuggled songs and literature. I'll never forget you. I'll never forget you. And we scattered about, on an infinite orange shore looking for each other, again. My love, come closer, now. I need you. Weave your arms through me. Pour your burning opal breasts into me; spin their twin halos inside me, glowing closer above the ruby forests of my soul. Forever. Kiss me. Listen to me. This is the most elegant nation in the world. I love the new fashions for '88. Don't you? All the floors are clean. Waxed properly. The aisle glistens. The Mayor dances to the numbers that are predictable. Minority Matthew says he will sell you the Real Last Letters of Slavery. The Rock top hit of the year—*Afrikan Murder*—blasts out. Everyone is feeling romantic. The hands of Victor Jara and the flayed heart of Rodrigo Rojas fall out of Nowhere, like phosphorescent meteors and explode into Red palm trees spurting gold honey

on the plaza. At the dark hour of five. *A las cinco de la tarde.*
¡Eran las cinco en todos relojes! ¡Ay que terribles cinco de la
tarde! ¡Que no quiero verla! Díle a la luna que no quiero ver la
sangre de Rodrigo sobre la arena. Can you hear the scream
from the basement of the General Hospital? A brown baby is
crying, standing, pointing at you. A wave of bees crashes out of
the billion watt Gibson amp in her chest.

Linda Hogan

LINDA HOGAN (1947–   ), a Chickasaw originally from Oklahoma, now teaches and writes in Colorado. A poet, playwright, essayist, novelist, she has published four volumes of poetry, *Calling Myself Home* (1978), *Daughters, I Love You* (1981), *Eclipse* (1983), *Seeing Through The Sun* (1985) and most recently, a novel, *Mean Spirit* (1990).

In an interview with Joseph Bruchac in his collection of interviews entitled *Survival This Way* (1987), Hogan says of her work:

> . . . There is a life deep inside of me that always asserts itself. It is the dark and damp, the wet imagery of my beginnings. Return. A sort of deep structure to myself, the framework. It insists on being written and refuses to give me peace unless I follow its urges. Then the earth opens and a memory comes out and says Write this. Or an old person says, 'Tell this: people need to know.' Or the creatures of the planet emerge beautiful and breathing—and who could omit them in all their grace?

It is this desire, this concern for preserving culture, land, and voice that defines Hogan's work. The public political commitment and the private creative world are one. Writer Paula Gunn Allen in *The Sacred Hoop* (1986) notes,

> The fundamental tribal understanding that Hogan possesses also protects her from falling into the simplistic rhetoric of activist propaganda; her politics are deeply knitted to her vision, and her vision . . . is a result of her being Indian. Being an Indian enables her to resolve the conflict that presently divides the non-Indian feminist community; she does not have to choose between spirituality and political commitment, for each is the complement of the

other. They are two wings of one bird, and that bird is the knowledge of the interconnectedness of everything.

—Shawn Wong

Planting a Cedar

From beneath a stone
the black ants hurry,
the old dark ones
fierce as slaves
protecting new white larvae
from danger or sun.

Let us care for those who protect.
They are blessed with numbered days
and labor.

As for the young in their cells,
they are surrounded by white swaddling,
by what they must swallow
and eat their way through.
Already they push at walls
like our own children
covered in so many words
there is nothing left for them to know.

I did not mean to disturb plain life
or sit this long
beside the stone's country. It is late
and the men have arrived home
with lunch pails rattling,
and the women have removed
laundry blowing from the lines.

I didn't mean to find myself
wrapped around the little finger of this town
I wear like a white lie.
I didn't mean to find myself
wrapped around the doubting finger
of these towns.

November

For Meridel LeSueur

The sun climbs down
the dried out ladders of corn.
Its red fire walks down the rows.
Dry corn sings, *Shh, Shh.*

The old sky woman has opened her cape
to show off the red inside
like burning hearts
holy people enter.

I will walk with her.
We are both burning.
We walk in the field of dry corn
where birds are busy gleaning.

The corn says, *Shh.*
I walk beside the pens holding animals.
The old woman sun rises,
red, on the backs of small pigs.

She rides the old sow
down on her knees in mud.
Her prayers do not save her.
Her many teats do not save her.

I won't think of the butcher walking away
with blood on his shoes,
red footprints of fire. In them
the sow walks away from her own death.

The sun rides the old sow
like an orange bird on its back.
God save the queen.
Her castle rises in the sky and crumbles.

She has horses the color of wine.
The little burgundy one
burns and watches while I walk.
The rusty calves watch with dark eyes.

The corn says, *Shh,*
and birds beat the red air
like a dusty rug. They sing
God save the queen.

My hair burns down my shoulders.
I walk. I will not think we are blood sacrifices.
No, I will not watch the ring-necked pheasant
running into the field of skeletal corn.

I will walk into the sun.
Her red mesas are burning
in the distance.
I will enter them. I will walk into that stone,

walk into the sun
away from night rising up the other side of earth.
There are sounds in the cornfield,
Shh. Shh.

Night and Day

At night, alone,
the world is a river in me.
Sweet rain falls in the drought.
Leaves grow from lightning-struck trees.

I am across the world from daylight
and know the inside of everything
like the black corn dolls
unearthed in the south.

Near this river
the large female ears of corn listen and open.
Stalks rise up the layers of the world
the way it is said some people emerged
bathed in the black pollen of poppies.

In the darkness, I say,
my face is silent.
Like the corn dolls
my mouth has no more need to smile.

At midnight,
there is an eye in each of my palms.

I said, I have secret powers at night,
dark as the center of poppies,
rich as the rain.

But by morning I am filled up
with some stranger's lies
like those little corn dolls.
Unearthed after a hundred years
they have forgotten everything
in the husk of sunlight

and business
and all they can do is smile.

Turning

The fevers of winter have flown away
and we rest in the empty palm of the house
like the shadows of animals
that lived here, chameleons
with starry fingers invisible on white walls,
deer breathing in the shadows.

We were almost
clenched in winter's fist
but the green leaves
are exploding from the trees.
Across the way, a woman's voice singing,
the song arriving like silk and spice
from Asia. Throw open the windows,
it's spring! All I held in
my winter breast turns back
into the world, an inverse body,
the universe turned inside out
singing and breaking through
the four red chambers of earth's heart.
Everything is alive.
The deer hooves clatter out of the shadows,
chameleons turn deep green.

I remember spring loves
and drunk kisses in the hills.
Things bloom in a woman's singing voice,
through open windows and longing.
Even nations are yielding

and there is the moonlight and her stars,
a flock of white cranes crossing the dark sky.

Tiva's Tapestry: La Llorona

For Tiva Trujillo, 1979

White-haired woman of winter,
la Llorona
with the river's black
unraveling
drowned children from her hands.

At night frozen leaves
rustle the sound of her skirt.
Listen and wind comes spinning
her song from the burning eyes of animals
from the owl
whose eyes look straight ahead.
She comes dragging
the dark river
a ghost on fire
for children she held
under water.

Stars are embroidered on the dark.
Long shadows, long like rivers
I am sewing
shut the doors
filling the windows in with light.
This needle pierces a thousand kisses
and rage
the shape of a woman.
I light this house,
sprinkle salt on my sleeping child
so dreams won't fly her into the night.

These fingers have sewn a darkness
and flying away
on the white hair growing
on the awful tapestry of sky
just one of the mothers
among the downward circling stars.

Susan Howe

"I WRITE to break out into perfect primeval Consent. I wish to tenderly lift from the dark side of history, voices that are anonymous, slighted—inarticulate" *(The Europe of Trusts).*

In midlife Susan Howe (1937–   ) turned from visual art to literary art, creating and publishing a singular and significant trio of books in the 1980s: *The Liberties* (1980), *Pythagorean Silence* (1982), and *Defenstration of Prague* (1983). It is her sense of history's presence, its illusions, deliberate confusions, emblematic and exclusively (and excluding) male motifs, that is the ground of her invention.

> From 1939 until 1946 in news photographs, day after day I saw signs of culture exploding into murder. Shots of children being herded into trucks by hideous helmeted conquerors—shots of children who were orphaned and lost—shots of the emaciated bodies of Jews dumped into mass graves on top of more emaciated bodies—nameless numberless men, women, and children, uprooted in a world almost demented. God had abandoned them to history's sovereign Necessity. If to see is to *have* at a distance, I had so many dead Innocents distance was abolished. *(The Europe of Trusts)*

Her interrogations of history (its dominant and dominating official versions) commingle with experimental and high lyrical richness. Howe shows that not only is the political personal but, obviously, history is personal as well. History's totalizing narratives, fascinating and revealing as they are, are fragmented, incomplete, partial. Not unlike H. D., Howe enters history to amplify it, personalize it, reinvest it with exiled presences and voices.

For me there was no silence before armies. . . . Malice dominates the history of Power and Progress. History is the record of winners. Documents were written by the Masters. But fright is formed by what we see not by what they say. *(The Europe of Trusts)*

Howe's three books of poetry are, I believe, a tiered declaration of a major post-modernist poet. I wince to use the word "post-modern" to describe a poet so deeply informed by the cultural history of modernism and the American Renaissance of the late nineteenth century, as well as earlier Anglo-Irish literatures. Nevertheless, while her experimentation avoids the de-centering or de-personalizing tendency of many post-modern poets, she uses many of their technical and structural devices. Despite the textured complexities and polyphonic voicings, Howe's work never loses direction or center.

Categories and hierarchies suggest property. My voice formed from my life belongs to no one else. What I put into words is no longer my possession. Possibility has opened. The future will forget, erase, or recollect and deconstruct every poem. There is a mystic separation between poetic vision and ordinary living. The conditions for poetry rest outside each life at a miraculous reach indifferent to worldly chronology. *(The Europe of Trusts)*

Howe's meta-history, *My Emily Dickinson* (1985), represents a landmark in creative scholarship and originality, matching the significance, a generation earlier, of Charles Olson's re-vision of Herman Melville in *Call Me Ishmael* (1947). It is a profoundly realized immersion into Dickinson's work and functions as a feminist critique as well, disrupting many normative feminist (and masculinist) readings of Dickinson. Informed by American spiritual rhetoric from diverse texts—Indian captivity narratives written by women, Jonathan Edwards's sermons, Shakespeare's poetry and plays—Howe widens the scope of Dickinson's work and grants her readers permission to reinvestigate the sociocultural world Dickinson inhabited. *My Emily Dickinson* is a work written in a language of quest and shared discovery, instead of in the vocabulary-barricaded, constipated language of works upholding the status quo and releasing little or no light.

> Poetry is the great stimulation of life. Poetry leads past possession of self to transfiguration beyond gender. Poetry is redemption from pessimism. Poetry is affirmation in negation, ammunition in the yellow eye of a gun that an allegorical pilgrim will shoot straight into the quiet of Night's frame. *(My Emily Dickinson)*

—*Shawn Wong*

From

THE EUROPE OF TRUSTS (1990)

The Liberties

her diary soared above her house

over heads of

those clouds
are billows below
spume
white
tossed this way
or that
wild geese in a stammered place
athwart and sundered
for the sea rose and sheets clapped at sky
and sleep the straggler led the predator away
(Say, *Stella,* feel you no Content
Reflecting on a Life well spent?)
Bedevikke bedl
bedevilled by a printer's error
the sight of a dead page filled her with terror
garbled version
page in her coffin. . . .
Do those dots mean that the speaker lapsed
into silence?

Often I hear Romans murmuring
I think of them lying dead in their graves.

Excerpt from
THEIR Book of Stella

trackless near sea   relating to sea
a sea of arms in my dispeopled kingdom
autumn till summer   homeland till dusk
      or whatsoever
plague   famine   pestilence
there in me   them in me   I
halted   I heard footsteps

fearsad bell   high stone wall
       evensong
    the blue of sweet salvation
such roads between the uplands
              over the lowered cols
eden éadan   brow of a hill
        as many lives
       as there are loaves
     and fishes
and O
     her voice
         a settled place
table spread   flesh and milk
        in mystery
      in the room
     in the sunlight
    about the dead
who come from west-the-sea
    raiment
        shirt-clad and light-clad

/   /   /   /

a
thin
nine
year
old
child

starlit
outlasting mother's hood

hereways
asquint
askew

(a
body
of
eyes
in shadow)

O cinders of Eve, what is my quest?

Kept watch
on the fixed promontory
of Howth

                          torches of dried bogwood
                          to light the bride over ravines
causeway
    stone-paved
      and others

                          memory written in meadows
              traditions still flit
                  he was born
                  kingly descent
                  made great progress
                  in learning
                  and loneliness
                  gave names
                  to different places
                  did not sleep here
                        Oldest idolatries called Arkite
the first danger
the first crossing

                hiatus
                chiasma
                a kind of death
John the Mad or Furious, fought like a true Berserker

a LEAP

      creates the pursuer
        stained mantle
crimson, blue, or green
           SHE DIED OF SHAME
           This is certain—
           That is mist—
           I cannot hold—
The sailors return
Did they really cross the sea?

        broken oar or spare
      healingly into a depth of
              hour
      or place
        or drifting face
     whomsoever
       even the least
     rowed as never woman rowed
     rowed as never woman rowed
through the whole history of her story
             through pain
    and peril
      the shores sang

The real plot was invisible
everything possible
was the attempt for the finest thing
was the attempt
him over the bridge into the water
her some sort of daughter

events now led to a region
returned in a fictional direction
I asked where that road to the left lay
and they named the place
Predestination
automaton whose veiled face
growing wings
or taking up arms
must always undo or sever
HALLUCINATION OF THE MIRROR

Excerpt from
WHITE FOOLSCAP

Book of Cordelia

            heroine in ass-skin
            mouthing O Helpful
            =father revivified waking when
nickname Hero men take pity spittle speak

            only nonsense
            my bleeding foot
            I am maria wainscotted
cap o' rushes tatter-coat
common as sal salt sally
S (golden) no huge a tiny
bellowing augury

                NEMESIS singing from cask
turnspit scullion the apples pick them   Transformation
wax forehead ash
shoe fits monkey-face oh hmm
It grows dark   The shoe fits   She stays a long something
Lent is where she lives   shalbe shalbe
loving like salt (value of salt)

Lir was an ocean God whose children turned into swans
heard the birds pass overhead
Fianoula Oodh Fiachra Conn
circle of One
threshing the sun
or asleep threshing nor
nor blood nor flesh nor bone nor
corona
chromosphere
Cordelia
no no no
the hoth(heath
sline(clear
crystal
song
le
lac
pure
semblance
aperçu

> giggling in a whistling wind
> unbonneted he runs

hrr
  hrru
    hurry
      hare
        haloo
          cry Whoop
          and cry Spy!
pauses   measures   feet in syllables   caesura   Copernicus
                                    the sun
                                    is a cloud
                                    of dust.
            has his children brought him to this pass?
                    Whowe
arrowy sleet
      bale the sea
      out and in
                stormstil stormstil
      shuttle and whiz

Excerpt from
III. Formation of a
Separatist, I

                                                                S

                        rebuke   boyne
             churn   alpha   bet   a   keep
    1727   expose   blade   broken   hid

    pierce   hang   sum
    clear   hester   quay   Liberties   46
    tense   whisper   here   libel   foam
    print   pen   dot   i   still
                 hole   yew   skip   1.

C

```
3.          bare          cube          arm          white
glass          weary          medium          verge
physic          stone          pane          golden
thin          swallow          concept          nor
dower          darker     ha          hue          yell
crisscross          luminate          wheel          a
up          wild          crown          flame          sa
tom          sa          nero          mum          mum
exeunt          fool          vault          tucket
clap          no          machination          fum          3
```

C

love	tongue	milk	pasture	words
bare	arm	cause	cube	words
inherit	cause	willow		words
barbary	sister	glade	he	words
say	nothing	verbatim	alarum	words
dower	cause	pierce	willow	words

bolt.
look.

leaves	sound	intonation	so	no
rustling	benediction	stain		no
broken	un	lips	here	look	no
stir	last	O	see	wal	no

I am composed of nine letters.
1 is the subject of a proposition in logic.
2 is a female sheep, or tree.
3 is equal to one.
4 is a beginning.
5 & 7 are nothing
6 7 & 8 are a question, or salutation.
6 7 8 & 9 are deep, a depression.

THE KEY

e n i g m a s t i f e m i a t e d c r y p t o a t h
a b c d e f g h i j k l m n o p q r s t u v w x y
                    z or zed
                    graphy
                    reland
                        I

Speak out.
Do not bawl.
Speak so   *What are eyes for?*
that all   *What are ears for?*
in the room   Tension
will hear   Torsion
you.   Traction
                                     Unction
                                     Vection
                                     Version
                                     Vision

(Vere passum, immolatum
O dulcis Jesu, Fili Maria
O distant
      Precipitant
Lord
    Word
  strew of words
Aine, the moon
        pleasure
            the sea
      An or Aon
(irish) One

blood and water streaming
swift to its close
ebbs out
    out
     of
    my pierced side
        not in my native land.

Across the Atlantic, I
inherit myself
semblance
of irish susans
dispersed
and narrowed to
home

Namesake
old Friends,
on the seashore at Irishtown

not in your native land.

Excerpt from HEAR

1.   antimony   one

two   antimony   2.

splash   atomies   dare

tangle   3.   trinity I

Liberties   sigil   C

willow   whitethorn   yew

1.   2.   3.   x

one   two   three   =

poesie   sign   wave   9.

(Aside.)   (Aside.)

(Grasping his sword.)
only   air   hear

SOJOURNER
—if that definition of truth is correct
that truth is what always remains—
(Pause.)
Peace at my tears for I am a stranger.

    Enter BASTARD, solus with a
                S
           (Horns within.

    Enter FOOL
    (Sleeps.)
    Here set at liberty

Tear pages from a calendar
scatter them into sunshine and snow

Robert Kelly

"Write everything."

—*Robert Kelly,* Kali Yuga *(1971)*

THE author's note to Robert Kelly's book, *Kill the Messenger Who Brings Bad News* (1979) begins somewhat querulously: "Everything that ought to be known about Robert Kelly can be found in his books, of which this is the fortieth." The photograph of Kelly printed there shows a long-bearded intensely staring man who is not smiling. The ending of the book, however, is prophetic, tender, and erotic—though perhaps tinged also with sexism:

> Go soft
> young man and she will love thee,
> exerting her own power to lift you both
> —that is how yearning is best satisfied,
> when the man sleeps and the woman labors
> making the mill turn round the stone.

Robert Kelly was born in Brooklyn in 1935, and he has published a great many books since his first, *Armed Descent*, appeared in 1961. Among them are *Her Body Against Time* (1963); *Enstasy* (1964); *The Common Shore* (1969); *In Time* (1971), for which he won the Before Columbus Foundation's American Book Award; *The Mill of Particulars* (1973); *Spiritual Exercises* (1981); and *Under Words* (1983). One book, *The Alchemist to Mercury* (1981), was edited by Jed Rasula as an "alternative opus" to Kelly's other work: twenty years of *un*collected work which Rasula had tracked down in magazines and in the poet's notebooks.

Kelly's poetry is, one feels, deeply sexual and, at times, deeply personal. Yet the poet insists that it is not at the personal level that he wishes us to confront him. Poets are, he writes in *In Time,* "the last scientists of the Whole":

> so
> these now, from us all,
> nothing personal. . . .The poet is "the
> DISCOVERER OF RELATION."
>
>
> redintegrator,
>   explorer of ultimate connection
> & connectedness in among & all

In search of what he once called "a polysyntactic liberty," Kelly's work ranges widely, both in form and in content, and he is highly aware of language and its etymology. The poetry which concerns him, he writes in his anthology *A Controversy of Poets* (1965), "demands everything the reader has. . . ." Poets, he says quoting Heidegger, are agents of a "multiple mobility": "The multiplicity of possible interpretations does not discredit the strictness of the thought-content" ("Texts: 16"). As he puts it in *In Time,* poets "do not have hobbies / they eat / everything." In this thrust towards the universe, Kelly places himself in the tradition of writers such as William Blake, Walt Whitman, Ezra Pound, William Carlos Williams, Louis Zukofsky, and Charles Olson—the "Charles of Worcester" to whom *In Time* is dedicated.

In his long poem, *The Loom* (1975), he quotes from an unnamed alchemist: "These discoveries have given rise to the idea that one substance can be transformed into another, so that a rough, coarse and beshitten substance can be transmuted into one that is pure, refined, and sound." And in his own "Alchemical Journal" he writes, "The anguish of the Work is the discovery of the correspondences." It is in this sense, I think, that Kelly wishes us to see "nothing personal" in his work. The poems are not confessional but are a continual assertion of, to use a term dear to both Swedenborg and Baudelaire, *correspondances.* Poetry is the exploration, not of selfhood, but of a world which is intensely *alive*, in which even the "rough, coarse and beshitten" may suddenly transform itself into pure gold. "Everything thinks," he writes in "Noemics" *(The Alchemist to Mercury)*, echoing Gerard de Nerval, who is himself echoing Pythagoras. Kelly's Irishness is complicated and has been explored in a number of texts, but surely a prominent aspect of it is related to the occultism of writers such as Yeats, AE, or even the Scottish Robert Kirk, whose researches into the lore of the Faery gave him a reputation as a "walker between worlds."

I mentioned to a friend recently that I had seen few of Kelly's poems in those little magazines by which poets communicate with one another. But perhaps I have been reading the wrong magazines. As we enter the confused and violent nineties, one senses the need for a voice like Kelly's, for "an explorer of ultimate connection / & connectedness." Kelly's work, which includes prose as well as poetry, speaks to the deep need for the poet to leap beyond the personal into the realm of myth—to reconnect the alienated, fragmented, separated "self" to nothing less than the universe as a whole. "A deep breath then," he writes in *In Time*, "Poets out in the open? The shadowy aimlessness of the poet's motive the driving force of everything that moves?" It is a question, not an assertion, but, as Kelly might insist, it is an *open* question, a question posed from neither a personal nor an impersonal standpoint but from the condition of openness itself. The twin axe, he writes ("labyrinth" means "palace of the *labrys*," "of the twin axe").

> chops all our wood
> to begin for all men the making new
>
> *(In Time)*

And from "Text 16":

> "We must stay with the question," says
> Heidegger at sunset on the ruined day.

It is at once this openness and this thrust towards wholeness which gives Kelly's work its richness and value. "Imagine Jesus without psalms without churches," he writes,

> a man on a winter road walking there is no decoding him
> the cipher of his passage is impeccable the wind
> is the dog at his feet the wind is the cat in his arms
> the wind is the breath that powers his walking
>
> I can hear nothing of him I can understand nothing
> but when I see him on the road there is a walking
> begins then inside me a hurrying in starlight a sunrise
> over frozen roads a midday scandal of luminous rushing

(Spiritual Exercises)

—*Jack Foley*

From
IN TIME (1971)

(pre f i x:

as (& not as)
the logographoi preceded Herodotos

but as (tho not as)
Novalis & Nietzsche preceded
Spengler & Kantorowicz

these gists in time, ours, these
as
   (& thus as)
chips or flakes
from our latest pleistocene,
craft,

the poets (now)
last scientists of the Whole

busy at their work

so
these now, from us all,
nothing personal,

shall precede some
formulator
            who will
be able to reckon,
                  in prose

(i.e., poetry an earlier form, embryologically,
         solid now,

but the prose of our horizon
            not yet made,

in prose,
later,
the dimensions of this
universal century & frontier time

re: Snow Jobs / we have got:

                    riding out over the whine
                    of the not-unjustified
                    universal bitching about
                    specialization
                    (in sciences & scholarship, as a bad thing)
                                                        is the fact
                    that there can be (& at historical times
                                    has been, now is)
                    a scientist of holistic understanding,
                    a scholar,
                                    a scientist of the whole
the Poet—
                    be aware that from *inside* comes
                        the poet, scientist of totality,
                                specifically,
                        to whom all data whatsoever are of use,
                    world-scholar
(from which infer the triviality of current trimmers & rhyme-
sters, viz that they are not interested or interesting themsel-
ves in anything everything &c)
                                Pound Goethe Coleridge (off
                                        the top of my head)
                            greatness from the breadth
of their *concerns,*
                    i.e. one (if only one) index is exactly

that breadth,
                    they do not have hobbies

they eat
                    everything
                        true index: breadth of radiance

  or splendor
                            poet as world-scholar,
                                holist,
      (poet here = maker (with words)
    (even as from the health of technology comes
                            information-theory

          & from computer praxis
        to unitize
                (as first steps (o = 1)
                    to unity, création du monde)
        poet then not the encyclopædia (à la McLuhan thesis)
                    but the DISCOVERER OF RELATION,
            redintegrator,
            explorer of ultimate connection
            & connectedness in among & all
      (& if we let teleology or divine providence in: that's why
        poets are hounded from place to place & job to job,
          to keep them moving over the whole earth
      whole surface of act & process & learning & doing,
                        children of Cain the wanderer
                            whence music & the fashioning
                            of metal
                            all
                                material
            for our use,
                    at-one-ing
                            the world

NINTH MATTER: Shape

schaft / scaap / scop

>   ('inscane' morphemically useful)

the function & meaning of *contour*

a) human, humanus, plausibly connects with
   humus, the ground, i.e., the intelli-
   gent animals that walk on the ground,
   that (to be specific)
   >   follow the contours
   or shape contours of their own.

>   Thus we are biologically bound to "shape"

b) Terminus : edge : limit : boundary

c) 'Platonic' solids

d) *topology,*
>   properties of contour,
>   as paradigm & paradise

e) here, if anywhere, to reassemble the
   old hierarchy of correspondences &
   signatures, the
   >   *Resemblances*
   by perception of which a man learns
   the world, his own attentions, his own
   capacities.
f) & learns to follow the lines that lead to Her.

TENTH MATTER: Story

(Narrative. How we tell. How is told.
What tells. What is told.)

muthos & logos do not separate in usage
                    till Pindar.

a word, what is it, a telling,
a science of utterance?

"Writing wants to go on"
                    (—Gertrude Stein,
in whose 4 essays in *Narration* we may
find a beginning).

a) Thousand nights & a night.
b) Mishle Sendabar & Petrus Alfonsi.
c) Jesus's parables.
d) Mulla Nasruddin
e) fabliaux
f) Miss Stein
g) Mr Dorn
h) is there any meaning to this phrase:
    experimental narrative forms?

Cf Stith Thompson's great *Motif Index*—is
        the motif then a germ of story,
& if so, what of the sense we have that the
story telling is the story told?

Maurice Kenny

"Set up the drum" begins one of Maurice Kenny's poems, conjuring up an image which fits both the sound and the sense of this Mohawk poet's work. The drum of that particular poem, "December," is both an instrument of music and a medium for healing prayers. So, too, are Maurice Kenny's poems prayer songs. Those songs may be celebrations of his heritage or laments, satires or paeans of joy and praise. The sounds of Iroquois social dance rhythms are in many of his lines, just as images of home, of loss, of longing, and of a heritage too long denied abound in his writing.

On one level, Kenny's work has been a journey towards the claiming of a name denied to him by parents who turned away from their Iroquois roots. Indeed, it was not until the publication of The Mama Poems in 1984 that Maurice Kenny began to be specific in his poems about his actual family and the precise "home" he alluded to in his work, even though his first book was published when he was twenty-eight, in the late 1950s.

Born in 1929 near the St. Lawrence River in the traditional lands of the "People of the Flint," his Mohawk ancestors, Maurice Kenny was taken south to Bayonne, New Jersey at the age of eleven to live with his mother. A year later, when he was in danger of being sent to reform school, Kenny's father came to New York to rescue his son, taking him back north to live with him and attend school in Watertown, New York. But Kenny's questing spirit led him to leave the north country after high school. He lived in Manhattan, where he worked in a bookstore, studied with Louise Bogan, and published poetry—though he was rejected by the Beats. He spent two years in Mexico as Willard Motley's personal secretary. He opened a night club in Puerto Rico. He wrote obituaries and handled classified ads for the Chicago *Sun-Times*. Finally, in 1967, Kenny settled in Brooklyn. This time it would not be until 1985 that he would return to the North Country. While in New York City he supported the writing of his poems with work as "Maurice, the French waiter," until he suffered a serious heart attack in 1974. That nearly fatal experience was crucial to Kenny, for it refocussed his attention on his poetry and on his Native American roots. The years immediately following would see the publication of some of his best-known work, including such chant-like and incantatory poems as "I Am the Sun." The impact of Kenny as a reader of his own work can only be compared to that of such gifted poetic performers as Dylan Thomas. Anyone lucky enough to hear one of his moving readings can easily understand critic James Ruppert's comment that "for Kenny, song/poetry is always religious." By the 1980s, his work had brought him such prominence that he was invited to teach, accepting appointments first at the University of Oklahoma and later at North Country Community College in the upstate New York town of Saranac Lake, which would become his new home—only an hour's drive away from the Mohawk Nation at Akwesasne.

Though he might joke about being an elder, few would deny that Maurice Kenny has been "setting up the drum" longer and more successfully than any other contemporary Native American poet. No Native writer has been more widely published. At last count, his published books numbered twenty-four and his poems have been translated into a dozen languages. With the exception of N. Scott Momaday, no Indian author has been more influential than Kenny in shaping the course of contemporary Native American writing. Through his poems and essays, through his encouragement of young Native American voices as editor of *Contact/II* and Strawberry Press, and through his example as a pathfinder and often outspoken voice, Kenny has been a seminal part of an American Indian literary blossoming which is as exciting and important for American writing as was the Harlem Renaissance of the 1920s.

This is not to say that Kenny's voice or his presence are always as lyrical and gentle as certain of his poems. His humor

can be satiric and biting, and the picture he paints of life—
both Indian and non-Indian—in the latter half of the twen-
tieth century is not a romantic one. It is the tale of our time
seen through the eyes of a wise person of Native blood attempt-
ing, against all kinds of odds, to understand, celebrate, express,
and claim his heritage. His work exposes the irony of a culture
which classifies a person as "black" if they have any touch of
African ancestry and yet says on the other hand that any Native
American person with white blood is no longer really Indian. In
the end, to quote his poem "For Those who Doubt," Maurice
Kenny proves that he is, indeed, "a man by any count or legal
declaration." Kenny's victory as a writer is an inspiration to all
those who long, despite being dispossessed and dismissed, to
find their strength in song.

—*Joseph Bruchac III*

Sometimes . . . Injustice

The day I was born my father bought me a 22.
A year later my mother traded it for a violin.
Ten years later my big sister traded that
for a guitar, and gave it to her boy-friend . . .
who sold it.

Now you know why I never learned to hunt,
or learned how to play a musical instrument,
or became a Wall St. broker.

Boy in the Bay Window 1939

Go out to play, she said!
          chickens pecking under rounds of peonies
          garter snakes hiding in vetch

Something about the morning . . .
          cold dew, the strut of the drake
          the fall of barn shadows

Something about the noon . . .
          hornets in tulips
          a hobo, the buzz of gnats

Something about the afternoon . . .
      aunts' gossip between kneading bread
        and rolling out pie dough
      grandma's snores in the parlor
        which mustn't be disturbed
      mailmen tipping the red flag with news

Something about the summer . . .
      he stared out: finch hunting lice
        in dusty feathers
      gobblers under currant bushes . . .
        bats wakened in the dimming light
      and uncles would come home drunk
        with a sunset glow of rouge on the chin

Joshua Clark

Three Mile Bay, N.Y. July 1979

> *"Kind and loving husband and tender to your
> flock."*
>
>   . . . *gravestone epitaph*

I

name stained in colored glass
on the Baptist window erected
in the English spirit of your fervor

let me tell you, Pastor Joshua,
great-great-great grandfather,
bred in the clover spring of 1802,
bed to Sybil, sire of Mary
sire to the stones of this
seedy cemetery bloody from veins
opened to the summer breeze,

let me tell you, Joshua,
even your bones are dust.
the headstone chips in the sun
white asters climb
moisture of the grasses
wending across your name

yes, let me tell you, Joshua Clark,
your great grandson married
the Seneca girl whose father's land
you stole, and his brother drunk
in the velvet parlor lifted cup
by cup the earth to the tavern keeper's smile
yes, my grandfather paid it away, too,
acre by acre to maids that came to dust
his wife's music room and to hired hands
who plowed his father's fields
until only your church and cemetary plot
were left and safe from their foolishness

Joshua, the apple trees have claimed
the house, sumac fill the cellar bins,
the stone foundations bed mice
and snakes prowl your yellow roses
where once you sat in the shade, counting souls
drinking ginger-beer
eyeing the westerly sun
black with barn swallows

your woods are cleared, hickory axed;
there is not a single creek
in those meadows, even bats
and hawks have fled;
your blood has thinned into a trickle . . .
I claim very little and pass nothing on . . .
not a drop to any vein.

your siring is finished, deeds done
and accomplishments or not only a name

remains penned into an old family Bible
and stained in glass, purple and green
of a church no one visits
but skunks and black spiders;
there's enough babies squawking anyway.

II

you were a strong man, strong as the elms
which once reared over the front lawn
and the white pine which fenced the fruit
orchard where ginghamed Sybil plucked
sweet cherry and damson plum
and teased your loins with her pretty English face
her thin ankle and narrow waist;
you were a strong man in the blood
your sap ran April
and you fathered our centuries, our wars
our treacheries, our lies,
our disappointing lives, loves; your fingers
coiled the rope which bound and trussed us all
on the hanging tree, the roots of our feet
dangling over the earth wet with blood
rockets exploding about our ears
deaf and blind as your drunken grandson
to the waste of blackberry brambles
and the loud gnawing of rats in the sweat
of your goose down mattress where Sybil birthed
Mary and all the dawns of your hairy thighs

old cats purr on the supper table
of cold beef; goats munch clean
meadows in the twilight of
birch bending to the rainbows of mornings past.

III

Patty-Lyn and Craig
never read your epitaph,
nor knelt in your Baptist church nor tasted
Sybil's plum preserves, nor haven't
the slightest thought that Ely Parker
was a great Seneca General who had little to do
with your Baptist God;
hands were unfinned, unwebbed for tools
to preserve and beget and protect
all that's beautiful in trout and mallard
all which is remarkable in fire and ice
all which is noble in blood and loin
all which births and dies
in the raging sunset, of dawn;

this half-blood Mohawk condemns your church
to ash and though I would not tamper with the earth
which holds your dust I would chip the stone
flake by flake that heralds your name and deeds
but carry pails of fresh water to the green cedar
rooting in your family plot where my bones
refuse to lay coiled and pithed in the womb
of a tribe which has neither nation nor reason nor drum

my father claims my blood
and sired in the shadow of a turtle my growls
echo in the mountain woods where a bear climbs down
rocks to walk across your grave to leave its prints
upon the summer dust and pauses to sniff a wild hyssop
and break open a bee hive for the honey of the years
and smack its lips on red currants

old cats should be wild and feed on field mice.
Joshua, I've nearly lost the essence of your name
and cannot hear the murmur of your time.
I stand throwing rocks at the stained glass
of your fervor knowing time ceases with the crash

the tinkle of the stones striking glass,
and all our blood between the installation
and the retribution has vaporized into the bite
of a single mosquito sucking my arm
in the summer breeze of this seedy cemetery

now sleep

Black River—Summer 1981

For Patti-Lyn

The evening river carries no sound . . .
not the bark of this fox whose skull
weights my hand,
nor the wind of this hawk
feather tucked into the button hole of my shirt

Rivers grumble and hiss and gurgle;
they roar and sing lullabys;
rivers rage and flow and dance
like unseen wind;
in the dark they carry the eyes
of stars and footprints of deer.

> I have slept on your arm,
> dawn sweetening my mouth,
> stiff in limb
> and rose to your morning song.
>
> I have watched geese fly over,
> eels slither down stream,
> bullheads defy rapids,
> spiders ripple waves
> in trapped inlets along the shore,

fireflies light paths
from murky banks
to mysterious islands
where witches live.

I have studied your waters:

Day-dreamed my watch to listen,
to feel your tremble,
to learn your summer,
touch your winter,
and be content.

Etheridge Knight

"I DIED in Korea from a shrapnel wound and narcotics resurrected me. I died in 1960 from a prison sentence and poetry brought me back to life." Thus Etheridge Knight (1933–1991) once explained how he came to write poetry. *Poems From Prison* (1968), Knight's first book of poems, was published one year before he was released from Indiana State Prison, and in her preface to this collection, Gwendolyn Brooks celebrated Knight's poetry as "a major announcement . . . certainly male—with formidable austerities, dry grins, and a dignity that is scrupulous even when lenient." Knight's reputation grew rapidly as his poems, essays, and short stories began to appear in *Negro Digest (Black World), Journal of Black Poetry, Prison Magazine, Cardinal Poetry Quarterly, Music Journal,* and other periodicals. *Poems From Prison* was a critical success, and between 1969 and 1973 Knight's work was included in many of the new anthologies of African-American literature: *Black Poetry,* edited by Dudley Randall (1969); *Dices and Black Bones,* edited by Adam David Miller (1970); *Black Literature in America,* edited by Houston A. Baker (1971); *The Black Poets,* edited by Dudley Randall (1971), *A Broadside Treasury,* edited by Gwendolyn Brooks (1971); *Afro-American Poetry,* edited by Bernard W. Bell (1972); *Black Writers of America,* edited by Richard Barksdale and Kenneth Kinnamon (1972); *The Poetry of Black America,* edited by Arnold Adoff (1973); and *Understanding the New Black Poetry,* edited by Stephen E. Henderson (1973), among others.

Born in Corinth, Mississippi, Etheridge Knight soon found himself snared by the racism and oppression of a closed society. In 1974 he provided this description of his education for Leonead Pack Bailey who was compiling her biographical direc-

tory, *Broadside Authors and Artists:* "EDUCATION: 'Drop
out. Education in various prisons and street corners thro-out
America,' " However, despite his difficulties—dropping out of
school at fourteen, substance abuse, and incarceration—
Knight managed to distinguish himself through literature. In
1990 he even completed his formal education by earning a
bachelor's degree in American poetry and criminal justice at
Martin Center University in Indianapolis. When his degree
was conferred, he was also named poet laureate of Martin Cen-
ter. Knight has also been awarded fellowships from the Na-
tional Endowment for the Arts and the Guggenheim Founda-
tion; and in 1985, he received the Shelley Memorial Award
from the Poetry Society of America.

An active advocate of poetry as an oral art, Knight quickly
mastered the art of "saying poems" (as he describes his deliv-
ery), and his passionate performances are legendary. He has
initiated a number of community-based activities in the past
two decades, the most successful of which is the Free People's
Poetry Workshop (Memphis, Indianapolis, Minneapolis, and
Worcester, Massachusetts).

Knight began his literary career as the Black arts movement
was emerging in America, and like poets Imamu Amiri Baraka
(LeRoi Jones), Sonia Sanchez (to whom Knight was once mar-
ried), and Haki R. Madhubuti (Don L. Lee), he embraced its
spirit and goals. "The Black Arts Movement," wrote poet-critic
Larry Neal in 1968, "is radically opposed to any concept of the
artist that alienates him from his community. Black Arts is the
aesthetic and spiritual sister of the Black Power concept. As
such, it envisions an art that speaks directly to the needs and
aspirations of Black America." Black Arts writers eschewed
"protest" literature. Implicit in the concept of "protest" litera-
ture, they argued, was an appeal to white morality. Knight, like
Neal, called for the development of a "Black aesthetic":

> Unless the Black artist establishes a "Black aesthetic," he will have
> no future at all. To accept the white aesthetic is to accept and
> validate a society that will not allow him to live. The Black artist
> must create new forms and new values, sing new songs (or purify
> old ones); and along with other Black authorities, he must create a

new history, new symbols, myths and legends (and purify old ones by fire). And the Black artist, in creating his own aesthetic, must be accountable for it only to the Black people. Further, he must hasten his own dissolution as an individual (in the Western sense)—painful though the process may be, having been breast-fed the poison of "individual experience."

Knight's commitment to this idea is evident in all of his creative efforts, not only as a poet-performer but also as an editor and teacher. In 1970 he edited *Black Voices From Prison,* an anthology of prison writing which is in part a strikingly vivid and rigorously clear indictment of the crimes of white society against Blacks. His vision and style inspired other Black prisoners to express themselves creatively and to strive toward a collective celebration of a new Black nationalism.

Since *Black Voices From Prison* Knight published three more volumes of his own poetry: *Belly Song* (1973), *Born of a Woman* (1980), and *The Essential Etheridge Knight* (1986, an American Book Award winner). Each volume demonstrates the poet's willingness to explore different forms and styles— praise songs ("Malcolm X," "Dinah Washington," "Langston Hughes," and "Gwendolyn Brooks"), love poems, portraits, and haikus.

—George Barlow

On Seeing the Black Male as #1 Sex Object in America

There / are / Black men in the south
Of America who / are soooooooo pretty
That their beauty
Sucks in fat gulps the breath from your mouth.
In Nashville, Memphis, Jackson, Lil Rock,
In spots that / are / just dots
On the hi / way to the south and sun—
Tall, "male" men—
Wearing flashing red caps, and hats
With wide brims in bold green, grin.
Black men in the south
Of America / are / soooooooo pretty—
In bright jeans, in tight jeans, bulging;
Shining their cars,
Hanging in the bars,
Leaning on the corners
Where the snow / janes pass
Stroking the Black male asses
From behind dark glasses,—
Where the crow / janes pass—and wonder too
And stroke too and gulp too and know too—
That it / is / true:
Black men in the south
Of America / are / soooooooo pretty
That men, and women, hide

Under sheets and masks and ride
And plot under the Alabama moon
How to "cut the nut."

For Malcolm, a Year After

Compose for Red a proper verse;
Adhere to foot and strict iamb;
Control the burst of angry words
Or they might boil and break the dam.
Or they might boil and overflow
And drench me, drown me, drive me mad.
So swear no oath, so shed no tear,
And sing no song blue Baptist sad.
Evoke no image, stir no flame,
And spin no yarn across the air.
Make empty anglo tea lace words—
Make them dead white and dry bone bare.

Compose a verse for Malcolm man,
And make it rime and make it prim.
The verse will die—as all men do—
But not the memory of him!
Death might come singing sweet like C,
Or knocking like the old folk say,
The moon and stars may pass away,
But not the anger of that day.

Talking in the Woods with Karl Amorelli

The old Toyota, green as a frog, coughs and clanks,
Shoots its last wad, throws its last rod,
Sighs and dies, bumps and hops to a stop on the Interstate—
Twenty miles from Worcester, the neat New England
City of three deck flats. Here my lover lives
And sets her plate, and lies late with me in the mornings.
The ride from Boston had / been / a merry-go-round of
    touching
And talking and wide-eyed smiles and body smells.
Now, like hail striking a tin roof, gravel pelts the fenders.
We get out and look around. There is a lake to our right
Surrounded by green: cedars, oaks, willows, ferns and lilies.
After consultations and imaginations, we decide
That she / could / catch a ride much better than I—
Being blond, blue-eyed, and a woman on the side.
"Well, catch a trucker then," I smarted, and turned
To Karl, this brown-eyed boy
With curly hair, this love / child of the woman
I love. "C'mon, Karl," I say,
"Let's check / out / the lake on this bright and good day."
We scramble over the fence and walk into the woods.
The beer bears on my bladder. We wander through the trees.
"I gotta pee," I say,—"what about you?"
"Me too."
Legs apart, urine splattering the dry leaves—
Me looking at the lake—
He looking at me.
"I can pee further than you, Eth."
"Yeah, I see."
"And *higher,* too."
"Yeah, Karl, the older you are—
The lower your arc."
"You mean, like flat feet?"

"No—like this." I make the motion with my hand,
And say, "Like a rainbow, boy."
"Well? why?—well? *why?*"
We dance, prance (the last few drops go down our pants),
Shake and zip.
"Well, dude," I say, "it's like this—speaking
from a psychological, physiological, chronological, and—
Sexiological standpoint of view . . ."
"*Eth* / ridge!"
I laugh. He laughs.
We crash outta the woods, tumble / over / the fence
And face our Lover.
Sunlight glints / off / her glasses.
"What were you / two / *doing* so long?"
"Well," I said,
"Karl was pissing—
Me?—I / was / peeing."

Alan Chong Lau

ALAN CHONG LAU was born in Oroville, California, in 1948. He grew up in Paradise, a small town north of Sacramento, at the edge of the Great Central Valley, just where the foothills begin their rise toward the Sierra Nevada range, an old gold-country town within view of sprawling croplands. Many of the poems in *Songs for Jadina* (1980) draw upon his early years, and the book is sprinkled with place names from this foothill-valley world—Paradise, Marysville, Lodi, Stockton. They mingle with the names of places the poet's family left behind two generations earlier, when they headed west across the Pacific—Szechuan, Chieh An, Taiwan, Kowloon.

It is very much a book of places and of lives tied to those places, lives of transplanted Asians yearning back toward the homeland while they strive to make their way in North America. The book is dedicated to Lau's grandmother, Jadina, and also to "the nameless ones." In a 1981 interview in Seattle's *International Examiner,* he said, "I wanted to give voices to those who came before, who couldn't tell their stories. I want to tell their story, that they *were* here and *did* exist."

Some poems reach back to the nineteenth century time of miners and fishermen and long lost sojourners:

> the book i am writing
> is full of postcards
> addresses of vendors orphans barefoot peasants
> people who don't exist
>
> wind sea grass fire leaves
> these form the other pages (a search for taiping ghosts)

Some poems pay tribute to Lau's immediate family, father, uncle, grandparents. In the geography of this book, each place on the map is a place in the heart. Poem by poem, a tale of generations unfolds, rich with affection and nostalgia. Throughout there is a generous compassion laced with grief, leavened with forgiveness.

The poet is the American-born son, the grandson, the one bearing witness. He cannot know China the way his grandfather knew it, but he knows the meaning of a photograph taken on the day "SUN YAT SEN COMES TO LODI." In this poem the grandfather, in pinstripes, is posed next to the celebrity-hero from China as he passes through that long ago valley farm town on a fund-raising trip. The grandson cannot translate the scrapbook clipping from the Chinese-language newspaper, but he can read the passion of the old man's memory and thereby translate, for us, something else—something about pride and community and loss and the way a man's identity can be pulled two ways across the world's widest ocean.

In the early 1970s Lau left California for four years of travel and made the first of several trips to Japan, where he met his wife, Kazuko. He came back home to enroll at the University of California at Santa Cruz, where he completed a B.A. in art in 1976. During this same period his poems began to appear in magazines and in such landmark collections as the Asian-American issue of the *Yardbird Reader* (Vol. 3, 1974), the Special Asian-American writers issue of *The Greenfield Review* (Vol. 6, Nos. 1 and 2, Spring 1977), *The Buddha Bandits Down Highway 99* (1978) (the volume he shared with Garrett Hongo and Lawson Inada), and in the 1979 anthology, *Califia: The California Poetry,* edited by Ishmael Reed, wherein the contributor's note says this about Lau's work: "Young Asian American poets are always quoting from his widely circulated but unpublished collection."

Songs for Jadina came out the following year from Greenfield Review Press, with funding from the National Endowment for the Arts. In the state of Washington, where Lau had by then settled, this book was the King County Arts Commission Publications Project Selection in Poetry for 1980. In 1981 it received an American Book Award. It is a collection that charts a profound journey in the history of a family and in the history of a people. At the same time something fresh and original appears on its pages. There is a new vocabulary, taken from both sides of the Pacific, made of idiom and foods and names and dreams.

In his 1981 interview Lau said, "Sometimes, especially with the second generation, people think acceptance means being white, so they drop their language and culture and try to become white. But this is impossible. People can't be white, and they can't be like they were in the old country. What has to occur is a new synthesis, a new culture created out of the old and the American."

Certain key works of the past dozen years have pointed the way, showing, in words and imagery, how this synthesis takes shape—works such as Shawn Wong's *Home Base,* Garrett Hongo's *The River of Heaven,* Maxine Hong Kingston's *Tripmaster Monkey. Songs for Jadina* is among them, a book that defines a way of seeing, a way of being in the world.

—James D. Houston

crossing portsmouth bridge

for grandmother and teru

*"the portsmouth bridge is a cement overpass
erected by the holiday inn and goes into ports-
mouth square, a park in the heart of san fran-
cisco's chinatown"*

over the bridge
your ghost
dries chicken wings
stretched across
a newspaper in october

so hot
the characters
dance
like a shimmer
of black ants
around food

each wing
well preserved
fingers of some child
embalmed
from a dynasty we never knew
or a boy shot dead in the street

with red twine
from bakery boxes
you fashion a necklace
for me to wear

i try to tell you
though a chicken
has wings
it cannot fly
but only flaps dust
into the eyes of ants

nothing i say
convinces

each wing
becomes a finger
attached to a hand

the twine
a line of blood
a circle
to connect memory to bone

we give
each of our lives
a name
and wear it

crossing this bridge
of cement
we enter a foreign land

these necklaces
our only proof
that we were ever
here

"Sun Yat Sen Comes to Lodi"

for my great grandfather, ou ch'ü-chia

I

SUN YAT SEN COMES TO LODI
grandfather in pinstripes
mouth sporting a toothpick
tells friends, "no sin, no sin,
no sir, no sin to get excited"

mr. yee's four-year-old beaming in a pink meenop
hair's done up in pinktails
sam wo has closed his laundry
only day of the year he would do this
excepting new year's

the good doctor smiles
from a sedan's back seat
cheers resound
delta dust flies

there is the speech
"china will be china again"
this brings tears

not losing a minute
to sip
he tells us all that money buys arms
money drives out manchus

most people understand, there is little hesitation
the new york yankees have not yet won the pennant
it is too early to predict weather or the lucky number
but money is dug from pockets
pulled from cloth bags

when the time comes
he says thank you
a cry of genuine sadness
a rush to take seats for a last picture

photographer tong yee
fumbles underneath a black shroud like a soul leaving body
poses change legs shift position
nobody seems to mind too much
only local banker wong hesitates
meeting the public often, he declines
offering a bigger contribution instead

grandfather sits by the doctor's side
pausing only to doff his hat
remove a coin from the ear
and drop a wet toothpick in a spittoon

2

he is proud of that picture
brown and bent in one corner
the only photo left in the family album
since big sister's marriage

there is also a newspaper clipping
with the headline
"SUN YAN SEN COMES TO LODI"
spread out all in characters
that could be relatives telling a story
or scales of a black bass dripping evidence of water

never having learnt the language
i just have to go by hearsay

home cooking

is it not the same
father
when crates of celery
bell peppers
parsley
green onions
beansprouts
arrive in the morning
and you sort things out
with your hands
redhard knuckles
soft fingers
arms splattered with grease burns
respecting each colour and shape
with proper names

is it not music
as you wash the bok choy
and they bubble and squeak
in submerged appreciation
as you cut the vegetables
just so
and the crisp juices
come out singing

as they simmer and swim in the pot
sizzle and flip in the wok of your imagination
does it occur to you
that you have created a poem
i am trying to recreate
with little success

treasure your hands
and delicate tongue of taste

Carolyn Lau

CAROLYN LAU'S poetry is like rice wine inside a new ceramic cup created by a Californian artisan. She has built a very reliable bridge to cross the older sources of Chinese philosophic traditions into the North American language: Mencius in Oakland taking a walk through the chatter of a coffee house. *Wode Shuofa (My Way of Speaking)* (1988), her first book, offers us small, tight, dense poems with multiple meanings. She is able to turn ideas into pictures, make thoughts visual. Her poems put you somewhere over the Pacific; they are not fully of here, of this place called America. They are not fully of there either, of inner Beijing. Her Sino-American conflict is a poetic delight, a room she has found full of surprises:

> First, you appear more
> furniture or sculpture than
> American, in two unbroken
> lines of brown and
> smooth, styled in curves.

You've got to focus your eye finely if you are reading and tune your ear precisely if you are listening; you must do both slowly like a peeling, but still you won't fall asleep. There are pins and pinches in the poems, an awkward drop changes from an idea to an image. She could use a launching pad of cerebral lavender, chase a rocket down an alley where a family or ancestral spirit oozes out of her fingers. She allows knowledge to make imaginative suggestions. Her poems unfold in layers; with a stroke, she escapes out of the ancient jails of masculine language. She says that Wode Shuofa is a secret women's language, a place where Confucious meets William Blake, and she makes them converse in silk; she pours into their cups not tea but Chardonnay. Their tongues loose, she can take them out of historic times, out of place, and use them as signals, as headlights for a California dreaming. Lau's is poetry in English with Mandarin sitting on the back porch. It describes the sensations of another language. In her poem "What Goes Down in One Written Character," she runs it down for us:

> . . . the wide street alters.
> The few cars putt nowhere arranging
> landscape, the sky in place.

She is wise and is not stuck on the popular superficiality of either Chinese or American culture. She is at the fountain drinking and inventing for us a new way of speaking. Y. H. Zhao of the Chinese Academy of Social Sciences in Beijing says of her work: "The poet who most successfully integrates the Chinese poetic and philosophical tradition into a post-modernistic mode is Carolyn Lau." Richard Silberg of *Poetry Flash* describes *Wode Shuofa (My Way of Speaking)* as "saturated with Chinese philosophy, calligraphy, landscape as well as references to Chinese language and translation. . . . a double achievement, a striking personal poetry, and a flesh born between cultures."

— *Victor Hernandez Cruz*

*WODE SHUOFA (MY WAY OF
SPEAKING) (1988)*

Kafka's Semen

Big cement mixer, green and brown, not moving.
This turtle belongs in the circus.
Going from small town to small town like Turlock or Barstow.
Happy to set up in the backstreet with the horse and gray
converted bread truck that are the show.
Very friendly, with time as the big top.
And as a ringmaster, a woman who waters her lawn
in front of her lighter green house, roof, and chimney
in her white print dress and blue sweater;
watering, watering,
a cigarette between her first and second fingers.

On the Fifth Anniversary of My Father's Death

Wandering into Mother's bedroom
after having bathed,
I see Father eyeing me
from the little glass coffin on the dresser.

I am naked.
Two breasts which I lotion.
My protruding pubic bone thinking.

If it is true that after a person dies
the spirit can hear and see its past life,
I want you to know, Daddy,
I'm glad you're dead.

The Last Time I Saw Jack

We sat across from each other in the dusk
with a blue tablecloth and white flowers
between. His fading blue shirt
and eyes making him barely visible.
The voice reasonable and slow. Giving
to me very small, the only way I can hear.
His hands holding the tea cup
and wiping his lips. He was his song.
Abundant among angels and beating
white light. Now without Michiko
and his forest burning,
he asks about my health and daughters.

We were confused by our charm
all that warm Sunday afternoon.
The flesh ready, but made distant
by politeness. I should have let him
put his fingers in me or see my breasts
at least. Instead, I walked with him
to the bus stop where we kissed like women
returning to our ruined lives.

Tato Laviera

JESÚS ABRAHAM "TATO" LAVIERA is the best-selling Hispanic poet of the United States, and he bears the distinction of still having all of his books in print, with his first work, *La Carreta Made a U-Turn* (1979), having gone through five reprints and a second edition (1991). In addition to publishing three other books of poems—*Enclave* (1981), *AmeRícan* (1986), *Mainstream Ethics* (1988)—all with the leading publisher of U.S.-Hispanic Literature, Arte Publico Press of Houston, Laviera has also written and published various plays and essays. His plays have been produced at the Henry Street Settlement's New Federal Theater on the Lower East Side, at Teatro Cuatro, at the Nuyorican Poets Cafe, and at Joseph Papp's New York Shakespeare Festival, all in New York.

Tato Laviera was born in Santurce, Puerto Rico, on September 5, 1950, and he migrated with his family to New York in July 1960. After finding himself in an alien society with practically no English, Laviera was able to adjust and eventually to graduate from high school as an honor student. Despite having no other degrees, his intelligence, aggressiveness and thorough knowledge of his community led him to a career in the administration of social service agencies. From 1970 to 1975 he was assistant director of the Association of Community Services and from 1975 to 1980 he was its executive director. He also served on the boards and was an officer of many other social service agencies during that time. After the publication of his first book, Laviera gave up administrative work to dedicate his time to writing. In the years since the publication of *La Carreta Made a U-Turn*, Laviera's career has included not only writing, but touring nationally as a performer of his poetry, directing plays and producing cultural events. In 1980 he was received by

President Jimmy Carter at a gathering of American poets at the White House.

All of Tato Laviera's books have been well received by the critics, most of whom place him within the framework of Afro-Caribbean poetry and U.S.-Hispanic bilingual poetry. But *La Carreta Made a U-Turn* has been especially acclaimed-it was the subject of an unheralded and surprising twenty-five page article, *"La Carreta Made a U-Turn:* Puerto Rican Language and Culture in the United States," by Juan Flores, John Attinasi, and Pedro Pedraza, in the prestigious journal, *Daedalus* (Spring 1981), which used his book as a paradigm of life and culture in Puerto Rican barrios in the United States. *La Carreta Made a U-Turn* is a sort of bilingual *salsa* poetry that presents the reader with a slice of life drawn from the Puerto Rican community of the Lower East Side. It examines both the oppression of the migrant community and its alienation through such popular-cultural genres as the soap opera; it acknowledges crime and drug addiction, while affirming the spiritual and social values of community and of art, poetry, and music in what many would consider the unlikeliest of social environments. Laviera, here as in all of his books, affirms and supports the existence of a true Puerto Rican-Latino culture within the heart of the metropolis and within the very belly of the United States. He further contends that there is no need to return to an island in the Caribbean or to a country south of the border to find a homeland, for Latinos have made their home here and are transforming not only mainstream U.S. culture, but also that of the whole hemisphere. This is a theme that dominates *AmeRícan, Mainstream Ethics,* and his forthcoming *Continental.*

Laviera's second book, *Enclave,* won a Before Columbus Foundation American Book Award in 1981. It was a celebration of cultural heroes, both real and imagined, including Alicia Alonso, Suni Paz, John Lennon, and Miriam Makeba, as well as the ficticious half-southern half–African American, half–Puerto Rican Tito Madera Smith, the barrio gossip Juana Bochisme, and the neighborhood tough Esquina Dude. As in *La Carreta,* Laviera's debt to Afro-Caribbean music and poetry is acknowledged in his eulogies to salsa composer and musician

Rafael Cortijo, to the famed *declamador* (or recitator of poetry) Juan Boria, and to master poets Luis Palés Matos and Nicolás Guillén.

AmeRícan, published on the occasion of the centennial celebration of the Statue of Liberty, is a poetic reconsideration of immigrant life in New York City and in the United States. After opening with a bitter-sweet eulogy to "Lady Liberty," Laviera goes on to consider success and accommodation in the United States from the vantage points of such marginalized urban dwellers as the homeless, the aging, and the poor, ending in the title poem with a challenge to American society to fulfill its promise of justice and equality for all of its people. The poems included in the first section of the book, "Ethnic Tributes," lists a representative sampling of the ethnic make-up of the country: "boricua," "arab," "black," "chinese," "cuban," "english," "greek," "irish," and so forth. *Mainstream Ethics* continues this development and posits an American culture that is being transformed from Eurocentricity to an ethnically and racially pluralistic society.

In his verse, Tato Laviera is an oral poet, a consummate performer of his poetry, which slowly but surely will finally constitute a living epic of Latino people in the United States. Laviera believes that poetry is essentially and irrevocably an oral art, one that must be shared in performance with a group or community. This commitment comes not from reading books and theorizing but from his observation of the power of poetic performance to move people and from his inheritance of the oral performance tradition from such *declamadores* and community bards as Juan Boria and Jorge Brandon. According to his masters and Laviera himself, to move people the poet must master certain physical and emotional postures, techniques, and devices for declamation. As does Jorge Brandon, an epic poet who also lives on the Lower East Side, Laviera memorizes and rehearses the poems before delivering them; neither Brandon nor Laviera is a *reader* of poems; both are creator-performers. Even Laviera's written and published poems have evolved from a process which attempts to recreate as closely as possible the oral performance. For Laviera, that includes the structure, spirit, and rhythm of popular and folk music, especially the

Afro–Puerto Rican *plenas* and *bombas* that have provided the
background music for the development of Puerto Rican culture
on the island and in New York.

By any measure Laviera is a virtuoso in his use of language
and in his combination of languages. He creates poems that
relate to his native Puerto Rico, to Spanish Harlem, Black Har-
lem, Africa, white America, ethnic America, the hemisphere.
He believes that he, as a black Puerto Rican living in New York
City and possessing two world languages, has many communi-
ties. In fact, he applies this to American culture as a whole:
There is potential here for reaching out to and embracing all of
mankind within our own national culture.

—Nicolás Kanellos

From
ENCLAVE (1981)

tito madera smith

for Dr. Juan Flores

he claims he can translate palés matos'
black poetry faster than i can talk,
and that if i get too smart,
he will double translate pig latin
english right out of webster's
dictionary, do you know him?

he claims he can walk into east harlem
apartment where langston hughes gives
spanglish classes for newly-arrived
immigrants seeking a bolitero-numbers
career and part-time vendors of cuchi-
fritters sunday afternoon in central
park, do you know him?

he claims to have a stronghold of the
only santería secret baptist sect in
west harlem, do you know him?

he claims he can talk spanish styled in
sunday dress eating crabmeat-jueyes
brought over on the morning eastern
plane deep fried by la negra costoso
joyfully singing puerto rican folklore:
"maría luisa no seas brava,

llévame contigo pa la cama," or
"oiga capitán delgado, hey captain delgaro,
mande a revisar la grama, please inspect
the grass, que dicen que un aeroplano,
they say that an airplane throws marijuana
seeds."

do you know him? yes you do,
i know you know him, that's right,
madera smith, tito madera smith:
he blacks and prieto talks at the same time,
splitting his mother's santurce talk,
twisting his father's south carolina soul,
adding new york scented blackest harlem
brown-eyes diddy bops, tú sabes mami,
that i can ski like a bomba soul salsa
mambo turns to aretha franklin stevie
wonder nicknamed patato guaguancó steps,
do you know him?

he puerto rican talks to las mamitas
outside the pentecostal church, and
he gets away with it, fast-paced i
understand-you-my-man, with clave
sticks coming out of his pockets hooked
to his stereophonic 15-speaker indispensable
disco sounds blasting away at cold reality
struggling to say estás buena baby
as he walks out of tune and out of
step with alleluia cascabells,
puma sneakers,
pants rolled up,
shirt cut in middle chest,
santería chains,
madamo pantallas,
into the spanish social club,
to challenge elders in dominoes,
like the king of el diario's
budweiser tournament

drinking cerveza-beer
like a champ,
do you know him?
well, i sure don't,
and if i did, i'd
refer him to 1960
social scientists
for assimilation
acculturation
digging
autopsy
into
their
heart
attacks,
oh,
oh,
there
he
comes,
you can call him tito,
or you can call him madera,
or you can call him smitty,
or you can call him mr. t.,
or you can call him nuyorican,
or you can call him black,
or you can call him latino,
or you can call him mr. smith,
his sharp eyes of awareness,
greeting us in aristocratic harmony:
"you can call me many things, but
you gotta call me something."

sky people
(la gente del cielo)

Eye-scratching mountain view
Puerto Rico counting houses
upon houses, hill after hill,
in valleys and in peaks,
to observe: la gente del cielo,
fingering on clouds,
climbing further and further,
to preserve taíno folklore,
gente del cielo,
toiling the land,
artcrafting musical symbols,
giving birth to more angelitos del cielo,
whose open-spaced hands captured moon waltz:
solemn serenity serenading life,
la gente del cielo,
who prayed in nature's candlelight,
galaxies responding with milky way guiñaítas
winked in tropical earth smile,
as God gleefully conceded,
what we had perceived all along,
that Puerto Rico is 100 by 35 by 1000
mountains multiplied by the square root
of many cultures breathing: ONE.

diega

diega llega, diega arrives, diega legacies,

diega llega, diega portrays, diega street-smarts,

diega llega, diega understands, diega loves. . . .

what more can i say about your soft strokes
caricias screaming gently on a smile.

what more can i say about your gracious
saludos hometown sentimientos mountain
jibarita romantic melody of songs streaming from your lips
    memories yearning from your
soul.

what more can i say, diega, how easy to say
your name, tu nombre, no pretensions, no
ornaments, saying simply diega, easy to
reach, easy to touch, dulce-soft silk
embroidered symphony your voice chanting
dancing living a call, your call, diega.

diega, you have arrived a otra etapa,
another time, but need not worry mamita,
you can sing to us the winds at night
are waiting, and we will speak your
caring phrases protecting our hands,
inspiring our eyes, stimulating our
senses.

diega, woman, mother, simplicity in
every sound you syllabled to us,
what more, diega, what more than
essence kissing petals on our
foreheads, never to be forgotten

affection, the rivers, the mountains,
the heavens, you touched us, you hugged
us, deeply, freely, diega, diega,
we respect your presence,
your children grandchildren
tátaranietos and chornos of the future. . . . .

te recordamos en el presente, bendición,
vieja, you diega, opening the door of
st. peter, festive celebration in the
gates of your eternity and this Barrio
that you touched.

just before the kiss

canela brown sugar coated bomboncitos
melting deliciously upon a sweet tooth tongue;
canela brown gold dust on top of tembleque;
canela brown fine sticks to flavored cocoa;
canela grounded into arroz con dulce;
canela melao
canela dulce.

canela browned in deep tan caribbean
sweet lips almost sabroso tasted by
a cariñoso sentiment, y buena que estás,
en gusto affection that cries
out loud: qué chévere tú eres,
como canela brown warrior woman diplomática
with her terms.

all of this canela,
inside your luscious lips,
smooth phrasing me deeeeply,
waking me up on the middle-night,

to change from exclamation mark
into an accent accenting:
canela, mi negra,
canela, trigueña,
canela, mulata,
canela, mi prieta,
bésame,
to taste your
cinnamon
powdered
tongue.

Wing Tek Lum

Wing TEK LUM was born in 1946, in Honolulu, Hawaii. Although he spent a number of years as a young adult on the U.S. mainland and in Asia, he is very much an island poet who finds his images, associations, allusions, and themes ready made in the local matrices of Chinese-American-Hawaiian cultural constructs.

Lum attended Brown University in Providence, Rhode Island, and the Union Theological Seminary in New York City and worked in New York's Chinatown for four years. During his stay in New York, he received the Poetry Center's Discovery Award in 1970. He then lived in Hong Kong for three years as a social worker before returning to Honolulu to help in the family business.

Despite Lum's various career moves, he has persisted in writing poems. In Honolulu, Lum has remained an active member of the literary community, and in 1987, his first collection of poems, *Expounding the Doubtful Points,* was published as a special double issue of *Bamboo Ridge: The Hawaii Writers Quarterly. Expounding the Doubtful Points* won the Creative Literature Award from the Association for Asian American Studies in 1988 and the Before Columbus Foundation American Book Award in 1989.

Lum's first book is a fairly ambitious collection of 105 poems arranged into four parts. Parts one and three are brief, composed of four and three poems each. They function almost as prologues introducing the much longer second and fourth sections. Part one. for example, is composed of poems that thematize an attitude towards the art of poetry. This attitude is never directly presented and only alluded to tactfully in the surrounding contexts of lives that proceed with or without poetry. Thus, the figures of a "classmate just dead" and that most famed Chinese poet, Li Po, play against each other. The poem for the dead classmate is paradoxically intended for the living: its significance, even as symbolic action beyond the temporal and physical, is outside the poet's purview. As a reversal of this thought, the poem "To Li Po" underlines the transformation of the physical and temporal worlds into the lasting artifact of words:

> In those days
> for every poem you wrote
> a million Chinamen suffered to die.
>   pen from bone
>   brush from hair
>   ink from blood. . . .

Similarly, Lum's poems negotiate between acknowledging the primacy of the immediate, sensual world with its transitory delights and a profound privileging of the act of poetry, an act that transcends time and transmutes the physical into the spiritual:

> And when the point scratches surface
> flesh is made word
> and these small truths of your existence
> illumine the page
> like laser light, scorching our hearts forever.

The bulk of Lum's poems treat familial and domestic experiences. Many record his struggles with a patriarchal father, a "gruff old fut," whose long death from cancer allows a final reconciliation. His poems to his mother, who also died of cancer when Lum was only sixteen, express a tender relationship that counters the mother-hate–filled works of some male Asian American writers. Lum attributes to this mother, who did not conceal her breastless right chest from her son, those lessons in love and happiness that surely have a connection to his later marital affection:

Love. my mother really knew,
was like these islands
formed in part
by tidal waves and hurricanes
and the eruption of volcanoes
which suddenly appear
and just as suddenly go away.

Besides these sharp, memorable family portraits and vignettes, Lum also writes pungently of socio-political issues. His book closes with a revised paradigm of the American melting pot, "The Chinese Hot Pot," which is

like a stew that isn't
as each one chooses what he wishes to eat
only that the pot and fire are shared
. . . and the sweet soup
spooned out at the end of the meal.

But this cheerful, optimistic, nourishing vision of a pluralistic United States must be balanced against a number of darker poems. These poems critique Eurocentrism ("Minority Poem"), insist on a difference between the dominant Anglo culture and the poet's particular and localized practice ("T-bone steak"), and suggest a more problematized understanding of pluralism than can be offered in the image of the Chinese hot pot.

Lum does not write from a stable ideological center. But his poems have been most publicly accepted when he is taken to speak for an ethnic program. The poems, however, collectively contruct a culture that is multivocal, one that speaks Chinese pride ("On the First Proper Sunday of Ching Ming"), American patriotism ("Grateful Here"), and Hawaiian sensibility ("Local Sensibilities").

—*Shirley Geok-lin Lim*

To a Poet Who Says He's Stopped Writing (Temporarily)

I don't care what you do for a living
sell stocks or bonds or both
drive a cab full time
wait on tables
    at that new jazz spot in Waikiki

I don't care what grand thoughts have moved you
the good image of your grandmother's smile
your delights at eating meatless meals
or that burning desire
    to let every child speak a language of his own

There have been the times
when those wishful sentiments aren't enough
when you must lay aside all other claims on your life
simply to satisfy
    that single all-consuming craving

And now you are waiting
not merely driving home at night with the radio off
or washing your hair in the shower
or lying in bed, face down,
    your lights out and the shades drawn

These periods are as essential
as that moment you sit down in a rush

your favorite pen in hand
pulling out that journal
    you've always carried for this very purpose

And when the point scratches surface
flesh is made word
and these small truths of your existence
illumine the page
    like laser light, scorching our hearts forever

To Li Po

I liked that poem
—the one about getting drunk,
three hundred gold cups of wine,
to drown away the sorrows
of generations.
           In those days
for every poem you wrote
a million Chinamen suffered to die.

    pen from bone
    brush from hair
    ink from blood

They were illiterate, you knew.
Better than words,
the liquor was solace enough for them.

To My Father

In our store that day
they gathered together
my grandfather among them
each in his turn
to cut off their queues:
the end of subservience.
They could have returned
the Republic just established
or, on the safe side,
waited a year
to grow back that braid.
No matter, they stayed.
Your father was young
and shrewd: the store flourished,
then the crops, the lands.

Out of your share
you sent us to the best schools;
we were to follow the dynasty
set by the Old Man.
But he had died
before I was born, his grave
all I could pay homage to.
I was freed from those old ways.
Today, unbraided,
my hair has grown long
because and in spite of those haircuts
you and he took.

It's Something Our Family Has Always Done

On every trip away from these islands
on the day of departure and on the day of return
we go to the graves, all seven of them,
but for one the sum total of all of our ancestors
who died in this place we call home.

The drive to the cemetery is only five minutes long.
Stopping by a florist adds maybe ten minutes more.
Yet my wife and I on the day of our flight
are so rushed with packing and last minute chores.
Why do we still make the time to go?

The concrete road is one lane wide.
We turn around at the circle up at the top,
always to park just to the side of the large banyan tree
as the road begins its slope back down.
I turn the wheels; we now lock our car.

As if by rote, we bring anthuriums,
at least two flowers for each of our dead.
On our way we stop to pay our respects to the "Old Man"
—that first one lain here, all wind and water before him—
who watches over this graveyard, and our island home.

Approaching my grandparents, we divide up our offering,
placing their long stems into the holes filled with sand.
Squatting in front of each marble tablet,
I make it a point to read off their names in Chinese.
My hands pull out crabgrass running over stone.

I stand erect, clutching palm around fist,
swinging the air three times up and down.
My wife from the waist bows once, arms at her sides.

I manage to whisper a few phrases out loud,
conversing like my father would, as if all could hear.

We do Grandfather, Grandmother, and my parents below
      them.
Following the same path we always take,
we make our way through the tombstones and mounds,
skirting their concrete borders, to the other two Lums
and to our Granduncle on the Chang side.

Back up the hill, we spend a few moments by the curb
picking off black, thin burrs from our cuffs and socks.
We talk about what errands we must do next.
I glance around us at these man-made gardens,
thrust upon a slope of earth, spirit houses rising to the sky.

As I get into our car, and look out at the sea,
I am struck with the same thought as always.
We spend so little time in front of these graves
asking each in turn to protect us when we are far away.
I question them all: what good does it really do?

I have read ancient poets who parted with sorrow
from family and friends, fearing never to return.
Our oral histories celebrate brave peasants
daring oceans and the lonely beds: they looked even more
to blessings at long distance from their spirit dead.

My father superstitious, even to the jet age,
still averred: but every little bit helps.
These sentiments I know, but I confess I do not feel.
Maybe it's for this loss that I still come here.
They are family, and I respect them so.

At a Chinaman's Grave

"Kingston, too, looked critically at it ['China-man'] as not being meaningful for her . . . She said she even tried 'Chinaperson' and 'China-woman' and found they didn't work either, the first sounding 'terrible' and the second being inaccurate."

—The Honolulu Advertiser, *July 22, 1978*

My grandmother's
brother here
died all alone, wife
and children back
in the village. He
answered to
"Chinaman" like all
the others
of our race back then.
The Demons hired
only lonely
men, not their
sweethearts,
tai pos, baby
daughters. They laid
ties, cut cane, but
could not
proliferate. They took
on woman's
work, by default,
washing shirts,
frying eggs and sausages.
Granduncle cooked.
From what he earned
he sent
money home,
gambled perhaps, maybe hid

some away—all for
one purpose. Those old men:
they lived
their whole
lives with souls
somewhere else, their hearts
burdened of
hopes, waiting to
be reunited.
Some succeeded
and we
are the fruits of those
reunions. Some
did not,
and they are
now forgotten, but for
these tombstones,
by the rest.

Minority Poem

Why
we're just as American
as apple pie—
that is, if you count
the leftover peelings
lying on the kitchen counter
which the cook has forgotten about
or doesn't know
quite what to do with
except hope that the maid
when she cleans off the chopping block
will chuck them away
into a garbage can she'll take out
on leaving for the night.

E. L. Mayo

E. L. MAYO (b. 1904) was, for a few of us, something of a father figure. He was a bit of the quiet shaman, witty and curative in his views, gentle and forgiving, sharp with insight but amused and nonacerbic. When we had the opportunity to talk with him, we experienced the satisfying of a deep and too-often-denied hunger. He offered us the views of a man who had achieved a disinterested and amused tolerance for the world and its disappointments, its sorrows, but also its small triumphs. No one who met him could doubt that he sought wisdom and had found some of its comforts and that he knew also of its denials. He asked very little for himself, but certainly he insisted on those basic necessities, his books and journals and pens and the time to do what he really loved to do, which was to think and to create poems. He embraced obscurity almost as a condition for his intellectual freedom; in turn that freedom was an essential condition for the creation of these poems.

Still, a few discerning critics noticed Ed Mayo's quiet achievement. In 1958, James Wright wrote in *Poetry* that the Mayo poems "smolder with a kind of subdued bitterness," and he praised the work as "unpretentious." He found the poet "daring and successful precisely because he does not overburden his language." The *Summer Unbound* volume, he said, was "severe, tough," with a natural modernity.

John Ciardi praised Mayo's "intellectual fire," "verbal felicity," and capacity to create symbols and images that conspire toward a "sudden burgeoning of second meanings." He saw in this work "happy evidence of how far poetry has come in a hundred years toward acquiring a wholly natural mastery of the commonest details of ordinary living." Ciardi put some of Mayo's work, along with an interview, in his influential anthol-

ogy, *Mid-Century American Poets,* and certainly from that
time Ed Mayo became for many of us "a poet's poet," not
widely appreciated by the general public, but certainly an ad-
mired craftsman, practitioner of the art of poetry at its best. All
too often in today's poetry there is nothing but surface mean-
ing. Mayo's readers, like Eliot's or Stevens's, had to go beneath
those surfaces, had to take a dive. Perhaps that's why Ed Mayo
named a poem and then an entire book, *The Diver.* He was
probably familiar with Neruda's "Ode to the Diver":

> Like all the things
> that I learned
> in my existence,
> studying them, knowing them,
> did I learn that to be a diver
> is a difficult
> profession? No!
> Infinite.

The wisdom of compromise and acceptance, adjustment
and yielding, was expressed in Mayo's "Iron Gate."

> Here Solomon perceives he is not wise
> And with an eye upon the second prize
> Divides desire with possibility . . .
> The sea gull in his proper breast
> Beats louder now against a thinner
>   door . . .

These lines do not, of course, share the much-lauded wisdom of
the suicide poets who, like Medea, eloquently announce that
"Life has been cruel to me" and then rush from one corner of
the stage to the other raging and murdering most glamorously,
till we forget that even self-murder is still "murder most foul"
and a hell of an example to the young, who after all watch us
more closely than the weather. Clearly Mayo realized, some-
where around midlife, that he would not have, could not have,
what Myra Mayo describes as: "not *acclaim,* but the knowl-
edge that his voice was heard—perhaps enough response to it

to reassure him on this point. He knew he was saying some-
thing important, but the feeling that he was saying it to no-
body—a vacuum—could be overwhelming." But that failure, if
it could be foolishly labeled such, drove him on and opened up
new wells of creativity. He said it in a poem, thanking those
powers that had denied his pettier, more selfish, quest. It is a
three line poem entitled "Failure":

> Failure is more important than success
> Because it brings intelligence to light
> The bony structure of the universe.

"Even the awkward song is excellent," the poet wrote, and
"from the bland, snow-crusted eminence / of sixty" he com-
pared himself to "a mild smiling Cheshire gentleman / cat of
sixty fading softly away." But like Williams in "The Descent"
he praised the process: "My vision will continue to expand /
Brobdingnagian / Until I comprehend all humankind /
Without being there."

Robert Hullihan, in a *Des Moines Register* profile in the
year of Ed's death, described the poet as something of a spy, a
man with a secret vision and a penchant for codes:

> When he was younger and deeply involved in espionage the
> authorities took little notice of him, even though he was one of the
> leading agents for a government unknown to this day.
>
> He walked about with a kind of ill-fitted vigor that made him
> seem harmless. He was skilled in seeming to approach some casual
> destination that would suddenly divide and become two destina-
> tions at once, or several.
>
> And so he was never captured even though he did not employ a
> cipher and always wrote his reports in clear language.
>
> That was dangerous but necessary for his mission was, as he
> recalls it now in retirement "to make things mean more than they
> mean; to compose a structure that common sense tells you just
> isn't there at all."
>
> It was hazardous, profitless work in a country intent upon mak-
> ing things mean less than they mean.
>
> But Edward Mayo persisted all through the 27 years when he
> seemed to be a professor of English at Drake University in Des
> Moines.

Of course, there was always some suspicion that he was some-
thing more than that. . . .

Edward Mayo is a poet who only called himself a spy once by
way of explaining where the poet is and what he does: "Someone
who watches and writes things down and sends in reports from the
midst of the human uproar. A spy, if you like."

"Yes, I remember. And I still believe that," said Mayo, nodding
into the smoke like a patriarch tending to a sacrificial fire. He has a
face molded for stern judgment except that it is incapable of re-
buke.

"A spy, trying to see through the apparent to the something
behind it that is something more," he said.

Mayo was a Metaphysical, and his poems gain in power
because of the tension between the metaphysical, the occasion-
ally obscure or at least demanding references, and the idi-
omatic. The poems "pretend to be simple prose-like utter-
ances," David Daiches noted, "whereas in fact the best of
them contain an echoing poetic meaning which begins to re-
lease itself a split second after we have read the words. There is
an assumed lightness of touch here, a note not quite of irony
but almost of timidity, behind which the richer meanings can
be heard. . . . He understands what form does to an idea, and is
not afraid to write something which is in itself trivial but in its
poetic context is not." Other critics tried to define that elusive
and unique quality not often found among "the clichés which
make much modern poetry seem a kaleidoscope in which the
same unevocative images and abstractions are constantly re-
shuffled into new patterns." Mayo followed up mysteries,
sought "the true, secret name of the river," opened up "the
mystery of better and of worse," negotiated with that angel
whose "name was Loneliness." And he knew that flesh is only a
door, behind which we hear the "Wind—I said—Breaker of
ties, breaker of promises." The human is always betrayed, and
yet "The jungles of the sea must flower still." Poetry, he said,
was a "mirror, showing / Clearer than to our shadowy sense,
the glowing / And waning of a more than mortal creature."
Just as "moles are very little / And worlds are very big," so the

poet and his world must work and live together, unfairly matched. Out of such tension an occasional miracle emerges, hence Mayo's "El Greco" sonnet.

Such poems must not be lost to future generations. It may seem extravagant to say so, but E. L. Mayo devoted his life to the purity of thought, and he generously passes on to us findings of great value. If we're into throwing away clear messages from the stars received on our most subtle astronomical telescopes, precisely beamed, then we should indeed disregard and tear up his poems or let them gather in out-of-the-way magazines and anthologies. But that queue of the generations coming will need all he has left them, and we must pray they will not forget how to read, not at all an unlikely possibility.

Ed Mayo was not, then, an idle collector of images, a man who sets his typewriter down on his crate and looks around the room for something to list. Nor was he a seeker of fashions; he didn't even live in the right place. And he had not the slightest idea of how to promote his own work. (I suspect that was itself one of his ideas.) Modesty made him rare. At last indifferent to acclaim he might have sought, he pursued his own light as devotedly as had Emerson; he gave everything he had to his writing, and because he was a learned man, that writing was an activity almost inseparable from his teaching. Not only did he teach for many years at Drake University, he is still teaching, through his poems.

Some of Mayo's poems of close family feeling, his elegy for his father and his "Letter to My Grandfather's Picture," are as vivid as Lewis W. Hine's photographs capturing the music of farm and mill. Mayo respects the crucial, inspiring link between generations, and he asks the ultimate question of our mission on earth:

> We never see the thing we have worked on
> Whirling from revolution to revolution
> Through the Mill's long explosion.
> Yet do not lean out of the picture, Grandfather;
> Though you cried out like Jesus and Jehovah
> I could not hear you through the spindles' roar.

A heavier worry runs through "A Reassurance," with its "Pre-
occupation / With liquefaction falling on our world," the
atomic nightmare that threatens to undo all philosophy:

> You can't unthink, you can't unlink again
> The Hiroshima chain. Our marriage rite
> Was the bridal of the earth and sky.

A persistent image for Mayo is that of the perilous perch, the
endangered grip. "Nature is innocent / Of nothing, nothing."
He compared our lives to those of pioneer children, ever vulner-
able. And yet the only solution is an affirmation of will:

> As pioneering children, when no rain
> Made water brackish in the last canteen,
> Went right to sleep, and just as seldom knew
> When guns were cocked and ready all night through,
> So do we ride the earth's revolving wheel,
> Moving across what prairies, to what wars,
> Against what ambush, eye does not reveal;
> Nor do we know what loyal outriders
> Swing on to clear our path across the plain,
> But drift to sleep where canvas hides the stars
> Of the long planetary wagon train.
>
> *("Wagon Train")*

Mayo was always a Platonist, knew that the eternal forms
were real, though threatened by "variably-defined Necessity."
Beauty and Love were the most threatened, and poetry aspires
not only to know them but to protect and perpetuate them.
Nature provides merely occasions for discovering truths:

> We neither knew
> A trumpet blew nor felt the whole world shake;
> Yet children playing with the evidence
> That soul is form and does the body make

Wake us with their shrill cries: the news is true:
The forms of things endure and glister
        through.

("Ice Storm")

E. L. Mayo has many such truths for us.

—David Ray

The Poet Who Talks to Himself

The poet who talks to himself
In despair
Or to an audience of
Air,

Married to the poem,
Knows once for all
What nagging lies between
The *will* and the *shall;*

Perceives that beauty is not
Thought, but the object of thought
And dances to its end
Hovering in the wind

Like doves, to settle down
About some casual man
Offering a casual crumb
Or not, as casual can,

Both being portion of
The carelessness of love
Which finds the perfect rhyme
Nowhere and in no time.

Poem for Gerard

Understand too late? Of course we can:
The love of everything, like winnowing,
Scatters the spirit like fine dust, plum-bloom
Over the world. Heart must be held, held down
Of its own will, chained, hooded and become
Deaf to itself and dumb

To hear things speak themselves in their sole tongue.
By stress and instress are their songs wrung
Out of them, scaped and bruited; to possess
Their breathing outwardness the eye must go
In to their root and onward to their end
Perishing with their vanishing to span

From germ to the full grain
Mountain or martyr, chestnut-leaf or man.
It makes the blood run cold, warm flesh glower
To think of you, Windhover,
Cleaving so bleak a wind, maneuvering
Sight more than any in how sealed an hour.

Anglo-Saxon

King Alfred sensed among his country's words
England's destiny;
But Caedmon, rapt, among his master's herds,
Felt all their history:
How all men, once, had owned a common tongue
And clumsy dialects the wide world over
Remembered music that the first had sung,
And would discover,

Through cries confused, the excellent, true stem
And scattered vowels of Jerusalem.

The Questioners

The sad sage-gray Dakota hills
That stood around me at my mapping table
Pestered with flies stay with me; the great moaning
Of wind that walks that country day and night—
The years of famine and the years of blight
Are in that wind, and all the helpless anger
That men defrauded turn against themselves
Before they lift their rifles from their shelves.
And I have seen the ghosts of the Dakotahs,
Out of revenge on white men, smut the corn,
Ride like Russian thistles on the dust storm,
Crack earth with drouth, as hoppers darken the sun.
And I have heard the foxes on the hill
Barking a question; insects at the sill,
Drawn by my lamp, as they flung themselves at the flame,
Whirred with their wings no other name but my name.
I have stepped from farmhouse kitchens and been drowned
In the great empty of the country nights
And seen the Northern Lights
Beam after beam shoot over, seeking me.
But I would not be found, and would not cry
"Here! Here am I! Send me!"
Or whisper from the ground,
For I knew I could not answer such hard questions
And better never heard and never found.
And yet I never cease to ponder the questions
Of the creatures of the country without trees,
But all the answers I know are wordy or bloody,
Sick with swords or social disease;

And though my country silence answered nothing
And vigilance and patience are unsure
I have given my love to the askers of hard questions
Till what discovers darkness finds dark's cure.

Colleen J. McElroy

IN the summer of 1985 the *Virginia Quarterly Review* described Colleen McElroy's "well-worked poems" in the collection *The Queen of the Ebony Isles* as having "a [lurking implication] that the reader may not understand. The poems contain detail in a way a logician's argument contains detail—as if clarity were the touchstone of persuasion." McElroy's creative imagination began being shaped during early adolescence when she sneaked moments to read Scheherazade's tales in the forbidden *Arabian Nights.* Like Scheherazade, she tells stories with her poetry and prose, and like Scheherazade, she frequently spellbinds her reader with the shock of detail, the simplest profundity. Like the words of the West African griot, of the old African-American men telling stories on the store porches in Hurston's *Their Eyes Were Watching God,* of the West Indian immigrant women chatting in their Brooklyn kitchens who inspire Paule Marshall's dialogue, McElroy's words help us remember the past, reflect on its meaning to the present and the future, and urge us to think and to act.

For most third world writers of the United States and abroad, clarity *is* the touchstone of persuasion. For most readers to enter into our worlds of mythology, they must be lured, cajoled, reasoned with, or convinced. Early slave narratives enticed readers with the style of the adventure story; sixties poets often brought their readers/listeners to a rapt attention with shocking language and shocking truths. Even third world audiences must at times be persuaded, for so many of us have been taught to devalue our own myths, our own worlds and truths. McElroy invites us to feel, see, hear, smell, and taste her worlds. And, as a close friend of hers observed, while she wants you to enjoy her romance with words, McElroy's clarity gives you worlds where oppression is a great part of the landscape, but where characters and personae are not oppressed. There is often satire, irony, and just plain fun in her worlds.

The name of the title poem of the collection from which these poems were selected came to McElroy when she found a postcard drawing by Edward Dulac from the *Arabian Nights* of the Queen of the Ebony Isles walking her panther in the moonlight. McElroy's book has three sections, each introduced by a quote. The first section, "In My Mother's Room," and its epigraph suggest the diaspora of the extended family of black people in Africa:

> "Surely I shall keep those who sit on my thighs" but no, even they, the children of her children were taken from her until it seemed that she herself was at last to be taken. But no, a change came over her and she grew younger. (*The Old Woman Who Tried to Find God,* a south African folktale)

The second section, "In Any Language," and its epigraph suggest tales, fables, poems of survival and sustenance, poems that teach, poems that explain:

> A wolf, peeping through a window, saw a company of shepherds eating a joint of lamb. "Lord," he exclaimed, "what a fuss they would have raised had they caught me doing that. *(Aesop's Fables)*

We should remember, of course, that Aesop was of black African descent.

The third section, "Queen of the Ebony Isles," and its epigraph suggest tales, storytelling:

> We sailed many days and nights, and we passed from isle to isle and sea to sea and in due course, came upon an island as it were a garth of the gardens of Paradise. ("Tales of Scheherazade," *Selections from the Arabian Nights*)

The five poems here are representative of each section: "My Father's War's," from section I; "The Poem I Never Meant to Write," from section II; and "Queen of the Ebony Isles,"

"The Dragon Lady Considers Dinner," and "The Dragon Lady's Legacy" from section III. McElroy's humor is apparent when we realize that her "model" for the Dragon Lady was the cartoon character in the comic book, *Terry and the Pirates.*

In a December 1990 discussion with me, Colleen McElroy explained why she wrote poetry. "The poem is drama, music, and dance. The way of doing variations on a theme. I push the limits in a poem in a way that I might not be able or willing ordinarily. There is a certain beauty that I don't find in other writing. I get high off poetry. I do. It elates me. It feeds me." A professor of creative writing as well as a poet, short story writer, and soon-to-be novelist, she urges her students to remember that "while the poem lets you stretch your imagination—while beauty may appear spontaneous—there is a craft. A poem is an instrument. You have to practice voice, piano, acting. You have to practice writing. Learning all you need to know about your instrument means that you must learn language and how the world and its history and its people change."

She says she writes for the eleven-year-old girl in Nachez, Mississippi, and for the ninety-year-old in Dubuque. She is always mindful that while she cannot (and would not want to) be anything but black and female in the twentieth century, she does not find that limiting. Neither does she "write for a particularly male or female audience. I have found that what I have to say speaks to both."

For Colleen McElroy, Black, African American is an ethnicity, not simply a skin color. Her poetry expresses love, joy, sorrow, and pain in the complex world of races, genders, classes, ethnicities, power, and politics. "Poetry", she says, "allows me to find myself in what in many ways is an intolerable world."

—*Johnnella E. Butler*

From

QUEEN OF THE EBONY ISLES
(1984)

My Father's Wars

Once he followed simple rules
of casual strength,
summoned violence with the flick
of combat ribbon or hash mark;
now he forces a pulse into treasonous muscles
and commands soap opera villains.
He is camped in a world regimented
by glowing tubes,
his olive-black skin begging for the fire
of unlimited color.
In towns where he can follow
the orders of silence,
gunfights are replayed
in thirty-minute intervals
familiar as his stiff right arm
or the steel brace scaffolding his leg.

By midday the room is filled
with game shows and private eyes hurling
questions against all those who swear
their innocence;
his wife is in full retreat
and jumps when he answers in half-formed words
of single grunts deadly as shrapnel.
He need not remind her
he is always the hero;
the palms of his hands

are muddy with old battle lines.
He has fallen
heir to brutal days where he moves
battalions of enemies;
his mornings are shattered with harsh echoes
of their electronic voices.

Here he is on neutral ground
and need not struggle to capture words
he can no longer force his brain to master;
he plans his roster
and does not attend to his wife's
rapid-fire review of the neighbor's behavior.
He recalls too clearly the demarcation of blacks,
of Buffalo Soldier and 93rd Division.
By late afternoon he is seen rigidly
polishing his car in broad one-arm swipes,
its side windows and bumpers emblazoned
with stickers: US ARMY RETIRED REGULAR

This Is the Poem I Never Meant to Write

my grandmother
raised me Georgia style
a broken mirror
spilled salt
a tattered hemline
all add up to bad spirits
when she died, I learned to worship
stranger things
a faded textbook full of bad theories
has no spirit at all
now I've gone full circle

in a town some still call Bahía
the drumbeat of the alabés
echoes my grandmother's warnings
I watch the daughters of the candomblé
dance to the rhythms of ancient spirits
as the ceremony begins
my lungs expand
like gas-filled dirigibles
stretched latex-thin

my grandmother spoke
the language of this scene
the mystery and magic
of rich colors in a tapestry
of brown and black skin
white candles
a small reed boat
six bloody gamecocks
all bind this church to its African source
I follow my people past spirit houses
past tight Spanish streets
where houses are painted blue and white
like any Moorish town
when we reach the sea
water seems to flow uphill
tropical landscapes turn mustard yellow
and above us the moon swallows the night

this is the poem
I never meant to write
I am learning to worship
my grandmother's spirits
an old woman
splinters of wood embedded
in her black leathery cheeks
three crosses tattooed
on the fleshy black skin
of her upper arms
draws my picture upon her palm

in blue ink
then tells me we are all strangers
bound by the same spirit
I have gone home
in the dim light
my grandmother smiles

Queen of the Ebony Isles

this old woman follows me from room to room
screams like my mother   angers like my child
teases me   rolling her tattooed hips forward
and out   steals my food   my name   my smile
when you call her I come running

when we were young and perfect
we danced together and oh we loved well
all the husbands and lovers   children and books
the sunshine and long walks on lonely nights
now she sucks me thin with her affairs

weaves romantic shadows over the windows
and curses my sober moods   kisses everyone
and insists on wearing red shoes
she hums the same songs over and over
something about love and centuries turning upon us

each time she changes the verse
shifting the words like cards in a game
of solitaire   the hot patent-leather colors
her mercurial moods as she flies about
her red heels glittering and clicking out of tune

she has seen too many comic strips
believes she's as deadly lovely

as Dragon Lady and Leopard Girl   I resist
but her limbs are daring   oiled for movement

without me who are you she asks   I am heavy
with silence   my hands are maps of broken lines
without her all sounds are hollow   I am numbed
cold and cannot read the cycles of the moon
even the sun   the sun cannot warm me

aloneness is a bad fiddle I play against my own
burning   bet your kinky muff she cackles knowing
the symptoms   then draped in feather boas
she drags me toward yet another lover   beckoning
with her brash reds pulsing like haunting violins

on midnight-blue nights she screams
into the eyes of the moon   twirling her war machine
like some Kamikaze pilot   her heat bakes my skin
even blacker   she's never happy unless we're falling
in love or hate   she grows younger while I

age and age   bandage wounds and tire too easily
she says   play the game   play the game she says
when I complain she says I'm hearing voices
she's hacked my rocking chair into firewood
I am the clown in all her dreams

when she looks into the mirror from my eyes
I want to float away unscathed
drift like patches of early morning fog
she thinks I stay because I love her
one day soon I'll move while she's sleeping

The Dragon Lady Considers Dinner

the next day I couldn't remember his name
there was that business with the flaming crepes
and the sea breaking around them
my fingers played a tattoo of ancient melodies
the oysters passed the tune to the lobsters
under the straw pattern of my wide black bamboo hat
I picked carrion from my teeth
it was all so boring
no amount of voodoo could save me
I dreamed of ghettos in revolution
he talked of contracts and commodities
I smiled at the oysters
they didn't smile back
the butter ran silently along the spine

he promised gold and all the exotic pelts
the world could offer
now more than ever I needed the loan
of his fleet of ships and long guns
I told him a lady flies low
and manages her own power
the sun nodded its approval
the waiter poured more wine
I wiped my lips pausing
as I rose to leave
the oysters chuckled inside me

The Dragon Lady's Legacy

years later, they could hardly remember her face
then a farmer plowing a tired field of soybeans
and lentils near Half Moon Bay
found her pearl-handled revolver
in a sump by a forgotten wellhouse
slit slid from the curve of metal
like folds in a silk dress and her initials
filled the dreary light with promise

for days, he carried the secret in his pocket
then his dreams infected his wife
she saw fires scorching the villages
in the valleys below them
the smell of strangers grew thick as napalm
and a slit of light, crafty as a woman's sigh
suggested battles yet to be planned
somewhere in the night she heard the lady speak

your breath will pulse in strobe-light patterns
of eight, she whispered
two for your husband and unnamed children
one for this house teetering
on its crumbling foundation like a child
one for that useless fence and barn
another for your sisters in other ghettos
the rest for yourself arising
gloriously, finally a rebel
alive outside yourself

each night, the lady returned
the farmer bathed himself in tales of love
where he was the hero
his wife pressed her onion-stained fingers
to her ears and begged for the old loneliness
the days pale as thin soup

the brief spate of evenings
still she saw the variegated shadows of sandalwood
so surprisingly delicate the lady took shape in them

her razor-sharp nails glistening like diamonds
come follow me, she said
it is an old story so foreign
it is typically Middle American, as always
when it is finally released to the public
everyone from lawyers to victims
will be FBI agents
but you are full of long-limbed seduction
and have nothing to fear

even now, soothed by the swell of adventure
there are those who say the lady is a myth
in these days there is no siren's voice
to lure men into battle or women
from the quicksand of supermarkets
there are no ladies of iron will or dark mysteries
and when you have settled into the safe corral
of your routine, *do not be deceived*
by the faint scent of our perfume

Thomas McGrath

WHEN Thomas McGrath (b. 1916) died at seventy-three on September 20, 1990, he received a three-inch obituary in the *New York Times* which said that he "wrote poems in a highly personal style about his own life and social concerns over the years from the Depression to the recent past." In my mind's eye I can hear McGrath's beautiful voice, with a hint of a brogue clipped clean by the harsh winds of his North Dakota birthplace, mocking the *Times'* prim effort to encapsulate and thus contain his authentic poetic legacy.

There's an echo of that voice in a eulogy by Lyle Daggett, which cites McGrath speaking to some "professors lounging at a meeting table" at "some sleepy gathering of these late years":

> Damn it, we don't need poems that are beautiful, we need poems that are useful, and if you can't write one that's useful, then steal one! Steal a poem, by Brecht or Neruda, and change a few words. . . .

The irony is that Tom did both truth and beauty exquisitely well. There's never been a stauncher advocate of American socialism than this farmer's son from the high plains; never a richer, fuller American poetic voice than this one, aged like good bourbon, mixing lyricism with bombast, high style with high dudgeon, and pleasure with political savvy.

McGrath was equally brilliant while writing a variety of pieces: an ode to his brother killed in World War II ("Blues for Jimmy" from *Longshot O'Leary's Garland of Practical Poesie*, 1949); a love song to a Communist organizer ("On the Memory of a Working Class Girl" from *The Movie at the End of the World*, 1972); a chapbook of fifty-eight haiku-like poems to his wife and young son (*Open Songs,* 1977); a paean in praise of beer ("Trinc" from *Echoes inside the Labyrinth,* 1983); or a great epic of American life (*Letter to an Imaginary Friend,* Parts 1–2, 1970; Parts 3–4, 1985). The quality of his work never flagged, despite physical excess and illness, personal tragedies, and a late, debilitating onset of nerve damage in both arms made worse by a botched operation.

Tom's life was full of incidents alternatively dramatic and difficult to endure. After a midwestern boyhood during the Depression, he graduated a radical from the University of North Dakota at Grand Forks in 1939 and served in the Aleutian Islands during World War II, isolated from combat in a unit full of radicals who were feared by the Army high command. He went on to win a Rhodes Scholarship to New College, Oxford University in 1947–48. Returning to the United States without a doctorate, he moved to Hollywood. In 1953, while married to Alice Greenfield McGrath, a Communist organizer in East Los Angeles and the true heroine of the play *Zoot Suit* by Luis Valdez, McGrath was called before the House Un-American Activities Committee, where he refused to cooperate on what he called aesthetic grounds. "Poets have been notorious non-cooperators where committees of this sort are concerned," he said; "I do not wish to bring dishonor upon my tribe." As a result he was blacklisted as a screenwriter and fired from his college teaching position in Los Angeles. Returning to the Midwest, Tom founded *Crazy Horse* magazine in 1961 and taught at North Dakota State University and Moorhead State University over the next two decades. In 1975 he was charged with third-degree murder in the shooting death of a Minnesota man, and though the grand jury returned a no charge verdict, this tragic incident scarred the rest of his life. By the late 1970s, however, he was beginning to be recognized for his life's work, especially for *Letter to an Imaginary Friend.* By this time he had received a National Endowment for the Arts fellowship, a Bush fellowship and a Guggenheim prize. In the 1980s he received a second NEA fellowship, a second Bush fellowship, and a $40,000 senior fellowship from the NEA. His book *Echoes Inside the Labyrinth* won an American Book Award from the Before Columbus Foundation in 1984.

There were many sides to Tom McGrath. His prose has been largely overlooked, though he is the author of a marvelous anti-utopian satire, *The Gates of Ivory, the Gates of Horn,* first printed by the Communist party's Mainstream Publishers in 1957. He also wrote a full length realistic novel of life on New York City's waterfront in the 1940s, originally entitled *All but the Last* and finally published as *This Coffin Has No Handles* by North Dakota Quarterly in 1984. Brief critical articles he published at random and the evidence of interviews suggest that McGrath missed a great career as a critic, but as he often noted, he had little taste for living off the works of others. Frequently honored for his work in the eighties, McGrath left, as one obituary has noted, "scores of writers afloat in his wake" and in fact spent considerable effort in his last years supporting the work of his young followers.

This extraordinary man lived a life full of the stuff of his poems, not always with prudence but with tremendous historical consciousness. His love of the working man and oppressed people of all races was always genuine. "Liberal" was a bad word to him; his on-again, off-again relationship with the Communist party came from his general support of its working class politics, coupled with his disgust with what he took to be its revisionism. (McGrath argued that the party made its major mistake in 1935 when it admitted middle-class intellectuals as a part of its united front against fascism.) Everyone who knew him must have remarked on his amazing probity and his "bullshit detector." He was *the* American radical poet of the decades 1940–1990, and his voice now becomes a part of our collective history.

—*John F. Crawford*

Revolutionary Frescoes—the Ascension

In memory of Walter Lowenfels

On that morning when the Unknown Revolutionary rises
From his bed in the Veterans' Hospital in Fargo, North
    Dakota,
There will be free cigarettes for everyone and no lumps in the
    porridge!
Trumpets will sound and resound from the four corners of the
    world!
The four blue-blowers and commissars of the vagrant and
    workless winds,
Standing at the round earth's blazing corners, in arms,
Will organize the demonstration: Marx, Engels, Lenin,
Che—the last and youngest at the western corner with
    machine gun.

Then, in the hospital corridors the walking wounded will fly
As a Blakean column of pure spirit toward the operating room
And the rotting flesh, bed-bound will rise up in song!
The walking delegates with wooden legs will race through the
    halls
And the wheel-chairs, now winged—the wheels within wheels
    of Fellow-worker Ezekial—
Will sport it in the very whiskers of Marx as he beams from
    his plinth

Near the ceiling of the north corner! And all four commissars
  will sound
The timbrel and the fraternal harp and the mouth organ and
  the guitar,
And the heavenly host will chant, led by Woody and Cisco:
Everything or Nothing, Comrades! All of us or none!

Then the rolling tomb will arrive blazing with slogans and
  flowers!
But *no gardenias,* dear Comrades! Damn all bourgeois
  conventions!
Let us have something simpler instead. Geraniums, maybe—
From the window-boxes of the poor. And, from the woods,
  red cardinals—and trillium!
To stand for the flowering unity of theory and practice and
  daring—
But leave it to the Mexican and Italian sections to organize:
  they *know!*
Finally the heavenly cadres have all in hand—no more
To do but fly up in a great hosting of real and hallucinatory
Light!
          They fly up . . .
                    Farewell, Comrade!
                              You did your share.

And now, in the pause that follows, I remember walking with
  you
And your other comrade, Walt Whitman, beside the Jersey
  shore
While he talked of news of these states and the foiled
  revolutionaires
Out of an earlier time; and we run to keep up with his stride.
Himself with his beard full of butterflies, you with the moon
  on your forehead!
Midnight ramblers and railers! By the cradle, endlessly
  rocking,
Of a fouled contaminant sea you both saw clean and young . . .
Father of the dream, you said he was; father of poets.
I see you now in the Shades, old Double Walt, dear outlaws.

And now we must straighten the chairs in the meeting room.
A few need dues-stamps to fill out their Party Books.
A few buy the works of the Lost Poet at the Literature table—
A bit dubious for all that the young Lit-comrade says.
Finally we divide the left-over cigarettes,
Cutting some in half so that everything comes out even.
All squared away. All in good proletarian order,
We leave the place ship-shape for the next delegation to
    use—
Though such uprisings don't happen every day . . .

Song: Miss Penelope Burgess, Balling the Jack

Barefaced baby with the three minute dream
Waking at morning with a soundless scream—
Not another ace in the dream-rigged packs,
Nothing but jokers and the non-wild jacks;

Oh baby, baby, when the light breaks clean
(And there's nothing to run on but a benzedrine)
It's back on the bricks and hustle the stem
Where the buffalo are thicker than the iron men.

Git it up, give it up, I hear you cry.
But one day and another and life goes by,
A little bit lousier day by day
But at last at last at last at last it's all gone away—

Then it will come easy, when there's nothing to lose,
Nothing to hope and nothing to choose,
No reason to cry, no reason to sing
Just nothing, nothing, nothing, nothing—

Oh, I hear you crying, baby, in your platform shoes,
With your Cadillac mutant or your cut-rate booze;
I hear you in your brogans or in sable or mink
Where the clubwomen chatter or the chippies swink.

Was it Prince Charming who deceived you from the age of
     ten
And threw you on the town in the world of men?
Did you look for honor and discover its lack
As you struggled for power from flat on your back?

Was it the books that tricked you or the priests that lied—
Promising, promising equality and pride,
While the boss demanded profit and the husband wanted
     more—
A dual purpose property both mother and whore?

We all helped to make you and the way you are:
Signed with our dishonor, an invisible scar.
Dream bitch-goddess, or terrible nurse,
On all of us who've harmed you I call down a curse.

Long gone lady with your three minute dream
Waking in a trap with a soundless scream
(As the child will scream at the terror of birth)
Where will be born your dignity and worth?
In what new heaven? On what different earth?

Josephine Miles

JOSEPHINE MILES enjoyed a long and productive life as a poet, teacher, and literary scholar. Born in 1911 in Chicago, she grew up in southern California and began writing poetry as a child, first publishing in the children's magazine, *St. Nicholas.* After receiving her Ph.D. from the University of California at Berkeley in 1938, she joined the faculty of the English Department there and spent virtually all her teaching career at Berkeley, retiring as a professor emerita in 1978. In early childhood Miles was severely crippled by rheumatoid arthritis and was turned down for teaching positions at several institutions of higher learning—including the noted women's school, Mills College—passed over as being too frail or more cynically a poor actuarial risk because of her disability. Her enduring professorial career at the University of California and the love and respect she earned as a teacher stand in noble refutation to such prejudice. However circumscribed her physical movement, and it must have been an arduous and painful task even to draw pen across paper, her mind ranged free, and she wrote and published prolifically throughout her life.

Miles published about as many works of literary criticism and analysis as poetry. Her literary studies ranged from the Elizabethan era to the present, and she developed a method of textual analysis the aim of which was to scrutinize poets' individual choices of words so as to trace "large evolutions in poetic language throughout history." Among her critical works are *Wordsworth and the Vocabulary of Emotion* (1942), *The Continuity of Poetic Language: Studies in English Poetry from the 1540s to the 1940s* (1951), *Eras and Modes in English Poetry* (1957), and *Style and Proportion: The Language of Prose and Poetry* (1967).

In 1935, while still a graduate student, several of her poems appeared in an anthology, *Trial Balances,* and in 1936 she was the recipient of a Shelley Memorial Award. The next year she was honored with a Phelan Memorial Award. She subsequently received a Guggenheim Fellowship and a National Endowment for the Arts award, among many others.

Miles' first book of poetry, *Trial Balances,* was published in 1935. She went on to publish a number of other books of poetry including *Lines at Intersection* (1939), *Poems on Several Occasions* (1941), *Local Measures* (1946), *Prefabrications* (1955), *Poems 1930–1969* (1960), *Civil Poems* (1966), *Kinds of Affection* (1967), *Fields of Learning* (1968), *To All Appearances* (1974), *Coming to Terms* (1979), and *Collected Poems 1930–1983* (1983).

Josephine Miles was known as a poet who focused on quotidian particulars. She had, as one critic stated, "an unfailing sensitivity to the large significance of the small." Miles characterized her writing as a search "to find the poetry in the common ordinary routine of the place" and found the source of her poetic language in everyday speech: "It is the poetry of talk that I like to think about: the line of conversation, a question or answer, a turn or intonation, the way somebody finds to say something." The poem "So Graven" from *Local Measures* distills the essence of her poetic insight and craft,

> Simplicity so graven hurts the sense
> The monumental and simple break
> And the great tablets shatter down in deed.
>
> Every year the quick particular jig
> Of unresolved event moves in the mind,
> And there's the trick simplicity has to win.

Miles also felt that growing up in southern California had given her a keen awareness of the artifice that surrounds us, and many of her poems call attention to those artifices that we unquestioningly mistake for substance. Though, as in the poem "The Plastic Glass," Miles questions the nature and value of things we take for granted—"And I would ask the saint at what expense / This incorporeal vision falls to the lay mind, / And search the breast / For revelations of unquietude"—and sometimes evinces a bleak, even bitter vision, when all is said and done hers is an expansively affirmative spirit, one in which ". . . the blessing / Falls not from above; the grace / Goldens from everyman, his singular credit / In the beatitude of place."

Poems such as "Government Injunction Restraining Harlem Cosmetic Co.," "Saving the Bay," the Vietnam War–inspired "Civil Poems," and many of the themes in the cycle "Neighbors and Constellations" (written in part out of her reflections on the McCarthy era), all illustrate how Miles's thought and poetry were shaped by social, political, and environmental concerns.

As a teacher and mentor, Miles gave special encouragement and support to young poets and scholars, particularly to women and members of minority groups who desired to pursue literary and academic careers, since her own experiences as a disabled person had made her acutely sensitive to the hurdles placed in the way of full participation.

Josephine Miles did not consider poetry to be something divorced from everyday life, but rather as something fixed preeminently in it. Using common speech, she explored and affirmed the commonality of our experience. Reading her poetry, one enters a place "Where we can ponder, celebrate, and reshape / Not only what we are, where we are from, / But what in the risk and moment of our day / We may become" ("Center").

—J. J. Phillips

Physiologus

When the mind is dark with the multiple shadows of facts,
There is no heat of the sun can warm the mind.
The facts lie streaked like the trunks of trees at evening,
Without the evening hope that they may find
Absorbent night and blind.

Howsoever sunset and summer bring rest
To the rheumatic by change, and howsoever
Sulphur's good medicine, this can have no cure—
This weight of knowledge dark on the brain is never
To be burnt out like fever,

But slowly, with speech to tell the way and ease it,
Will sink into the blood, and warm, and slowly
Move in the veins, and murmur, and come at length
to the tongue's tip and the finger's tip most lowly,
And will belong to the body wholly.

Dream

I see you displaced, condensed, within my dream,
Yet here before me in your daily shape.
And think, can my dream touch you any way
Or move you as in it you otherwise moved?

I prosper in the dream, yet may it not
Touch you in any way or may you move.
It is the splendor of the possible
Not to appear in actual shape and form.

It is the splendor of the actual
So to be still and still be satisfied,
That any else or more becomes a dream,
Displaced, condensed, as by my dreamed regard.

Tide

From the flood of tide to the shore edge how withdraws,
From the full consonance of waters at the brim how starves
    and stands away,
How chafes and shallows upon scraping stones,
Belief, belief.

Now in the night the vessel of sea
Brims with the waters we taste in our life
Cool to the curve and the clear
Of belief,
And runs over.

Now in the day the shocked rubble of stone
Scrapes at the ebb, and the real
Bristles of barnacle shells clash in the draining
Down of belief
Out of brine.

And I cannot learn

How in the flood of tide the shells implicit
Grate in the sand, how the rocks
Rack in the stillest full the fact of the ebb

But in ebb
Drains down to loss the fiction of belief.

My Fear in the Crowd

The thousand people stand in the sunlight,
They are taking in the messages of the speakers
Deliberately, they are weighing the judgments,
They are making up their minds.

The sun is on their shoulders, weight of the earth,
They know it, and they are not despairing.
Against odds, they may consider quietly and freely
What they will do.

Who knows then, not I,
And I am desperate in no knowledge,
If later, somewhat dispersed, they will yell
And turn and burn the place where they stood.

But look, the May light
Outlines each shape, each moving
Out from the crowd, each carrying
In his own mind the place where he stood.

Doll

Though the willows bent down to shelter us where we played
House in the sandy acres, though our dolls,
Especially Lillian, weathered all the action,
I kept getting so much earlier home to rest
That medical consultation led to cast
From head to toe. It was a surprise for my parents

And so for me also, and I railed
Flat out in the back seat on the long trip home
In which three tires blew on our trusty Mitchell.
Home, in a slight roughhouse of my brothers,
It turned out Lillian had been knocked to the floor and broken
Across the face. Good, said my mother
In her John Deweyan constructive way,
Now you and Lillian can be mended together.
We made a special trip to the doll hospital
To pick her up. But, They can't fix her after all, my father
    said,
You'll just have to tend her with her broken cheek.
I was very willing. We opened the box, and she lay
In shards mixed among tissue paper. Only her eyes
Set loose on a metal stick so they would open
And close, opened and closed, and I grew seasick.

A friend of the family sent me a kewpie doll.
Later Miss Babcox the sitter,
After many repetitious card games,
Said, We must talk about bad things.
Let me tell you
Some of the bad things I have known in my life.
She did not ask me mine, I could not have told her.
Among the bad things in my life, she said,
Have been many good people, good but without troubles;
Her various stories tended
To end with transmigrations of one sort or another,
Dishonest riches to honest poverty; kings and queens
To indians over an adequate space of time.
Take this cat coming along here, she said,
A glossy black cat whom she fed her wages in salmon,
He is a wise one, about to become a person.
Come to think of it, possibly Lillian
Is about to become a cat.

She will have different eyes then, I said.
Obviously. Slanted, and what is more,
Able to see in the dark.

Larry Neal

LARRY NEAL was one of the most influential writers of the
1960s and 1970s, before his untimely and tragic death from a
heart attack in early January 1981. He was 43 years old, much
too young to have left us.

His death, for me, was doubly shocking and frustrating, be-
cause I found out about it over the telephone while trying to
reach him. I had just returned from a visit to Lesotho, a quasi-
independent Black African country surrounded by the menace
of white South Africa. Before I had left New York in mid-
December, Larry had asked me to bring him back some infor-
mation on the Basotho, the native people of Lesotho.

My telephone call to him on that extremely cold, snowy
January morning was to let him know that I had gotten the
information he wanted. But his number was busy every time I
dialed it, so I phoned my friend Barbara Masekela, the sister of
South African trumpeter Hugh Masekela, instead. Before we
could get deep into our conversation, her call-waiting let her
know there was another call coming in. She excused herself and
went off the line. When she came back after a brief pause, she
was crying hysterically. I was stunned. What could it be? She
told me in a trembling voice wracked by sobs, almost wails, that
Larry Neal had died just the night before of a heart attack.

"Larry's dead!" she kept shouting into the phone. "Larry
Neal is dead! Can you believe it?" she kept saying over and over
again.

No, I couldn't believe it. Needless to say, I was more than
stunned by this news. I was devastated. Now I understood why
I couldn't get through to him; everybody and his mother was
trying to do just that. But more than anything I felt a profound
sense of loss and pain, because along with Jayne Cortez, Larry

was responsible for helping to pave the way for my coming to live in Harlem. Harlem was where Larry Neal lived and felt most at home. He convinced me that I should live there too, and I felt right at home, just like Larry had said I would, just like Larry had said.

I spent many, many nights talking with Larry Neal—at his home, at my home, in bars, at poetry readings, anywhere we could get in a word with each other. We discussed everything from poets and writers to basketball and football; from musicians and painters to politics and religion; from women and clothes (see, Larry Neal was a "clothes junkie" who liked himself "clean" and in fashion) to "street brothers" and why they felt it was necessary to sell drugs. Larry knew and understood that if America respected them, held out a life that included them, that they would be more than happy to give up their lives in drugs. But Larry also knew this wasn't going to happen, and he accepted these "street brothers," carried no animosity towards them.

Larry Neal was also one of the people who turned me on to the visual arts. His Jumel Terrace brownstone was full of the works of great African and African American painters, photographers, and sculptors. Larry loved art, though I think he loved music more. Indeed, he took piano lessons at the baby grand he had ensconced in his living room. I remember one day coming into Larry's home and finding the great drummer, Max Roach, sitting at Larry's piano fingering some chords with a big grin on his face. But then this was the way it was at Larry's house. You might meet anyone there: the late Romare Bearden, Ralph Ellison, Charles Fuller, Amiri Baraka, Vincent Smith, Toni Morrison, Maya Angelou, Albert Murray, Gwendolyn Brooks, Sonia Sanchez. I met them all (and too many more to mention here) at Larry's home—over food, over music, over love.

But if Larry loved music and wanted secretly to become a musician (and he did), it was as a writer that he had an impact. He was a seminal figure in the 1960s and 1970s, as a poet, essayist, playwright, and critic. And while I think he was very fine in all of these genres, for me it was as a critic that he had made his greatest contribution. His penetrating, insightful ideas on literature, music, and art made talking to him an excitingly, pleasurable experience. He was always, in my estimation, fair in his comments and judgments, almost never allowing his feelings to get in the way of his analysis. This is rare (as he was rare) and is much needed today.

At Yale, Larry Neal had been the mentor of Henry Louis "Skip" Gates, perhaps the foremost African American literary critic and scholar writing today. It was Larry Neal who laid the groundwork for much of the work that Skip Gates and Houston Baker are doing today in the area of folkloric language and the signification of folk forms. They both owe much to Larry's ground-breaking work.

Larry was stylish, urbane, and positively hip. It was always a pleasure to be in his company. His New Year's Day parties were especially memorable because he knew so many people, from every level of society and from practically every racial group. He'd always invite a lively crowd including people like Charles Fuller, Amiri Baraka, and Paul Carter Harrison for a feast, including drinks, conversation, and football games.

While I considered Larry a better critic than a poet, he was still a fine poet. His poem "Poppa Stoppa Speaks from His Grave" is reminiscent of Langston Hughes, and "Don't Say Goodbye to the Porkpie Hat" (the porkpie hat was one of Larry's trademarks) and "Ghost Poem #1" also represent some of his finer efforts at poetry. The conclusion of "Ghost Poem #1"—"Is that my Junie Boy running/with that fast crowd?"—is just about every mother's nightmare.

Larry Neal's absence from the literary scene today affects me profoundly in many ways, yet his spirit is forever present. His work, his vision, and his writing—his essays, his poetry, his plays—help us to keep on keeping on, doing the work, getting the writing done. It is what he would have wanted for himself had he lived, and I'm sure it is what he would have wanted—would have expected—from us, wouldn't have had it any other way.

—Quincy Troupe

From

VISIONS OF A LIBERATED
FUTURE: BLACK ARTS
MOVEMENT WRITINGS (1989)

Don't Say Goodbye to the Porkpie Hat

Mingus, Bird, Prez, Langston, and them

Don't say goodbye to the Porkpie Hat that rolled
along on nodded shoulders
                    that swang bebop phrases
                    in Minton's jelly roll dreams
Don't say goodbye to hip hats tilted in the style of a soulful
     era;
the Porkpie Hat that Lester dug
swirling in the sound of sax blown suns
                    phrase on phrase, repeating bluely
                    tripping in and under crashing
                    hi-hat cymbals, a fickle girl
                    getting sassy on the rhythms.
Musicians heavy with memories
move in and out of this gloom;
the Porkpie Hat reigns supreme
smell of collard greens
and cotton madness
commingled in the nigger elegance of the style.
                    The Porkpie Hat sees tonal
                    memories of salt peanuts and hot
                    house birds the Porkpie Hat
                    sees . . .
Cross riffing square kingdoms, riding midnight Scottsboro
trains. We are haunted by the lynched limbs.

On the road:
It would be some hoodoo town
It would be some cracker place
you might meet redneck lynchers
face to face
but mostly you meet mean horn blowers
running obscene riffs
Jelly Roll spoke of such places:
the man with the mojo hand
the dyke with the .38
the yaller girls
and the knifings.

Stop-time Buddy and Creole Sydney
wailed in here. Stop time.
chorus repeats, stop and shuffle.
stop and stomp.
listen to the horns, ain't they mean?
now ain't they mean
in blue
in blue
in blue streaks of mellow wisdom
blue notes
coiling around
the Porkpie Hat
and ghosts of dead musicians drifting through
here on riffs that smack
of one-leg trumpet players
and daddy glory piano ticklers
who
twisted arpeggios
with diamond-flashed fingers.
There was Jelly Roll Morton, the sweet mackdaddy,
hollering Waller, and Willie The Lion Smith—
some mean showstoppers.

Ghosts of dead holy rollers ricocheted in the air
        funky
with white lightnin' and sweat.

Emerald bitches shot shit in a kitchen smelling
of funerals and fried chicken.
Each city had a different sound:
there was Mambo, Rheba, Jeanne;
holy the voice of these righteous sisters.

Shape to shape, horn to horn
the Porkpie Hat resurrected himself
night to night, from note to note
skimming the horizons, flashing bluegreenyellow lights
and blowing black stars
and weird looneymoon changes; chords coiled about him
and he was flying
fast
zipping
past
sound
into cosmic silences.
And yes
and caresses flowed from the voice in the horn in the blue
of the yellow whiskey room where bad hustlers with big
coats moved, digging the fly sister, fingerpopping while
tearing at chicken and waffles.

The Porkpie Hat loomed specter like, a vision for the world;
shiny, the knob toe shoes,
sporting hip camel coats
and righteous pin stripes—
pants pressed razor shape;
and caressing his horn, baby like.

So we pick up our axes and prepare
to blast the white dream;
we pick up our axes
re-create ourselves and the universe,
sounds splintering the deepest regions
of spiritual space
crisp and moaning voices

leaping in the horns of destruction,
blowing death and doom to all who have no use for the spirit.

So we cook out of sight
into cascading motions of joy delight
shooflies the Bird lollygagging
and laughing for days,
and the rhythms way up in there
wailing, sending scarlet rays, luminescent,
spattering bone and lie.
we go on cool lords
wailing on into star nights,
rocking whole worlds, unfurling song on song
into long stretches of green spectral shimmerings,
blasting on, fucking the moon with the blunt edge
of a lover's tune, out there now, joy riffing
for days and do
railriding and do
talking some lovely shit and do
to the Blues God who blesses us.

No, don't say goodbye to the Porkpie Hat—
he lives, oh yes.

Lester lives and leaps
Delancey's dilemma is over
Bird lives
Lady lives
Eric stands next to me
while I finger the Afro-horn
Bird lives
Lady lives
Lester leaps in every night
Tad's delight
is mine now
Dinah knows
Richie knows
that Bud is Buddha

that Jelly Roll dug juju
and Lester lives
in Ornette's leapings
the Blues God lives
we live
live
spirit lives
and sound lives
bluebird lives
lives and leaps
dig the mellow voices
did the Porkpie Hat
dig the spirit in Sun Ra's sound
dig the cosmic Trane
dig be
dig be
dig be
spirit lives in sound
dig be
sound lives in spirit
dig be
yeah ! ! !

spirit lives
spirit lives
spirit lives
SPIRIT ! ! !

SWHEEEEEEEEEEEEEEETTT ! ! !

take it again
this time from the top

The Life: Hoodoo Hollerin'
Bebop Ghosts

We walked the bar
        the neon world of hip players judged us in the
afterhours
            spot where they busted Booney, and where Leroy was
            blasted in the chest, in the john where we snort
            coke from tips of Broadway polished switchblades,
            talking shit, high on the ego trips.

The fly world in action
            our bitches turning Seventh Avenue tricks;
            whipping her pussy with the coat hanger,
            and saying: stop jiving bitch, get me
            the motherfuckin money now.

We walked the bar
            trying to get it together—
            ghosts of men, but men just the same.
            Yeah . . . this world judging us
            marking our progress from cradle
            to cane, laughing, wishing us luck
            while we hover over pits of dry bones
            laughing like forgotten pimps—we so hip.

It's all here
            all down here in the neon world of flash
            and-let-me-fuck-you bullshit.

Even in our weakness here, somewhere we are strong some
        snake-skinned god hisses here:
            hoodoo hollerin' bebop ghosts
            some eternal demon squirming
            in his head—that's why he be bad
            and all them things.

Some of us
            teetered on the edge of the Life like peeping
            toms; teetered maneuvering for the grand score
            that came every night, but every night, came late.
                        dope pushers
                        take-off goons
                        Murphy-working old ladies
            one used to dance in the high yaller chorus
            of the Cotton Club;
            one, a nympho, claimed once to have graduated
            from Vassar. (If you can dig it?)
            Scenes like that were quite common.

One, a singer, a Chanel No. 5 freak from South Philly called
    herself the Duchess, spoke with an English accent.
                        Lois
            the envious one, frail hunk of bones
            and cigarette holder, wraps spider legs around dull
            honky sailors; likes going down on Market Street
            cowboys.

                    Up under it all
some ancient memory trying to break through the
perpetual high:
            He be hoodoo hollerin' bebop ghosts
            some awesome demon twisting close
            curling in the smell of beer
            and reefer; some dick strong god
            hissing softly in his ear
                        Hey!
            And he is mean with his nigger rod
            thus note the smell of sen-sen on his breath
            but dig how he teeters on the edge of death. . .

Ghost Poem # 1

You would never shoot smack
or lay in one of these Harlem
doorways pissing on yourself
that is not your way   not the
way of Alabama boys groomed slick
for these wicked cities momma
warned us of

You were always swifter than that:
the fast money was the Murphy game
or the main supply before the cutting—
so now you lean with the shadows
(at the dark end of Turk's bar)
aware that the hitman is on your ass

You know that there is something inevitable
about it
You know that he will come   as sure as shit
snorting blow for courage
and he wil burn you at the peak of your peacocking
glory
And when momma gets the news
she will shudder over the evening meal
and moan: "Is that my Junie Boy runnin
with that fast crowd?"

Can I Tell You This Story, or Will You Send Me through All Kinds of Changes?

> *Summer city,*
> *asphalt memory*
> *of blood and pain,*
> *night game*
> *the eerie rain;*
> *we had no pity*
> *on the weak ones . . .*
>
> *—Charles Neal*

                              Stiff old Philly saints dripped gold
into the arms of Georgia Queens; Columbia Avenue was
      snake
eyes and the hussy in red.
                              In those days, the avenues were
nigger cops, like Reedy who thought he was the Durango Kid;
we shot him in the doorway of a mean loud party.
                              These were the days of the bebopping
house of blue lights.
                              Bird gained weight; we meet our
                              turnpike death clutching our
                              instruments.

Places got turned out then—
heads were busted and lips swelled purple;
we were blind.
we stayed high on Mexicano marijuana,
drank wine in narrow alleys,
and Lady Melody, the blue spirit breezed
in every now and then.

                        We were killed in weird ways,
puked guts, stabbed heads, bleeding marcels,

cursing each other's mothers and fathers and sisters and
brothers;
old dribble-lipped drunks high on tokay spewing and pissin
on themselves.
And Daddy Grace mad with power, shoving pigfeet and
    barbecue
down the throats of shouting soul sisters.
Preachers dreamed yellow Cadillacs,
waiters pretending doctor,
mailmen pretending lawyer,
doctor and lawyer pretending Negro society.

These were the Eisenhower years—the landscape of the
    fifties.
                    The whole thing was a skunky bitch,
legs in a putrid spread, obscene these Northern cities.
                    And no prophets walked these streets;
                    or at least, we did not know them.

Can I tell this story?
We slow-dragged, our do-rags wrapped, like Harlem sheiks,
a thin swish of sweat darkening
the edge of silk scarfs.

Horns on bats' wings hollered high,
the saxes seemed to carry the deepest tales;
and even the smells had meaning.
our rhythms played stink finger with the moon.
we died bullshit deaths
behind urinating staircases.

                        High yallers moved to Germantown;
and Summer saw an invasion of Southern dark brown
    chippies.
                        Each king's reign ended in the
slick slash of air-teasing razors.
                        But boiling lye was the weapon
of lonely plump old maids.

We formed nations, and bopped all over the city,
   gang-warring.
we were blind then, and even now the light is hard to take.
For some the winters were blue lights, the slow grind,
Johnny Ace dying of Russian roulette, cocaine, and the hawk-
eyed, the hawkeyed wind tearing at our asses; home was candy
stores, stuffy rooms, the burning incense of shattered bebop
poets who had seen Bird and wanted to be Bird in all the
ways that Bird was.

So they spread their asses
for the Scag God to fuck them;
and so, some nights they sat high
in the Diamond Street cemetery
talking to Yoruba ghosts.
It was not our time or place;
it was an empty time,
an asphalt bridge stretching into nowhere
some words
some deaths
somebody pinned
against the wall
gun up under his throat.

               And all we wanted
             to do was sing like *moonglow*
           ravens or raspy-voiced old
         blues singers, times we wanted
       to be killers slouching treacherous
     under broad skies.

So we twisted our dreams and shaped
our worlds out of lean fables
and awesome toasts that sucked
us into streams of moody anger—
to turn our lips down and be
angry was at the pit of the style.

So, we danced, switchblades nestled
in socks or back pockets
as we   as we   as we glide
under the mystic aura
of black Buddhas and voodoo gods
Whole chunks of life lay chopped up in alleys—
fresh-born babies wrapped in the classified
pages of the *Philadelphia Tribune;*
in our boredom, we allowed streetwalkers
to seduce us while the smells from fish n' chips
drifted into two-room apartments adorned
with velvet Jesuses.

God bless this house of body and of desperation
of blood and of story of gesture and of nighttime hassles.

We died and killed for our puny reps:
"Shove that punk in his chest, break his
head, blast that motherfucker," sez Camel
Hair Benny, the no-tooth killer.

Spring was loose, the surge of color
                    the park
                    and her body
                    as holy object,
                    walks along
                    the Schuylkill,
                    love hard today
                    cause death
                    rules the avenues
                    as do
                    rhythm and change
                    kiss
                    under the Japanese gazebo
                    kiss
                    smells, soft plunge
                    wet joy and all
                    moans and the clutching fingers

> screams
> tears when you first split her.

It was not hard to be tender when
the heart like wide boulevards lay exposed
for the shuffling armies and the demon preachers
who would soon descend upon us flailing whips,
cursing, teaching submission to a bullshit god.
Parents and uncles would join the act, too;
the whore aunt would argue the virtues
of virginity, fat and high on beer, sucking reefer.
Their nights would end in spilled wine
and the lonely odor of cigarette butts—
their curses would greet the sun;
but most of our spring nights would end
in mellow morning songs and soft rain . . .

Duane Niatum

Few contemporary writers find as much lilt and music in their work as does Duane Niatum, and yet his music is informed by perceptions unfogged by romantic notions or easy answers. His lines may seem soft as branches moving in the wind, but they are also as tough and stubborn as deep-rooted cedars. Ocean wave and sea wind and the thrust of the salmon upstream against the current are part of the voice of this poet whose words "Give you the Duwamish River's way/ Of offering it all to the sea,/ Offering it all to the sea" ("Owl").

First published under the name of Duane McGiness, Niatum was born in Seattle in 1938 and raised by his maternal grandparents. The author of six major collections of his own poetry and several chapbooks, Niatum also worked for a time as an editor at Harper and Row. While there he put together one of the earliest and most significant anthologies of Native American poetry, *Carriers of the Dream Wheel,* published in 1975. In 1988, he updated that work by editing *Harper's Anthology of Twentieth Century Native American Poetry.* Not long after the publication in 1970 of his first book, *After the Death of an Elder Klallam,* he took the name Niatum. Not only was this to honor his Klallam Indian ancestry, it was also to make a statement about the direction of his work.

Like many other contemporary Native American writers. Niatum's childhood was not an easy one. He spent time in reform school and later, in the Navy, was sentenced to a month in the brig. There was not much in those early years which would have led one to expect his flowering into a serious student of literature, a trail-breaking anthologist, an award-winning poet, and a gifted university teacher. Yet even in those dark times he carried with him memories of heritage and images of dream which protected him like totems. His awareness as an adult of the drastic contrast between the urban settings in which he was forced to live and the old Klallam ways which depend on a balanced relationship between human beings and their environment—both ocean and land—would prove his salvation as a person and the driving force behind his poems. It helped shape a consciousness which can present not only celebratory, sensual songs of ancestral dream animals, but also visions of the bitterness of human separations and losses in a city world which has little time for tenderness. As he said in *Survival This Way: Interviews with American Indian Poets*, "Art gives the individual a chance to deal with the complexity and the chaos. . . ."

There is, despite the accessibility of his poems, no lack of complexity in Niatum's prosody. A student of Theodore Roethke, Niatum's work draws easily on the forms of European literature, while remaining rooted in the imagery and the spiritual vision of the Native American universe. The brevity and clarity of his lyrics are not only an indication of his awareness of the great classical poets of Japan, but also proof of his familiarity with the form and content of the songs of Klallam oral traditions. Though his poems go through numerous revisions and his devotion to craft is as great as that of any contemporary poet now writing, the world in which his poems exist is one in which human beings are *not* at the center of the universe. The cedar tree and the whale are as alive and as full of wisdom as any ancestor and, in a real sense, are ancestral beings themselves.

One of the great traditional tales of the Native peoples of the Pacific Northwest is of the salmon boy, a young man who scorns the salmon and as a consequence drowns and must live for a time as a salmon himself before being allowed to rejoin his human relatives in his original human shape. Niatum's vision in the best of his poems is, to my mind, the kind of vision that the salmon boy brought back to his people. It reminds us of the terrible dangers of human pride and self-centered actions, while also conveying something of the dignity and the beauty of the oldest natural rhythms. His harvest of dreams is one

which can give nourishment, not only to our ears and our imag-
inations, but also to our everyday lives.

—*Joseph Bruchac III*

The Musician

You often played
On sheets of dawn,
Your notes building
A room in our house.
Your visits were brief
Retrievals lost to dusk,
Our coming of age,
Time's eraser.

We miss you most
When the snow falls
And hardens to crystal,
When the attic mice
Sleep in the candlelight
We burn on stairways
And in the room
They nest in all winter.

You're the secret sharer.
What moon went bronze,
What measure surrendered
The colors of the peonies
At the concerto's end?
Your sound, a sapphire fountain,
Transparent as the river.
What warmth of place

In our hearts explodes
With your absence. Oh
Why did you leave
The piano, the city
Unannounced? What melody drove
You from our lives?
We feel marginal. Yet,
The lines on our faces

Keep returning the hours
You composed the silence.
In our imperfections
And the pizzicato refrains
Of adventurous leaves, we wait
For the piano to open
The window, our souls
To skip on water.

First Spring

Drifting on the wheel
Of a past looking like
A redskin American gothic,
Staring through forty-one years
Of rain-pelted windows, I bear
With modest grace, diminished nerves,
Narrowing light, half-formed figures:
The memories floating in purgatory.

Renting a small house,
The first in fifteen years, I
Admire each hour the diffidence
Of the elders walking by,
Their eyes of snow-caves,

Their hands dancing like puppets.
When a lost love calls,
Having abandoned another,
I say, *Sorry, sorry, I'm*

Too busy with the friends
Still left. I'll call you.
The lie of copper on my tongue.
Why tell her they are
The birds at the feeder,
Bees in the lilacs and roses,
Books on the shelves,
Paintings on the walls,
Wind in the roof?

It is called giving your body
A field to get lost in.
It is called standing on your head
Before the women you lost.
It is called sleeping
In the embers of your name.

John Norton

JOHN NORTON was born into a Boston Irish family and edu-
cated at the Jesuit-run Boston College. He subsequently earned
a Ph.D. in eighteenth-century literature at the University of
Pennsylvania, and he has gone on to work as an editor and a
technical writer in San Francisco. Norton's poetry, fiction, and
criticism have appeared in a variety of journals and magazines,
and *Posthum(or)ous,* a chapbook of his poems, was published
in 1986.

More recently, he is the author of *The Light at the End of
the Bog* (1989), a series of prose-poetic sketches, dialogues, and
meditations in which Norton probes the psychological, genera-
tional, and often ethnic mysteries of a father-son relationship.
As he explains: "My natural father was born in Ireland and died
when I was in my late teens. We never knew each other as
adults, never had time enough to talk intimately as father and
son. In these pieces the voices of father and son sometimes
merge, sometimes diverge. These are records of conversations
never held."

These prose poems seem deliberately prosy, for Norton con-
sistently withholds the grace of lyricism. This stylistic austerity
is appropriate for the dour heritage of a certain sort of New
England Irish Catholicism which both father and son struggle
to chronicle, to understand, and ultimately to repudiate. In-
deed, the Puritanical/Jansenist "Land of No" from which the
father figure emerges bloody but unbowed has much in com-
mon with the classic theatrical embodiment of a similar terrain,
Eugene O'Neill's *Long Day's Journey into Night.*

Norton's work is also in the Irish tradition of Seamus
Heaney's bog poems, that now famous series of meditations on
ritual violence provoked by the uncannily preserved prehistoric

bodies found in Danish bogs. Norton's pieces, like Heaney's, embody an Old World habit of mind. As Heaney puts it in "Bogland," Irish perspective is not expansive and horizontal, because "We have no prairies / To slice a big sun at evening." Instead, "Our pioneers keep striking / Inwards and downwards, / Every layer they strip / Seems camped on before." The characteristic movement is vertical, down to the roots of thought and feeling.

Similarly, in Norton's book the son calls his father "an anthropologist of ideas," and in the title piece, "The Light at the End of the Bog," the father is confronted as a young man in Ireland with the palpable mystery of a body surfacing in the bog near his home. The experience prompts a lesson in burrowing tenacity that exemplifies the effect of Norton's writing: "Never back away, Jack, never try to unthink what's already grabbed your attention." And again, in the book's last piece, while surveying the "suburb of cemeteries" outside San Francisco, the speaker exposes the "straight rows" of "marble crypts and memorials" as a sentimental fiction: "That's not the way it is, he said. Roots head for each other, tendrils reach for anything, try to make some possible connection. Everything makes the same mouldering way into earth, turns into the stuff of future lives."

—Charles Fanning

From

THE LIGHT AT THE END OF
THE BOG (1989)

The Family at Christmas

MY father sensed Christmas approaching, like a pip on a radar screen. He opened every December in character. He would read aloud from "Scrooge and I," a favorite romance. He sang carols dolefully like a stage tenor. Bleak Christmas, he would croon. Let me go to my bed and wake on the 27th. This was his star role.

My father grew a strong shell and mimicked the ways of high-minded Brahmins in sentimental Irish Boston. He took an aristocrat's pleasure in displeasing the masses. Three days before Christmas, SH-T appeared on the front pages. A censored photo of my father carrying a large sign NO SHIT ON MY LAWN to picket the city's Nativity creche on the Boston Common with its array of larger-than-life figures and penned animals. Arrested for littering papier-mache cow chips with green and red bows and disturbing the peace.

You call this peace, he said to the police. My father was playing to the overburdened shoppers and purse snatchers, but his principal audience was that floating pack of hecklers found at every religious freedom and civil liberty event on the Common the last 350 years. You call this peace? The crowd got noisier and began grabbing for him, thus the police escort to the Charles Street Jail. My father made Eyewitness News on two major channels. I watched him hold a handcrafted turd up to the cameras. You call this litter?

My father adopted pagan darkness. My father lobbed symbols back at the believers. Few got his point. Encapsulated in each painted turd was a signed folded document where my father rationally presented his argument against public celebration of religion. Few bothered to break theirs open to read it. My father wanted a federal case, all the way to the Supreme Court if needed. My mother feared these shenanigans. What will he get but more trouble? She *had* to disapprove because of the children. We didn't have our father's tact.

Start by the enemy's perimeter. Knock that over first. My father's strategy for all wars, literal or symbolic. Rent a monk's costume and browze the adult book stores and arcades.

An ominous report followed his preliminary hearing and psychiatric evaluation. One more arrest or one more public episode and he'd find himself in Boston State Hospital, where the staff was Jungian and, my father presumed, unsympathetic to his causes. He could be shut away for all holidays. Bleak Christmas, he moaned and pulled the blanket over his head. Wake me on the 27th.

A Com/Plaint

A DIFFICULT people the Irish. Difficult stuck in the past. Stuck in the arse people who emerge out of the bogs, look around long enough to go back, farther inside than they ventured out, farther inside father. A hidden man hurt in a prideful tumble. The pain broke him. Mother cheerleading, not the collegiate type yelling Yea Tim, Yea Tim. Raising her general's cheer from a seat far back in the stands. Encouraged him in a way he never noticed. Let him feel the ideas were his. My presence will never be fully realized, she vowed, until Tim and I have separated. One will die and leave the other. God rest her, my father would say, she saw to that.

Commuting

progress is slow
we could go faster
two years from now
each must have a valid ticket
the system relies upon
compliance not trust
the conductor coaches me
into learning the stops
my father lets me drive the train
the fat woman I don't like gets on
this ride lasts fifty years
from Sunnyvale to Boston
the romance of trains
speaks of journeys
which close at home

Work Rules

For there is my father
who calls the sheep-
like passengers aboard
he speaks of tickets
For my father assigns seats
above to the gallery or below
he is the travelling judge
crew and passengers follow
his work rules
all under his care and stern eye
no wrinkled transfers and no change
you shall not disembark before your stop
For violations pain my father

his rules are clear and on time
For we run by schedule
For I praise his high name
and fear his loathing

William Oandasan

WILLIAM OANDASAN is a member of the Ukomno'm tribe, popularly known as the Yuki, at the Round Valley Reservation in the coastal ranges of northern California. He is also a tribal historian, the author of *A Branch of California Redwood* and *Sermon & Three Waves,* and a teacher of Native American literature and poetry. He has taught at colleges and universities in California, Chicago, and New Orleans. As editor and publisher of *A, a Journal of Contemporary Literature,* he has featured the work of many major Native American authors. He once jokingly referred to his choice of the name for the journal as being intended to make sure that it would always be the first among any directory's listings. But the significance of the name also relates to the first Americans and to contemporary ties with ancient traditions.

Trees figure prominently in Oandasan's poetry. Like the ancient redwoods and giant sequoias that grow in California's north coast and are probably the oldest living things on this planet, Oandasan's tribe has lived in that region for over 10,000 years. His roots are strong and alive, and like his people he continues to struggle and survive. "One Native American cultural value is a reverence for the earth" he notes, and in his own poetry he eloquently displays "the knowledge of [this] organic relationship to the life of the land and the need to express this unique relationship." Oandasan has stayed true to this natural spiritual linkage, whether in Chicago editing an anthology of uptown urban Indian poets ("Chicago" is the Potawatomi Indians' word for "where the onions grow") or in New Mexico living at his wife's grandmother's house on the Laguna Pueblo Reservation where, he writes in the poem "Acoma," "For many distant travelers / The way to Acoma is merely/Interstate-40./. . . But for those who still / travel the four directions / The way to Acoma / Is always the way."

Round Valley Songs maintains strong links to the oral tradition from which contemporary American Indian literature grows. The four "songs" consist of twelve four-line verses that are written not only to be read as poems by themselves or as parts of an orchestrated whole, but are also meant to be rearranged with the other verses to create still more original poems according to a tribal tradition of song renewal. In the same way that many tribal songs were inspired in the past, these poems derive from dream experiences. From his opening invocation, "first there is the word / the word is the *song,*" Oandasan fluidly blends past and present, dreams and reality. But underlying the creation of each song, there are always the hopes for the future and the sense of responsibility for contributing to the creation of that future. Oandasan is not an individual who simply pays eloquent homage to his past; he is an integral part of its landscape, a part that helps keep it alive.

—Gundars Strads

Excerpt from The Past

1

from heart through mind into image:
the pulse of the four directions
the voice of our blood
the spirit of breath and words

2

in chipped and tattered
weavings of a willow basket
the voice of an ancient age
dreaming of breath

3

in a chert arrowhead speckled with quartz
i have seen our grandfathers
along a stream east of the valley
lancing salmon and deer

4

swimming up the Eel
a spirit sings   *acorn-*

pound-the-old-way-draws-
the-milk-of-Earth

5

from fresh currents of night air
above manzanitas near the cemetary
the words of ancient lips
turn in our blood again

6

a few traditions live
alongside a garden walk
in two large stones
now called mortar and pestle

7

for three days before and
after summer's new and full moons
beneath ripples near the head of the Russian
bass will spawn beside sandbars

8

long ago black bears
sang around our lodge fires
tonight they dance
alive through our dreams

9

when we spoke we spoke
the mother tongue of the valley

and counted the spaces between our fingers
today metrics cut underneath the pounds, feet and quarts

   1 0

the woman with white hair
only whispered   *Tatu*
but through my ears
30,000 years echo

   1 1

skirmishes leading to blood and death
have marked Hachet Ridge for centuries
but no one *just* killed before
like at Fish Town on the South Fork!

   1 2

on the summit of Blue Nose
night wind races through long hair
and tears stream down laughing Yuki faces
tens of thousands of years old

Hilton Obenzinger

THE title of the first book by Hilton Obenziger (1947–   ),
The Day of the Exquisite Poet is Kaput (1972), immediately
declares itself political. Its themes of personal and social re-
sponsibility, the marginality of oppositional art in a monocul-
tural stranglehold, are announced in the flow of poems of sim-
ple everyday pleasures. Reflecting an insouciance associated
with the New York school of poetry, his work in California
begins to address themes central to his identity as a Jewish
American radical poet. *This Passover or the Next I will Never be
in Jerusalem* (1980) brings together poems, autobiographical
narratives, and charged polemics focusing on an interrogation
of the Zionist nation of Israel. It is an extraordinary and coura-
geous work, problematizing knotted themes of exile and home-
land from the twice-removed Jewish American vantage point.
Drawing metaphors from the white Anglo-American usurpa-
tion of the American continent from its indigenous people,
Obenzinger accuses Israel of a similar theft and a similar (and
familiar) demonizing of a native population. Obenzinger is, to
this day, a Jewish activist in the struggle for Palestinian rights,
and the groundwork for his moral rationale is laid in this book
and the questions it asks.

—*David Meltzer*

From

THIS PASSOVER OR THE NEXT I WILL NEVER BE IN JERUSALEM (1980)

Sweat-lodge

Hot—my lungs on fire, my hands, knees,
burned alive, hunched in an oven—
scalded, crouched, naked, crowded with others knee-cap
    to knee-cap,
sweat-lodge hot rocks so close my scrotum retreats.
I slap my shoulders to cool them as the sweat-lodge
    leader prays,
*"Grandfather, remember our Indian brothers & sisters
    in the White Man's jails,
Grandfather, help us to remember the four colors of man,
help us to remember Mother Earth and all our relations. . . ."*
He splashes more water on the rocks we inhale
    as excrutiating steam.
I slap & squirm as each takes a turn for prayer.
Now comes my turn to pray. . . .

What can I say?
Should I sing *Shma Yisroel?*
Hear, O Israel . . . that we are one among many?
Perhaps I am of that lost tribe now found.
By chance I came to Yurok land, landed
a teaching job—*sure, Indians, why not?*—
far from New York, far from myself, just
    passing through,
now to find myself in the heat of a struggle
of all Indians, all people.
It was just an accident.

I needed a job, that's all.
I didn't realize it would come to this!
To be a Jew naked in an oven, alive with fire!
Is this the Goldeneh Medina?
So much has been torn in the name of gold
that only silt remains, scars
to which I came with flowers in my hair, almost a fool,
but it is everything that we've known before,
massacres that have come before.
I am the evidence of Eastern Europe.

Yes We have No Bananas

"Yes, we have no bananas."
That's what they sang as my father clung
to the rails of the steam ship
pale from the depths of steerage.
Ellis Island has no bananas?
No bananas in this, the Goldeneh Medina?

In Lublin he wanders through the woods
with his friends to picnic.
Pounced upon by thugs—*"Jews!*
Out of our woods, you dirty Jews!"—
they were chased back towards the ghetto
until he grabs some acorns, fires
them back, cracks some heads:
"I'll teach you to beat on Jews!"

"Yes, we have no bananas"
was what they sang
on the Lower East Side.
"Apple pie & coffee" was all the English he knew.
"Apple pie & coffee," he said
& others they laugh, these Americans,

they call him a *"greenhorn,"*
& they sing "*Yes,*
we have no bananas,"
as he wanders the garment district
looking for work,
eating apple pie & coffee
day after day in the automat.

I'm a Yurok Indian & I'm Proud & You Can Take Your Goddam White Man's Religion Back Over the Ocean Where It Came from & Shove It

He tipped the Oly up to the blue
& polished it off.
I steered the beat up Caddy
away from ruts & he
flung the can out the window
into a confusion of manzanita & oak & second growth

"Ya know why I did that?"
he asked like a bark.
"Uh no, why?"
"Cause this is *my* land
& I can do any goddam thing I *want*
on *my* land!"
& then his anger subsided.

What's his he'll take, unashamed, like
spotlight a deer, blind it & blow it away.
"Yer a printer. Print me
a bumper sticker says:

I'M A YUROK INDIAN & I'M PROUD
& YOU CAN TAKE YOUR GODDAM WHITE MAN'S
RELIGION BACK OVER THE OCEAN WHERE IT
CAME FROM & SHOVE IT!"

Sometimes anger & hope & shame spun together
can get longer than a 65 Caddy bumper.
He's been saying the same things for years.
It explodes, tears through imported Scottish weed
& Himalaya berries, goes crazy.
Original redwood has been cleared for
long rows of sublets in San Jose
& the 2nd growth is unruly & a tangle.

Being white & in endless supply
I need to check my own panic
or my own paternal winks.
He don't know all the answers
except his—
& even those don't come with instructions
on how to assemble
an authentic model of a nation.

He's been saying it for years:
"We are the evidence of this
Western Hemisphere."
We swerve down the road, him
pulling out his 38
taking pot shots at beehives
& laughing it up.

The X of 1492

Columbus?

I leaf through the books, randomly skimming,
looking to discover Jews, not Columbus.

"In the same month
in which Their Majesties
issued the edict that
all Jews should be driven
out of the Kingdom
and its territories,
in the same month
they gave me the order
to undertake with sufficient
men my expedition of
discovery to the Indies."

Columbus, his diary.
Or, as they called
him in Spain, Cristobal Colon.
1492: the year of the Great Expedition;
and the year the Jews were expelled from Spain.

Jews again, even as America is hunted down.

1492: the year Spain is one, wed
by Their Catholic Majesties,
Ferdinand & Isabella.
Heathen Islam, after hundreds of years,
is driven out, gone.
I scratch my head, astonished:
Jews again, gone with the Arabs.
Spain was whole, Holy, Catholic, and
pure—and financially precarious.

With the Jews also went Spain's vehicle
for the passage of gold and trade,
as that was much of the role they played.

This was a bold step for Their Catholic Majesties.
Trade with Asia was essential, but the Arabs
had control of Palestine despite Holy Crusades,
while the Italians monopolized trade with the
        Arabs.
Spain and Portugal faced out, on the
cusp of the Mediterranean:
They sought another route.
Portugal surmised they could inch around Africa
to reach India—and they were closing in.

Enter pushy Columbus upon the Spanish Court
with his business scheme.
He could reach Asia via the West—
and take a sizeable cut of the profit
accrued from the seizure of the fabled
gold mines of Genghis Khan.

There was no question among scholars:
The world *was* round.
Too round in fact.
They computed that Columbus
would die of thirst
before reaching Asia.
How could they know
an entire hemisphere
stood in his path?
They cried objections.
But Spain was desperate, and risks
needed to be taken, especially
in regards to the grabbing of gold.
The Jews were expelled,
a whole civilization ejected.
The confiscated Jewish wealth
was used in part to finance

Columbus's enterprise.
How strange, even the first
to step ashore as the
Discoverer beached was a
merchant Jew, brought to
translate Oriental tongues:
unfortunately, he was
ignorant of Arawak.

Courtiers rumored that Cristobal
himself was a Jew.
Wasn't the leading Jewish
scholar of Italy named
Rabbi Joseph Colon?
How else could a mere son
of a weaver find such access
to the Royal Court
(and to the Royal Purse)?
Such mobility in feudal times
smelled suspiciously of Jew.
Perhaps the Inquisition missed
inquiring of such a one.
Perhaps it was just the hint
of what the voyage heralded—
a new world, a new class.
And, in its own way,
the expulsion of the Jews
heralded the same.

Columbus's fleet and the boats
of Jewish refugees fleeing East
all left from Palos harbor,
their wakes crossing,
a gigantic X
of the Jews and Columbus
crossing: X

as in X marks the spot
or the unknown of a vast algebra.

Two distinct and diverging directions,
a watery X washed over and dissolved.

The bows cross, and the Jews,
leaning against masts and railings,
wail at the last of Iberia.
Rabbi Jacob Habib of Salamanca,
may his memory be blessed,
prays, weeping.
He stares at his congregation
on the verge of delerium,
raises his arms to quiet them.
The boat sways, he glances
at the passing Santa Maria.
Only the boat creaks
in silence as the Rabbi speaks:

    "It is so hard to leave home.
    We lived well, not so poverty-stricken as those of
      Palermo,
    despised by the Christians because they are all tattered
      and dirty
    and forced to do hard labor with their hands at the King's
      incessant bidding;
    nor were we so blessed as our brethren in Alexandria
    who sit on rich rugs and drink raisin wine deep in study of
      the Torah.
    Yes, we have transgressed to be cast so far, and we must
      look deep within for our sin.
    We will find it fathomless,
    though we have kept apart in the light of the Torah. . . .

    "Mourn our dead, those who perished in the Arms of the
      Lord, killed by riot.
    Myself, I mourn my sister Rachel and her children she
      sacrificed before God, the High & Exalted;
    Rachel put her children next to her body, two on each side,
    covering them with her two sleeves.

There they lay struggling in the agony of death,
and when the enemy seized the room they found her sitting
    & wailing over them—
'Show us the money that is under your sleeves,' they
    commanded.
But when it was the slaughtered children they saw,
they struck her & killed her,
& her spirit flew away & her soul found peace at last.

"I mourn them all, yet those who took their own lives,
    themselves dead
rather than to die at the hands of the unrighteous
they shall sit forever, basking in the light of the Lord,
  with crowns of righteousness upon their heads. . . ."
The crowded deck of Jews
heaves up with cries.
Rabbi Jacob raises his head,
pointing to the three caravals of Colon:

"So there sails on that rumored Jew, Colon,
  kept in the light of the King & Queen by his wild schemes.
I only hope that neither of us return.
Perhaps our mutual passing in our affliction is a sign
as once a rainbow stood as a sign.
We are cast to the sea,
spit out by our occupation of gold imposed by the state,
expelled by our steadfastness in the Law
the Lord Our God commands us to obey
& for which he sets apart our fate.
For what Christians and Our Lord demand of us
we receive such wealth of hatred.
So be it. We are chosen to be set adrift,
& through our suffering the whole world is uplifted.

"But this Colon, what of this Italian, this Jew?

"If he is one of us, his direction is opposite.
I think the rumor is not true.

We are forced to our money-lending, banned from other
    pursuits;
yet he embarks on his bold Enterprise by choice to loot
China, Sumatra, & all other Asian destinations.
He has cast himself to the sea, elected by his own gross
    ambition.

"We pass—my brethren, note this passing in our affliction.
Our wakes swamp over in conflicting directions.
We sail off to a new world holding fast to the ways of
    our fathers;
he to usurp the old.
Pray that we never return, but that by scorn & sacrifice
we endure as sheep in Abraham's fold.
Pray also that this Colon drowns,
    dies of thirst & hunger with his crew,
    never to port home with his calf of gold."

Salamanca's Rabbi Jacob Habib
implores Israel to remember
God is one.
Without hesitation, Colon sails on,
holds steadfast to his task
as stipulated by the Crown. . . .

Columbus? The myths on
elementary-school windows;
a man in tights with a telescope
staring off into eternity
as soldiers drive a cross
into a beach with Indians
keeping a cautious but curious
distance; him, the one
on the school window
after the turkey and Pilgrims
and those other Indians
come down? But how
did the initial step
mark the whole journey?

I turn the page, whereupon
enter Friar Bartolome de las Casas.
The Friar was there, saw the
expedition's success.
He was witness,
Jesus's servant sent to bless
Asiatics with mysteries
of Catholic holiness.
A reformer, he still sought
colonial possession,
but for years
he walked the Spanish Court
seeking adjustment of the
policy blazed by Columbus,
the policy of bestiality.
There he is now, stopping a
nobleman passing in the halls.
Breathless, the Friar
makes his appeal;
and by so doing hopes
to make his memory heal.

"I was there!

"I saw it, saw the Devastation of the Indies.

I chronicled that Cristobal, that whore Italian—
Viceroy of the Indies, Admiral of the Ocean Sea—
the titles so lately bestowed upon him.
No! Admiral of Death, Admiral of Mosquitoes!
I know. I saw it.
I went to preach the Cross—& I beheld again our Savior die.
Again His Life was sold for a measure of gold.

"Those gentle people came to greet us.
We towered like gods with our shields and swords.
In wonder & faith they made us welcome.
But Colon spied his prey early, whispering,
'That heathen, see, in his ear one gold pendant!

That one over there, seashells & gold around her neck are
    hung!'
Colon, his eyes grown wild, made his declaration:
This very isle was the secret gold mine of Genghis Khan
now under Spain's direction!

"Such playful jewelry, such little dabs of vanity
became the spark to light the fires of their misfortune.
With haste, he ordered Pacification.
Those newfound subjects who resisted burned
slowly over fires of green branches.
Shrieks & howls filled the air day & night.
The Admiral of Hell pitched arms & legs to his dogs
that prowled the hills so they could better
learn the taste for native flesh.
So horrible these screams that it became impossible to sleep,
& when I objected to the tumult
& for mercy made Holy plea,
he chose such nicety
as to gag his victims.
In silence they could weep.

"Certain this was the great Khan's secret mine, he made
    decree
that around their necks each of these unfortunates
must wear medallions to be notched at every appointed date
upon receipt of one whole measure of gold.
When the appointed day arrived his fearful subjects dutifully
    returned
with buckets of earrings, pendants, & other minor treasures,
and dutifully in turn Colon notched their coins & saved a few
    from being burned.

"But came the next date & fewer came with gold, mere flakes
    from streams.
Those that could not match the measure
instantly were dragged to the block, their hands severed.
Dismayed, they stared at chopped arms.

"This Admiral of Mosquitoes & Worms, this Plague,
could not see, would not believe what soon we learned.
Viceroy of Gnats! There was no more!
There was no gold on this isle, only a trinket's worth.
Yet this Admiral of the Ocean Sea
poured blood ceaselessly into that sad earth.
The truth left his madness undeterred.

"What tortures these poor people were cast;
to be made slave is enough,
yet more to be slave to the impossible task.

"I saw it.
As well I saw these people in such distress
that they rebelled
& fought steel swords with clubs & wood spears.
When revolt seemed hopeless mothers with awful tears
took the lives of their own children
so that by themselves choosing doom they held
a measure of dignity to their nation.

"A few years have gone, but in that meagre time
millions butchered.

My Lord, do you hear me? I know I speak long,
but stay so that you might stop this wrong.
Perhaps it didn't happen, only a friar's dream,
I pray—but my ears are filled with hideous screams.

"Cristobal Colon, Christopher!
Spain is amazed at his great new find.
They murmur he is kin to his namesake, St. Christopher,
who carried Our Lord Savior Jesus Christ
across the river on his back to save him from the flood.
They fancy this Christopher is also a ferryman of the Lord
as he carries blessings of Christ to new lands.
Oh yes, on his back he carries Christ's Body across the sea—
& there he dumps the carcass down for his dogs. . . .

I was there. I know.
I saw the Devastation of the Indies. . . ."

This Passover or the Next I Will
Never Be in Jerusalem

The clan is all together, eating Passover matzoh, joking.
At the head, the old Patriarch makes his blessing; he collars
me, & he imparts wisdom:
"Is it so bad to be a Jew?
In Israel even the street sweeper is a Jew, not that anyone
should be a street sweeper, but
nobody yells 'Dirty Jew!'
After 2,000 years we have something finally. Isn't it about
      time?
We are not taking any Arab land from anybody.
This is the land that belonged to our forefathers,
& we came only to take up our inheritance.
Can anyone say we are *stealing* what is already *ours?*
Why don't you go to Israel, learn something about your
      people?
Can it be nothing but good?"

I fidget & nod politely at his references to Abraham & other
      long-lost relatives.

"So you move so far away from your parents in New York,
you move to California to live with the Indians.
You decide to be so noble to be a schoolteacher with the
      Indians.
Nu, I wish them well, but what is this with the Indians,
aren't they so different & so wild?"
                              "Actually,

Indians are not what you see on TV . . ."

"Nu, but are they your own people? Your own flesh & blood?
Do you hate New York so much you have to live with
      Indians?
What is this Indians? You can work in your father's store,
make a good life. He is getting old, and you need gelt in life,
right?
Is it so bad selling rags?
Can't you be writer all you want, love Indians all you want,
& make money too?
What's this, Indians and California?
If not Israel, shouldn't you think New York maybe to live?"

The young couple across the table from me, recently married
(& living just a few blocks away as does all the family
peppered throughout the Brooklyn neighborhood
so as better to visit one another on Shabbas when one can only
walk & by injunction is forbidden to drive),
these young marrieds smile good-naturedly & ask,

"Don't you feel strange living so far away from your family?"

Why is this Jew different from all other Jews?
I sip my wine. The white table cloth is a vast Jordan.
This Passover or the next I will never be in Jerusalem.
The Jordan flows between me and the land I never remember
      anyone promising me.
No sound can be heard except the occasional wail of some
      wild animal.
I will never step across the shore. *Am I the anti-Moses?*

I jump up from my plate, startled.

"Uh, no, I don't feel strange at all. . . ."

Charles Olson

IMMEDIATE and apparent was his physical presence: the size of the man, nearly seven feet tall, a height matched by his wide-ranging mind, a genius of correspondences and linkages, his resonant New England voice unfurling multilinear pronouncements that acolytes and peers followed as if implicated in a divinatory rite. His influence was pervasive on those who sought it: a poet whose metaphors included an emphasis on "energy," that dynamic transforming stuff unable to stay still long enough to be framed, a Heraclitan stance rooted to layered pasts yet also embedded in present-tense alertness. Both a classicist and Yankee historian, his work bridged both domains with ease. Olson sought to mythify America, especially his adopted home site of Gloucester, and to Americanize mythology, working almost twenty-five years on his New World epic, *The Maximus Poems.*

Born in Worcester, Massachusetts, in 1910, son of a Swedish father and Irish-American mother, he attended Wesleyan, Yale, and Harvard, focusing on American studies, and taught at Harvard from 1936–39. Until 1948 he worked in diverse jobs, winding up in political work for the Democratic party and as an official in the Office of War Information for the Roosevelt administration. In 1947, his first book, *Call Me Ishmael,* was published. It remains a strikingly unique work of history, theory, and criticism; as well, it invigorated the Melville scholarship of that period. It marked the arrival of a distinctly "outside" voice, i.e., an independent intelligence unaffiliated with institutionalized dogmas and strictures. While working in Washington he regularly visited Ezra Pound confined at St. Elizabeth's; a document of that relationship, from Olson's vantage, can be found in *Charles Olson and Ezra Pound: An Encounter at St. Elizabeth's* (1975).

He quit politics to write and study, spending some time in the Yucatan, investigating the persistence of archaic culture (which yielded the unique poetic-linguistic quest documented in *Mayan Letters*). He returned to the States to replace Edward Dahlberg—a friend and mentor—as rector of the experimental Black Mountain College, 1951–56. There he initiated his influence as teacher and theoretician of the Black Mountain movement, which included Robert Creeley, Denise Levertov, John Wieners, Robert Duncan, Fielding Dawson, Edward Dorn, Merce Cunningham, John Cage, Buckminster Fuller, and Robert Rauschenberg. One of Olson's major theoretical salvos, "Projective Verse," was published in 1950 and offered, in its way, the same emancipatory provocation that the paintings of the Abstract Expressionists announced.

In the tradition of Pound's *Cantos* and Williams' *Paterson*, Olson's counter-epic, *The Maximus Poems* (1953–75), remained unfinished, impossible to close, embodying as its forebears had an open-endedness impossible to resolve. (A similar inability plagued both Wordsworth and Coleridge.) Like Pound and Williams, Olson understood the bardic function of poet as historian. His history was strongly rooted in geography, in place, as well as in time: "I am an archaeologist of morning. And the writing and arts which I find bear on the present job are (I) from Homer back, not forward; and (II) from Melville on, particularly himself, Dostoyevsky, Rimbaud, and Lawrence. These were the modern men who projected what we are and what we are in, who broke the spell. They put men forward into the post-modern, the post-humanist, the post-historic, the going live present. . . ." The reclamation of history and the repatterning of myth and symbol in the everyday—as played by Joyce and Eliot—is an aspect of the modernist project which Olson took on, as he writes, from beyond the Greeks and to the Pleistocene. There was a Whitmanesque democratic élan to Olson's reclamation of poet as citizen, speaker, and recorder engaged in immediate public discourse and in fused connection with a plurality of historic and prehistoric voices and signs,

traces and clues. The range of his sources and the resourceful-
ness of his inventive intelligence permeate his poetry and prose.
Human Universe (1965) is a major collection of his essays.
Since Olson was a brilliant improvisatory talker, transcripts of
his lectures are often dizzying in their range. *Muthologos*
(1978) in two volumes, is also a prime and influential gathering.

The University of California Press has issued—under the
scrupulously attentive editorship of the late George F. But-
terick—the complete *Maximums Poems* and *The Collected
Poems of Charles Olson.*

—David Meltzer

From

THE COLLECTED POEMS OF
CHARLES OLSON (1987)

In Cold Hell, in Thicket

In cold hell, in thicket, how
abstract (as high mind, as not lust, as love is) how
strong (as strut or wing, as polytope, as things are
constellated) how
strung, how cold
can a man stay (can men) confronted
thus?

All things are made bitter, words even
are made to taste like paper, wars get tossed up
like lead soldiers used to be
(in a child's attic) lined up
to be knocked down, as I am,
by firings from a spit-hardened fort, fronted
as we are, here, from where we must go

God, that man, as his acts must, as there is always
a thing he can do, he can raise himself, he raises
on a reed he raises his

Or, if it is me, what
he has to say

I

What has he to say?
In hell it is not easy
to know the traceries, the markings
(the canals, the pits, the mountings by which space
declares herself, arched, as she is, the sister,
awkward stars drawn for teats to pleasure him, the brother
who lies in stasis under her, at ease as any monarch or
a happy man

How shall he who is not happy, who has been so made
        unclear,
who is no longer privileged to be at ease, who, in this brush,
        stands
reluctant, imageless, unpleasured, caught in a sort of hell, how
shall he convert this underbrush, how turn this unbidden
        place
how trace and arch again
the necessary goddess?

2

The branches made against the sky are not of use, are
already done, like snow-flakes, do not, cannot service
him who has to raise (Who puts this on, this damning of his
        flesh?)
he can, but how far, how sufficiently far can he raise the
        thickets of this wilderness?
                    How can he change, his question is
                    these black and silvered knivings, these
                    awkwardnesses?

                    How can he make these blood-points into
                        panels, into sides
                    for a king's, for his own
                    for a wagon, for a sleigh, for the beak of, the
                        running sides of

a vessel fit for
moving?

How can he make out, he asks,
of this low eye-view,
size?
And archings traced and picked enough to
    hold
to stay, as she does, as he, the brother, when,
here where the mud is, he is frozen, not daring
where the grass grows, to move his feet from
    fear
he'll trespass on his own dissolving bones, here
where there is altogether too much
    remembrance?

3

The question, the fear he raises up himself against
(against the same each act is proffered, under the eyes
each fix, the town of the earth over, is managed) is: Who
am I?

Who am I but by a fix, and another,
a particle, and the congery of particles carefully picked one by
    another,
                    as in this thicket, each
                    smallest branch, plant, fern, root
                    —roots lie, on the surface, as nerves are laid
                        open—
                    must now (the bitterness of the taste of her)
                    be isolated, observed, picked over, measured,
                        raised
                    as though a word, an accuracy were a pincer!
                                                        this

is the abstract, this
is the cold doing, this
is the almost impossible

So shall you blame those
who give it up, those who say
it isn't worth the struggle?

(Prayer

Or a death as going over to—shot by yr own
    forces—to
a greener place?

Neither

any longer
usable)
    By fixes only (not even any more by shamans)
    can the traceries
    be brought out

I I

ya, selva oscura, but hell now
is not exterior, is not to be got out of, is
the coat of your own self, the beasts
emblazoned on you   And who
can turn this total thing, invert
and let the ragged sleeves be seen
by any bitch or common character? Who
can endure it where it is, where the beasts are met,
where yourself is, your beloved is, where she
who is separate from you, is not separate, is not
goddess, is, as your core is,
the making of one hell

where she moves off, where she is
no longer arch

(this is why he of whom we speak does not move, why
he stands so awkward where he is, why
his feet are held, like some ragged crane's
off the nearest next ground, even from
the beauty of the rotting fern his eye
knows, as he looks down, as,
in utmost pain if cold can be so called,
he looks around this battlefield, this
rotted place where men did die, where boys
and immigrants have fallen, where nature
(the years that she's took over)
does not matter, where

> that men killed, do kill, that
> woman kills
> is part, too, of his question

2

That it is simple, what the difference is—
that a man, men, are now their own wood
and thus their own hell and paradise
that they are, in hell or in happiness, merely
something to be wrought, to be shaped, to be carved, for use,
    for others

does not in the least lessen his, this unhappy man's
obscurities, his
confrontations

He shall step, he
will shape, he
is already also
moving off
        into the soil, on to his own bones

he will cross
            (there is always a field,
            for the strong there is always
            an alternative)

                            But a field
                        is not a choice, is
                        as dangerous as a prayer, as a death,
                            as any
                        misleading, lady

He will cross

                    And is bound to enter (as she is)
                    a later wilderness.
                                        Yet
                    what he does here, what he raises up
                    (he must, the stakes are such

                                            this at least

                    is a certainty, this
                    is a law, is not one of the questions, this
                    is what was talked of as
                    —what was it called, demand?)

He will do what he now does, as she will, do
carefully, do
without wavering,
without
            as even the branches,
            even in this dark place, the twigs
                                        how

            even the brow
of what was once to him a beautiful face

as even the snow-flakes waver in the light's eye

as even forever wavers (gutters
in the wind of loss)

even as he will forever waver

precise as hell is, precise
as any words, or wagon,
can be made

At Yorktown

I

At Yorktown the church
at Yorktown the dead
at Yorktown the grass
are live

        at York-town the earth
piles itself in shallows,
declares itself, like water,
by pools and mounds

2

At Yorktown the dead
are soil
at Yorktown the church
is marl
at Yorktown the swallows
dive where it is greenest,

the hollows
are eyes are flowers, the heather,
equally accurate, is hands

at York-town only the flies
dawdle, like history,
in the sun

3

at Yorktown the earthworks
braw
at Yorktown the mortars
of brass, weathered green, of mermaids
for handles, of Latin
for texts, scream
without noise
like a gull

4

At Yorktown the long dead
loosen the earth, heels
sink in, over an abatis
a bird wheels

and time is a shine caught blue
from a martin's
back

Knowing All Ways, Including the Transposition of Continents

I have seen enough: ugliness
in the streets,
and in the flesh I love

I have gone as far as I will go: justice
is not distributable, outside
or in

I have had all I intend
of cause or man: the unselected
(my own) is enough
to be bothered with. Today
I serve beauty of selection alone
—and without enormous reference to stones
or to the tramp of worms
in the veins. Image
can be exact to fact, or
how is this art twin to what is,
what was,
what goes on?

America, Europe, Asia,
I have no further use for you: your clamor
divides me from love,
and from new noises.

Sonia Sanchez

SONIA SANCHEZ (1934–   ) was born in Birmingham, Alabama, and has spent her whole life pursuing peace, freedom, and justice as a poet, playwright, fiction writer, teacher, lecturer, and mother. She is the author of several volumes of poetry including *Homegirls & Handgrenades* (1984), which won an American Book Award. She has given the keynote address at two of the Before Columbus Foundation's American Book Awards ceremonies.

The easiest thing to do in presenting Sonia Sanchez's work is to allow Sanchez to speak for herself. Zala Chandler's interview with Sonia Sanchez in *Wild Women in the Whirlwind*, (1990) allows Sanchez to define her world with immediacy and accuracy:

> I maintain that I will never in my life walk secondarily again—or even appear to have any secondary views. If you approach me, you must approach me on an equal level. If I see your stuff is incorrect, is racist, then I will tell you. And when I hit the stage, I know that I am just as tough as anyone there. People aren't accustomed to that kind of behavior. That is a legacy that we've gotten from Malcolm, from Fannie Lou, from DuBois, and from Ida B. I am aggressive, I will not deny myself. I will not be one of those people talking about they need to get some training on how to be aggressive. To them, I say, all you have to do is come into a sense of yourself, announce that you are an African and intend to "be." That is some automatic aggression. And you will see that in order to defend yourself, you will have to move in an aggressive fashion. Because the moment you say that you're not sure of who you are, people will slap you down, will attempt to slap you to the right and the left, tear you up!

The power in Sanchez's voice in this interview is what Haki R. Madhubuti (formerly Don L. Lee), in his essay "Sonia Sanchez: The Bringer of Memories" (*Black Women Writers*, 1984), called her respect for the power of Black language:

> More than any other poet, she has been responsible for legitimizing the use of urban Black English in written form. Her use of language is spontaneous and thoughtful. Unlike many poets of the sixties, her use of the so-called profane has been innovatively shocking and uncommonly apropos. Her language is culturally legitimate and genuinely reflects the hard bottom and complicated spectrum of the entire Black community. She has taken Black speech and put it in the context of world literature.

—Shawn Wong

Blues

i love a twenty yr old weekends
dig him way down until he's glad.
yeh. i love a twenty yr old weekends
dig him way down until he's glad
you see what my wanting you has
done gone and made me badddddd.

watched for you each evening
stood right outside my do
said i watched for you each evening
stood right outside my do
but you never came in and
i couldn't stand still no mo

what do you do when you need
a man so much it hurt?
i say where do you go when you
need a man so much it hurt?
you make it down to the corner
and start digging in the dirt.

yeh. i love a twenty yr old weekends
dig him way down until he's dry
yeh. i love a twenty yr old weekends
dig him way down until he's dry
you see what my needing you
has done gone and made me try.

you see what my needing you
has done gone and made me try.

A Letter to Dr. Martin
Luther King

DEAR Martin,

Great God, what a morning, Martin!

The sun is rolling in from faraway places. I watch it reaching out, circling these bare trees like some reverent lover. I have been standing still listening to the morning, and I hear your voice crouched near hills, rising from the mountain tops, breaking the circle of dawn.

You would have been 54 today.

As I point my face toward a new decade, Martin, I want you to know that the country still crowds the spirit. I want you to know that we still hear your footsteps setting out on a road cemented with black bones. I want you to know that the stuttering of guns could not stop your light from crashing against cathedrals chanting piety while hustling the world.

Great God, what a country, Martin!

The decade after your death docked like a spaceship on a new planet. Voyagers all we were. We were the aliens walking up the '70s, a holocaust people on the move looking out from dark eyes. A thirsty generation, circling the peaks of our country for more than a Pepsi taste. We were youngbloods, spinning hip syllables while saluting death in a country neutral with pain.

And our children saw the mirage of plenty spilling from capitalistic sands.

And they ran toward the desert.

And the gods of sand made them immune to words that strengthen the breast.

And they became scavengers walking on the earth.

And you can see them playing. Hide-and-go-seek robbers.

Native sons. Running on their knees. Reinventing slavery on asphalt. Peeling their umbilical cords for a gold chain.

And you can see them on Times Square, in N.Y.C., Martin, selling their 11-, 12-year-old, 13-, 14-year-old bodies to suburban forefathers.

And you can see them on Market Street in Philadelphia bobbing up bellywise, young fishes for old sharks.

And no cocks are crowing on those mean streets.

Great God, what a morning it'll be someday, Martin!

That decade fell like a stone on our eyes. Our movements. Rhythms. Loves. Books. Delivered us from the night, drove out the fears keeping some of us hoarse. New births knocking at the womb kept us walking.

We crossed the cities while a backlash of judges tried to turn us into moles with blackrobed words of reverse racism. But we knew. And our knowing was like a sister's embrace. We crossed the land where famine was fed in public. Where black stomachs exploded on the world's dais while men embalmed their eyes and tongues in gold. But we knew. And our knowing squatted from memory.

Sitting on our past, we watch the new decade dawning. These are strange days, Martin, when the color of freedom becomes disco fever; when soap operas populate our Zulu braids; as the world turns to the conservative right and general hospitals are closing in Black neighborhoods and the young and the restless are drugged by early morning reefer butts. And houses tremble.

These are dangerous days, Martin, when cowboy-riding presidents corral Blacks (and others) in a common crown of thorns; when nuclear-toting generals recite an alphabet of blood; when multinational corporations assassinate ancient cultures while inaugurating new civilizations. Comeout comeout wherever you are. Black country. Waiting to be born . . .

But, Martin, on this, your 54th birthday—with all the reversals—we have learned that black is the beginning of everything.

it was black in the universe before the sun;
it was black in the mind before we opened our eyes;
it was black in the womb of our mother;
black is the beginning,

and if we are the beginning we will be forever.

Martin. I have learned too that fear is not a Black man or woman. Fear cannot disturb the length of those who struggle against material gains for self-aggrandizement. Fear cannot disturb the good of people who have moved to a meeting place where the pulse pounds out freedom and justice for the universe.

Now is the changing of the tides, Martin. You forecast it where leaves dance on the wings of man. Martin. Listen. On this your 54th year, listen and you will hear the earth delivering up curfews to the missionaries and assassins. Listen. And you will hear the tribal songs:

Ayeeee	*Ayooooo*	*Ayeee*
Ayeeee	*Ayooooo*	*Ayeee*
Malcolm . . .		*Ke wa rona**
Robeson . . .		*Ke wa rona*
Lumumba . . .		*Ke wa rona*
Fannie Lou . . .		*Ke wa rona*
Garvey . . .		*Ke wa rona*
Johnbrown . . .		*Ke wa rona*
Tubman . . .		*Ke wa rona*
Mandela . . .		*Ke wa rona*
(free Mandela,		
free Mandela)		
Assata . . .		*Ke wa rona*

As we go with you to the sun,
as we walk in the dawn, turn
our eyes
Eastward and let the prophecy
come true
and let the prophecy come true.
    Great God, Martin, what a
morning it will be!

*he is ours

Edward Sanders

BEING at the forefront of American counterculture is, of course, an ironic position to occupy especially when one advocates "Total Assault on the Culture." Ed Sanders (1939–   ), with his wide range of influence in the music and literary worlds, certainly defines the time and place when a word like "counter-culture" was suspect. His first book, *Poem from Jail* (1963), was the result of his being sentenced to jail for his involvement in a peace vigil at a Polaris submarine base. In 1962 he founded *Fuck You: A Magazine of the Arts* to pursue anarchy, pacifism and a "Total Assault on the Culture." The magazine was eventually shut down by police in 1965 on obscenity charges. In the mid-sixties Sanders, along with Tuli Kupferberg, formed the musical group, The Fugs (derived from the word Norman Mailer used in his novel, *The Naked and the Dead*, for "fuck" in order to sidestep censorship). His works include, *King Lord/ Queen Freak* (1964), *The Toe Queen Poems* (1964), *Peace Eye* (1965), *Shards of God* (1970), *The Family: The Story of Charles Manson's Dune Buggy Attack Battalion* (1971), *Vote!* (with Abbie Hoffman and Jerry Rubin, 1972), *Egyptian Hiero-glyphs* (1973), *Tales of Beatnik Glory* (1975), *20,000 A.D.* (1976), *Investigative Poetry* (1976), *Fame & Love in New York* (1980), *The Z-D Generation* (1981), and *The Cutting Prow* (1981). *Thirsting For Peace in A Raging Century* (1987), his most recent work, is a collection of selected poems from the works listed above. He also founded the Peace Eye Bookstore on New York's Lower East Side in 1964, and the proprietor listed himself as "Ed Sanders—book creep, grass cadet, fug poet, editor, squack slarfer, madman composer and poon scomp." Fuck You Press set up operations in the backroom where books were "printed, published, zapped and ejaculated"—forefront indeed.

—Shawn Wong

THIRSTING FOR PEACE IN A RAGING CENTURY: SELECTED POEMS 1961–1985 (1987)

A Flower from Robert Kennedy's Grave

> During demonstrations at Nixon's second inauguration, we watched his limo pass, on the way to the White House; then I drove over to Arlington Cemetery

January 20, 1973

After
a winding walk
up past the white stones
of snuff,

past the guardhouse
circling circling
around the Catholic henge
to John Kennedy's bright taper
burning on the ground
in windy cold winter after-speech
afternoon

    then walk down
    to the left-hand

        edge of the hill-
    ock—there in speechless serenity,

built onto the steepness
a small
elegant
perfectly proportioned
white cross 'bove
white flat marble marker

Robert Francis Kennedy

nearby a fount jets horizontal
over a slab o' stone

water curving down abruptly on the
rock front lip

R.F.K.'s words of race heal
writ upon the rock above
the flat-fount.

Across the walkway
by the grave
a long red rose
with a vial of water
slipped upon the stem end
& wrapped with shiny tape
lay singly
& to the left of it a
basket of yellow chrysanthemums

and this: that
only a whining hour past,
Richard Nixon
oozed down Pennsylvania Avenue
flashing V's from a limousine
behind a stutter-footed wary pack of Marines
their
bayonets stabbing the January
in a thickery of different directions
like small lance hairs
pricked up on the forehead of a

hallucinated drool fiend
during a bummer

but big enough to stab the
throats of hippie rioters

buddy.

I picked a yellow petal

from thy grave
Mr. Robert Kennedy

& brought it home
from Arlington, where many young mourners
stood crying quietly this inauguration day

Picked a dream
Mr. Robert Kennedy
brought it home in our hearts
burning like a brand in a fennel stalk

Picked a thought-ray
Robert Kennedy

brought it back from this
henge of park-side
eternity

buses of protesters parked
in the lots beneath your hill

Tears splash
in the vessels
of the sun

Picked yellow
molecules bunched
in beauty
from the beauty fount
Mr. Robert Kennedy

The peace-ark
glides in the vastness,
though weirdness clings to your death.

But nothing can touch the ark
sails through the trellis of evil
brazen American wrought of light hate

Nothing can touch it
not even pyramidal battlements of gore-spore
nor tricky's pitiless flood
of dungeonoid luciphobian losers.

The Chain

For 15-thousand years
the plutonium
in the smoke detector
lay in the Woodstock dump

till the day
the grade-blader scraped it out
& smashed it to chiplets
the chipmunk pulled
to the pouch of his cheeks

& during
the next 200
            years

it caused
        6 cancers

in a skunk
a crow   a deer
a dog   a dog
and Johnny McQuaife

Leslie Scalapino

"No one to hear me: those warnings coming by strange absences."

—from *"Water, A Poem for Virginia Woolf,"* in O and Other Poems *(1976)*

THE "abscences," the "strange absences," announce the agenda of Scalapino's (b. 1947) intensely focused body of work. The "absences" are present. They are presences pushing against boundaries of private and public self, not so much by metaphysical encounters or through seductive reveries of abstracted philosophies, as through the disjunctive flow of the everyday that her poems contend with: everyday strangers—the homeless, the bums, the intruders, the other. Neither iconic nor theoretical, her presences intrude, yet remain to be known. If her poems are emblematic, they are emblematic of a fall, a fall tied to economy, loss of "place" and "face," poverty, resistance to scrutiny, the paralyzing terrors and romances within a self walking down an urban street or looking out an apartment window.

Boldly experimental with syntax and in recombining circular permutations of repetition, Scalapino's use of these devices never obstruct the actual but, instead, intensify the reader's discomfort at confronting the real presences, the absented and strange. A subtext of sexual ineffability is most directly present in her first omnibus volume, *Considering How Exaggerated Music Is* (1982); edgy, wry, sometimes malevolent narratives voice themselves in the sequences "hmmmmm," "The Woman Who Could Read the Mind of Dogs," and "Instead of an Animal." They challenge and displace the dominant phallocentrism of sexual narration in modernist poetry. Dark ridges of Scalapino's work cluster at cores of possible violence—mugging, rape, battery—which she writes in discrete units that assume a neutral voice. This distant and distancing voice describes, then redescribes, shifts emphasis from one event to another, telling what seem to be everyday events, urban commonplaces, normative terror zones where women walk at risk within culturally targeted bodies. The person, the personal, the absences and presences in her poetry enable both her aesthetic and political sensibilities to coexist and interact in a significant ensemble of texts.

—David Meltzer

From
WAY (1988)

the men—when I'd
been out in the cold weather—were
found lying on the street, having
died—from the weather; though
usually being there when it's warmer

the men
on the street who'd
died—in the weather—who're bums
observing it, that instance
of where they are—not my
seeing that

cranes are on the
skyline—which are accustomed
to lift the containers to or from
the freighters—as the new
wave attire of the man

though not muscular
—but young—with
the new wave dyed blonde
hair—seeming to
wait at the bus stop, but
always outside of the
hair salon

the bums—the men—having
died—from
the weather—though their
doing that, seeing things from their view when
they were alive

so not to
be upper class—the new
wave baggy pants—the
man with the dyed blonde
hair—who's always standing in
front of the hair salon on
the corner

the public
figure—as gentle—as
the freighter and
their relation

that
of the man with the dyed
blonde hair and
new wave attire—and
the freighter

of our present
president—who doesn't
know of the foreign
environs—as vacant—and
to the freighter and
his and its relation

                           when our present
                           president is in an inverse
                           relation to them—when there's
                           a social struggle in their
                           whole setting, which is
                           abroad

the bums—who've
died—but could be only when
they're living—though it
doesn't have desire, so inverse in
that one setting

to their
social struggle in their
whole setting, which is
abroad and its
relation to the freighter

                              to the person of
                              new wave attire—that
                              person's relation to
                              the freighter

when the bums are not
alive—at this time—though
were here, not abroad—and
not aware in being so of a
social struggle

the man in the new
wave attire—as the relation
of him
being another person—as
the freighter and
his and its relation

                              the inverse
                              relation to the freighter
                              only occurring when that
                              person is living

the man—who's
accustomed to
working in the garage—
as having
that relation to
their whole setting

I have been—am—
dumb—as the way
in which that would occur—the
bums—not their existence or
dying from the weather—though
the effect of that

            for me to
            be dumb—to have
            been actually stupid—so that
            really could occur—the
            bums—in an event

so—dumb as an
active relation to
the bums or to the freighter and
the still oil
rigs—on the ocean

to the repair of
the car—so inverse in that
setting—though
it doesn't have desire—of
the present

                                    as the oil rigs—which
                                    are the freighter—on the
                                    ocean—pushed
                                    up to be the relation
                                    with me, by my
                                    being—am—dumb—their
                                    to have that occurrence

to have that—for them, some
people who'd had an attitude
of snobbery—always—so that they're dumb—when it's
senseless—that relation with
them

                              I almost
                              froze—and realized I
                              could die from it—when the
                              bums
                              were in that situation—and
                              then not
                              caring, though that's not
                              possible

which had been repaired
—to the car—as I
am—when that's
senseless—though
it doesn't have desire—of
the present

the bums—
found later—in the whole setting
—though when the car
hadn't been repaired—and so
their grinding and
movement in relation to it

Gary Snyder

GARY SNYDER (b. 1930), along with his colleagues Robert
Haas, Kenneth Rexroth, and Carolyn Kizer, has effectively ex-
plored cultures outside those he was raised in, and has, through
his work translating Zen Buddhist texts, managed to bring back
to the rest of us folks some ideas from a culture mightily differ-
ent in its approach to life and to creation.

Snyder has been involved in cross-cultural pollination since
his graduate studies at the University of California at Berkeley
in oriental languages, preparatory to spending twelve years in
Japan studying Zen Buddhism. When asked about his work
habits, he answered, "I'm always working." Indeed, we see the
effects of meditation, as well as the daily reporting of a man
earning a living alongside others, in his poems. Like many writ-
ers, he has worked a variety of jobs: he has been a seaman, a
carpenter, a reporter, and now a teacher at the University of
California at Davis. He uses the voices of those he encounters
to record the histories of people who might never record their
own.

> Jimmy Jones the cook said "I
> used to do that, run the ridges
> all day long—just like a coyote."
> When I built a little sweatlodge
> one Sunday by the creek
> he told me to be careful. . . .
>
> *("Look Back")*

He has also been involved in the ecology movement since his
late teens and has consistently incorporated love of the earth
into his work. His well-earned reputation as a voice for the

earth is still justified, as we see in this poem, "All in the Family":

> . . . Full moon, warm nights
>   the boys learn to float
> Masa gone off dancing
>   for another thirty days
> Queen Anne's Lace in the meadow
>   a Flicker's single call
>
> Oregano, lavender, the *salvia* sage
>   wild pennyroyal
>   from the Yuba River bank
> All in the family
>   of Mint.

("All in the Family")

But there is a new note in his work as well, one that I find most endearing and rare, and that is in fact the reason I nominated Axe Handles, a book by an already well-respected American writer. Because of the habit of blame we have established in our culture, we blame white men for the visible destruction of our planet, as if anyone else with access to such power would have remained compassionate. This cultural blame, along with their often religiously-based, habitual self-hatred, makes many white male writers in the United States either boring or unreadable. Gary Snyder has learned to express himself as a white American male who loves his own children and himself. He has learned to do this without acquiring an arrogance about his own cultural past. If we are ever to heal as a nation, these are the keys.

> How intelligent he looks!
>   on his back
>   both feet caught in my one hand
>   his glance set sideways,
>   on a giant poster of Geronimo
>   with a Sharp's repeating rifle by his knee.
>
> I open, wipe, he doesn't even notice
>   nor do I.

Baby legs and knees
    toes like little peas
    little wrinkles, good-to-eat,
    eyes bright, shiny ears,
    chest swelling drawing air,

No trouble, friend,
    you and me and Geronimo
    are men.

("Changing Diapers")

Some of my colleagues were concerned that the American Book Award should always go to a younger or less well-recognized writer. This is a vital point, because what we are demanding is that the mainstream take the work of talented writers seriously, even if their style is unfamiliar or their ideas exceptionally challenging, I stood by my nomination, however, not only because *Axe Handles* was the best book I'd read that year, but also because Snyder has continued, in spite of great success, to explore his own soul and the cultural soup of living in the United States.

Somehow the children will be taught:
How to record their mother tongue
    with written signs,
Names to call the landscape of the continent
    they live on
Assigned it by the ruling people of the last
    three hundred years . . .

("Painting the North San Juan School")

Always a realist, Gary Snyder advises young writers to "learn a trade," and when asked "How do you view the writer's role in the 1990s?" he responded, "Same as the last 4000 years."

—Alta

From
AXE HANDLES (1983)

Strategic Air Command

The hiss and flashing lights of a jet
Pass near Jupiter in Virgo.
He asks, how many satellites in the sky?
Does anyone know where they all are?
What are they doing, who watches them?

Frost settles on the sleeping bags.
The last embers of fire,
One more cup of tea,
At the edge of a high lake rimmed with snow.

These cliffs and the stars
Belong to the same universe.
This little air in between
Belongs to the twentieth century and its wars.

VIII, 82, Koip Peak, Sierra Nevada

Talking Late with the Governor about the Budget

for Jerry Brown

Entering the midnight
Halls of the capitol,
Iron carts full of printed bills
Filling life with rules,

At the end of many chambers
Alone in a large tan room
The Governor sits, without dinner.
Scanning the hills of laws—budgets—codes—
In this land of twenty million
From desert to ocean.

Till the oil runs out
There's no end in sight.
Outside, his car waits with driver
Alone, engine idling.
The great pines on the Capitol grounds
Are less than a century old.

Two A.M.,
We walk to the street
Tired of the effort
Of thinking about "the People."
The half-moon travels west
In the elegant company
Of Jupiter and Aldebaran,

And east, over the Sierra,
Far flashes of lightning—
Is it raining tonight at home?

"He Shot Arrows, But Not at Birds Perching"

Lun yü, VII, 26

The Governor came to visit in the mountains
    we cleaned the house and raked the yard that day.
He'd been east and hadn't slept much
    so napped all afternoon back in the shade.

Young trees and chickens must be tended
    I sprayed apples, and took water to the hens.
Next day we read the papers, spoke of farming,
    of oil, and what would happen to the cars.

And then beside the pond we started laughing,
    got the quiver and bow and strung the bow.
Arrow after arrow flashing
    hissing under pines in summer breeze

Striking deep in straw bales by the barn.

Summer, '76

Frank Stanford

In Frank Stanford's twenty-nine years (1949–1978) he published nine collections of poetry including a 542-page opus *The Battlefield Where the Moon Says I Love You.* He was the adopted son of Dorothy Gilbert, at that time Firestone's only female manager, and of Albert Franklin Stanford, a levee contractor. Just prior to middle school young Stanford left the Tennessee delta with his family for the Arkansas Ozarks. The Benedictines are partially responsible for his education, but no more so than the levee hands along the St. Francis River. He was twice married. He earned his living as a land surveyor. He was founding editor of Lost Roads Publishers, a book press which issued twelve titles under his direction.

Most of Frank's experience was kept within the borders of four contiguous states: Mississippi, Louisiana, Tennessee, and Arkansas. With his original publisher, Irv Broughton, he did tour the country once, making documentary films that featured prominent poets. Malcolm Cowley was the subject of one such film. According to Frank, Cowley initially eyed him with suspicion, seeing in him an uncanny resemblance to a young Hart Crane who had deprived Cowley of his first wife. Also according to Frank: when the younger poet pressed his first collection *The Singing Knives* upon the venerated editor of Faulkner, Cowley barked, "My boy you know what Art is?" Young Stanford was quick to admit, "No Sir, not I Sir." And Cowley quick to bark, "It's an ostrich, sticking its head in the sand, shitting bricks"—followed a lengthy pause—"Thus the pyramids." Together Broughton and Stanford produced an award-winning short about Frank's own life and work entitled "It Wasn't A Dream It Was A Flood."

By his choice Stanford earned no academic degrees, taught

at no college. Nor did he give public readings. In the main he avoided cities, published with obscure presses. Save for placing fourth in a contest sponsored by the Ninth District Tennessee Federation of Women's Clubs in 1958, he went unhonored. Any of these decisions could have guaranteed his enduring invisibility as a writer. Yet he acquired a sizable, devoted readership in his lifetime. And it would be unwarranted to think his reputation profited by his premature death. On the contrary, the work suffered and to some degree remains tainted on this account because death was his subject. He has rightly been called one of its great voices.

While the surveyor was shouldering his transit to clear a fenceline, the poet was drinking in the afternoon; when he was breaking up with one woman to take rooms with another, his poems slowly moved out. For months at a stretch he cached himself in the woods, emerging to pass night after night in bars listening to local bands and people's talk. He was a major listener. Art, high and low, held the better part of his attention most of the time. He was a philanderer; consequently he lied. Men sometimes envied, always protected him, which is not to say he was not bitten by a righteous order of politics as well. Injustice—on a large, impersonal scale—was an intense preoccupation. Religion was not, although Zen suited him. Literature bracketed everything. He was spare of the spoken word—but killingly funny and purposeful. He both read and wrote prodigiously and evidently at all his ages, under every condition. There are poems in his published collections dating from 1957 when Frank was preposterously only nine years old. The work is that continuous. In addition to the books his legacy entails several dozen manuscripts in various states of completion: poems, translations, stories, interviews, essays, filmscripts. Thus the pyramids.

At his best, Stanford was a poet abundant in word and scope. Out of this cornucopia have come scores of poems I would not hesitate to call faultless. For a fact, faultlessness was not a virtue in which he put stock. Style he had to burn. Once the poet had achieved fluency, which he did at a precocious age, there boomed the weight of what he had to say, the matter of urgency. Finally there is the work.

Stanford's first nine titles are now effectively out of print. However, his selected poems are due out in the spring of 1991 from the University of Arkansas Press. In addition a collection of stories, *Conditions Uncertain and Likely to Pass Away,* will be released early in 1991 from Lost Roads Publishers.

—C. D. Wright

From

THE BATTLEFIELD WHERE THE MOON SAYS I LOVE YOU (1977)

I still got hope Tang says
Jimmy was looking at the pictures trying to read James Dean's
   lips
there were for real tears coming out his eyes
the man turned up the volume folks we want you to
   remember our sunrise service
tomorrow morning we'll stop whatever is showing as soon as
   the preacher
gets here we would ask your cooperation in picking up the
   bottles and cans
under your vehicles before the preacher arrives
there will be he asked me to announce a collection taken up
aw shut up Clyde Miller a kid says
hymnals will be passed out at the concession stand after five
   o'clock this
morning thank you now back to our feature
honk honk honk he switched the mike off
and with a quick glance he reached in the till and got the two
   dollars Jimmy
give him and give it back to Jimmy saying sorry you can't
   bring those niggers
in here tonight son we got a religious service at daylight
and turned his back to Jimmy and says to his wife
Ronnie don't pay no tention to what the customers say I'm
   running this Drive Inn
Jimmy yelled what'd you say
the man's wife said honey you should a heard what some those
   people called you
the man turned around said get it they ain't coming in here
the woman said colored night was last night

Jimmy said we drove a long way ma'am
sorry she smacked her gum
Tang said un huh what I say now what I say
the woman said ya'll come back on another night and me and
    Clyde will be happy
to let you in see tomorrow's Easter and it just wouldn't be
    right
be too much scuttlebutt wouldn't honey say boy didn't Ray
    Charles record that
I just love Ray Charles he's one of my favorites next to Hank
did you know he's not really blind I read in a magazine it was
    a gimmick
hey Jimmy I said tell that motherfucker who I am
and tell that lady Ray Charles's blind as a bat
and while you're at it tell her she's batfucked too
sorry but you can't bring them boys in here I don't care what
    your name is
that didn't work either
the woman chewing gum said the others are welcome to come
    in she smiled
ya'll go head and go Charlie said
Jimmy rattled the two bills in his hand like he was going to lay
    down and bet
ask him if we can come in just to see Baby Doll I said
what about me Tang said
ask him about Hallelujah too I said
he asked Clyde Miller
he was getting mad at Jimmy he said get on out the niggers
    couldn't come
they was having a revival service in the morning he said
the man said hold on cause his wife says it's time honey
he picked up the microphone and was about to talk
but Jimmy yelled out why don't you and Mrs. Miller go get
    fucked
the both of you I added Amen Tang and Charlie B. said
it carried over the sound system to every white man's car and
    truck
I know there must have been a tense moment for a moment
in the moom pitchu Drive Inn

cause all the peoples turned around and looked out they cars
I figured we'd be dead inside a minute but those folks had
    more sense
than I ever give them credit for I know them like the back of
    my hand I thought
but I guess I don't cause they just passed the two brown faces
    on
they must of know'd who we was although I'd like not to
    think so
yessiree they commenced to honking and yelling and laughing
    at Clyde Miller
it was a sight to see Tang looks over my direction he say smart
    cracker jacks
Jimmy shoved it in reverse and scratched out backwards
he left two dollars worth a rubber in the man's Drive Inn
    driveway
he runned into his ticket shed on account of the slipping and
    sliding
then he hit another man's car he said get your ass out the way
Jimmy should never have riled the white man like that cause it
    riled all of them
he peeled out forward and we tore up some dead bushes Clyde
    Miller had planted
Jimmy was mad I guess before long we was doing a hundred
    miles an hour
fucking shithooks he was mumbling
I didn't think that car would do a hundred you drunk Jimmy I
    said
sorry bout that he told Charlie B.
Tang was laughing to himself saying told you so
he touched Jimmy on the shoulder slow this thing down boy
    he hit him in the head
you crazy or something
we cruised on some more
boy that pisses me off Charlie B. says
don't it though Charlie Jimmy says
shuckit I says
goddamn motherfuckers Jimmy says

be what I told you wouldn't it Tang said ya'll won't listen to
    an old man
shit ya'll just whipsnaps I rode a hundred mules
you want to go back and shoot him Jimmy I said
nah could of done that then
open me nothin Tang said
say what about my supper
we stopped off on the way home about the time he said it
can a buy some firecrackers with the change Tang I said
yea but you better get me some soda crackers
I got some under the seat Jimmy says
good then they'll do he said
Jimmy gave me a dollar and told me pick some shells up
they had a sale on fishing worms and hooks so I took
    advantage of the bargain
I got enough to eat alright
so did Tang and the rest
drive up to the levee I want to yell a little bit Charlie B. says
the night got darker and we drove up there and parked
turn the damn radio back on Tang said
going to run down the battery if I do Jimmy said
piss on it you can coast start it if you have to
I got out the car and drunk me a lemon lime
lemme have the pistol I want to shoot tin cans
don't shoot yoself Charlie B. said
give me that box of shell too I just bought
don't shoot up all my bullets Jimmy said
I walked down the levee the high road
now it is getting cooler and I am getting madder but an idea
    will come I thought
I'll dream something up
here I am saying this and still ain't off the mule yet
I ain't hit ball one ain't caught one either
I kept shooting at the can keeping it on top of the levee
    sometime having
to reel off some mighty quick shots to keep it from rolling
    down
whenever I missed I yelled missed

I didn't miss too much
after I'd shoot a full round I'd eject the empty cartridges out
    of the chamber
into my palm I'd warm my hand on them and and smell the
        gunpowder smoke
it curled out of the brass like a garbage fire
I walked way down to a place I hadn't been before
some clearing had been done
the remains of snakes that had been cut in two by the
    bulldozer blade
stunk to high heaven the flies was buzzing like a radio station
    that won't come
in the trees were like wounded soldiers bent over on a
    battlefield
men that knew they had lost the fight and were going to die to
    boot
I can't see it but I know it's there
gaunt and gallant like an old man with a pistol and an ace up
    his sleeve
reserved and noble with a silver moustache
mean as a convict's widow the river
I can smell it

Askia M. Touré

In his career as a writer, editor, poet, and activist Askia M. Touré has mastered the art of the metaphor. The piercing effectiveness of images he creates comes full circle in his latest work, *From the Pyramids to the Projects: Poems of Genocide and Resistance!* It creates in verse a vision of genocide as the willful intent to destroy, in whole or in part, a national, ethical, or racial group. Through menticidé (cultural genocide) to devastation to rebirth (resistance) Touré has catalogued the history of the world's first holocaust (the destruction of over 100 million Africans) and the continuing methods surgically used to destroy members of the African race.

In the introduction he speaks forebodingly of the wanton cultural destruction of Africa's cities, and universities and the new genocide of AIDS, along with the plague of drugs, which he captions "holocaust two of the twentieth century." Touré quotes the the legendary Paul Robeson's statement concerning the United States's refusal to ratify the United Nations Genocide Treaty. He discusses as well the mental games, such as colorism and unconscious self-hatred, that African-Americans are subjected to in order to divide their communities.

There are lessons to be learned in his searing images of a people lost in negative images, needing to understand the intrinsic beauty of their true and natural selves. He captures the depth and complexity of our cultural heritage, from Della Watson to the ancient imagery of Khemit (ancient Egypt):

> ". . . because knowledge, like our children,
> was sacred then, in Ipet Isut [Karnak],
> in the royal city Waset [Thebes]
> . . . when our great Masters taught

Geometry, Medicine, Algebra,
Astronomy, Chemistry, Philosophy,
Trigonometry, Engineering, Music; all the
basis of
Civilization; in Afrika, in Khemit,
the Black Land where we built
the Sphinx, the Great Pyramid,
charted the stars, the calendar,
led mankind on new roads into
bright tomorrows"

*("From the Pyramids to the Projects,
from the Projects to the Stars!").*

From the Pyramids to the Projects should be welcomed as an addition to the critical body of research on genocide along side Walter Rodney's *How Europe Underdeveloped Africa,* Chancellor Williams's *The Destruction of Black Civilization: Great Issues of a Race, 4500 B.C. to 2000 A.D.,* Ayei Kwei Armah's *Two Thousand Seasons,* Yambo Ouologuem's *Bound to Violence,* Samuel Yette's *The Choice: The Issue of Black Extermination in America,* Frank C. Tucker's *White Conscience* and S. M. E. Bengu's *Chasing Gods Not Our Own.* While these works are dispassionate scholarly studies, Touré's book shocks your mind into visualizing the full pain and unforgetable sorrows of genocide.

Askia M. Touré's work, while intense, also speaks of gentleness in its tributes to African women in poems like "A*boriginal Elegy,*" "Ifé: A Bronze Lament" and "Nzingha Revisited." He gives us new avenues of hope for liberation in the final section entitled, "Bennu/Phoenix: Rebirth: The Naked Sword Of Resistance!" As a writer and literary craftsman realizing that culture identifies a people, Askia Touré utilizes the ancestral names of African American people: the Mande, Ibo, Fulani, Asante, Ewe, Wolof, Dogon, Bakongo and others. As the historical notes in the work attest, the author has studied the work of the late Cheikh Anta Diop, Chancellor Williams, John G. Jackson, Sterling Stuckey, and George G. M. James.

In the poem "Groovin' on a Sunday Afternoon," (dedicated to the prima donna of the sixties movement, Aretha Franklin), he poses pertinent questions for a people as we look toward the twenty-first century. He asks, "Can you imagine a world where/we hold the balance of power? . . . Imagine Jesse Jackson, Frances Welsing/Queen Mother Moore running the world!" His belief in and love for African people suffuses his work. He envisions the unlimited possibilities of African men and women.

Askia M. Touré can be seen a griot, a word spinner-weaver. *From the Pyramids to the Projects: Poems of Genocide and Resistance!* must be celebrated as a masterpiece of African literary expression reminiscent of African proverbs, the role of which were to give counsel and guidance. As students of African and African-American culture, we can use *From the Pyramids to the Projects* as a manual of teaching and to gain insight into our struggles to be a free and independent people. Ngugi Thing'o has said, "Poetry is a distillation of human wisdom and thought." He believes that a writer's pen both reflects reality and also attempts to persuade us to take a certain attitude toward that reality. Not only does Touré force us to be realistic and conscious, but he also forces us to see that literature is important in a people's cultural education. The ultimate message of Touré's novel-in-verse is that awareness is never a given.

—*Larry Oba Dele Williams*

*FROM THE PYRAMIDS TO THE
PROJECTS: POEMS OF GENOCIDE
AND RESISTANCE! (1988)*

Ifé: A Bronze Lament

(This is Malkia's)

Somewhere in
                the tidy collection
of a distinguished citizen
                                lies
the bronze head of an Ifé princess . . .
                        She whose
                                full lips
mouthed oaths or curses which
                        for some were the
                                        cycles
                        of the very heavens,
now lies dormant like frozen fire.
                        Siren-eyed beauty,
whose sensuous curves titillated god-kings
                                and
influenced the fates of empires   so curiously
                        mute upon the bland shelf of
                        a Scarsdale banker.

Your Highness;
                in temperate climes
far from your tempestuous
                        Niger Age,
do you scream through the mask of regal
                                bronze

accusing long
                    dead
                        gods
    of arcane betrayals?

Scarsdale in temperate zones
    oblivious
        to silent
            Afrikan queens   screaming!

Blackbelt Rhapsody/A Redemption Song

"Please won't you sing these songs of freedom,
They are all I've ever owned . . .
Redemption songs."

—*Bob Marley*

Return to the Womb/the Source
of your legends defying seasons of agony.
Here,
        among these ebon multitudes—among
        resisters of the lash, iron chains,
        aeons of slavery—find
        the Anthem of your rebirth,
                            Afrikan!
        aroused from milleniums of oppression
                            fighting
                                to restore your
living history, your own heartbeat,
collective tred upon the crimson soil
            of this legendary entity,
            this zone of triumph/agony,
                this

gory
womb, this
prime-

val Blackbelt Nation!

O joy! that
our Fathers Mothers
unsung forebears
gave of their
flesh their blood-rhythm
sweat-song
genius to nourish it
make it a
living
whole
ripe with
destiny:
rhythm-breath of living, toiling
beings bearing the marks of pariahs
moving beyond the zeroes of a famine
existence
to embrace Tomorrows & zones of feeling
beyond colonies of gain/

into the flame
of human passion: revolution!
triumph of
broadbacked dreams scribbled in sweaty dawns
breaking hotly
across horizons of cotton, cane, tobacco
baptized in the grim bio-rhythms of our
awesome heritage/
To emerge from ashes of martyred
centuries—alive:
Phoenix of
Afrikan spirit!
triumphant
Gospel-song of transformed
pariahs

                    Avatar of communal compassion
Passionate Griot-voice
    of oracular vision/ reborn in
          transcendental bloodstorms: Furies
              Whirlwinds of Redemption
                blasting misbegotten
                Citadels of gain!

Transcendental Vision: Indigo

for Malcolm X & Dr. M. L. King, Jr.

And
    there
          are
              Whirlwinds embodied
in
    the
        minds of
Visionary griots/singing:
                    Tomorrow!
                        Tomorrow!) Language of
transcendental passion-flame
                    (spirit-tongue. Surreal
                            Saint-
inflected solo) motivating warrior
                    generations
                    venerating liberation
                            in
                    primary language of
                            forever.
Seize
    this
        instance
            of

indigo/your martyred
prophets
      challenging in lucid
               moralities/O
multi-rhythmed multitudes. Multi-
               visioned
               Negritude
    invisible in this
    travesty of ironies: A-
      merikkka:
unholy paradox writhing in
          explosive
             cataclysms/
               deemed
"Criminal
    violence of
    degenerate
      pariahs."   A-
        merikkka
     chants in Viking-vision
        Aryan in-
      humanities (Swastica-intoxicated
        burning
          crucifix/ed in
    the consciousness of
     red-haired
     politicians
     spawning
        red-necked
aspirations: Reaganomics.
    Reaganomics—jackbooted,
        lean,
         ubiquitous—
    envisioning
       an era
musclebound with
    repression/O
    huddled masses
    screaming

in
urban
junglescapes)
"High crime"
reservations
liquidate Bantu populations/
frozen
media blitz of
infamy
rationalizing genocide.
Blizzard morality/
frosty
mentalities: forever
"Born Again"
Forever
$tar-$pangled.
"Pure".

And
there
are
Whirlwinds (bearing
Griot-vision: ghosts
of
flame-tongued
prophets
alive/in
multi-rhythmed multitudes
multi-
visioned
Negritude
Mamas/Papas strong
and . . .
Loving Liberation: Forever
(Transcendental Vision)
Loving
Liberation: Forever
(Transcendental Vision)

Loving
Liberation:
Forever!

Nzingha Revisited

Mould me a face in
gleaming bronze, a rare one;
mobile, sensitive, strong.
Female and gentle
with full lips and
classical Afrikan
feature: nostrils
chiseled from
Yoruba forms.
Place above it a crown of cornrowed hair;
adorn the ears with bright, golden rings;

Place gentle, placid eyes
large beneath arching brows;
a glowing smile usually
lighting up this face.
A beautiful, Afrikan
woman, smiling—or
dreamy-eyed, lost in
precious thoughts.
Bathe her in the vermilion light of a
glowing sunset, shifting its colors to
canary horizons beneath tangerine skies.

She is walking at sunset,
in autumn, bathed in the day's
dying brilliance. A tall, radiant
beauty adorned with kinte
robes above sandaled feet.

Though our setting is not
Afrika, but North America.
She is seed of the lost
tribes in Diaspora, who
formed a nation in the U.S. Southland.
This tall, beautiful woman walking in autumn

is a living miracle: a testament
of a race's drive for survival.
She is intelligent, artistic,
lovely. She is modern,
dedicated to her people's
freedom; educated to
know that it is a bitter,
protracted struggle,
lasting centuries.
She is determined that her children
will drink from cooling waters

of that freedom, and is sacrificing
to make that dream a reality.
She is building institutions, organi-
zing, educating, demonstrating,
by example, how a Black woman
should conduct her life in this
age of the U.S. empire falling.
She is giving her all—her
life, honor, energy, above
all, undying love—to make
this Black freedom blossom in the West.

Black man; working your shift,
fixing your car, walking your dog,
I didn't mean to interrupt, but
a few words in passing. Please
know that she is the most vital,
precious glory of your life.
This woman was always
yours—from the slave-

ships to the hot
cottonfields and beyond. She is your
dignity, and the only Afrika you'll ever know!

Rebellion Suite/Straight. No Chaser.

(for Thelonious Sphere Monk
and the Bebop Rebellion)

No trumpets announce
                    this
Maybe skies   hero's
          toned   arrival.
            a deeper
            sapphire.
                        Intense the days
brimmed with his sacramental hipness. Stride.
            elemental
                    vision.
The world we recognize
                    takes on
additional tones. textures. colors.
                        (Language
            conveys our usual coded
                        sophisticated
                            overtones.
            But another dynamic strikes the depths:
            our rhythms lyrics harmonies
                    vibrate
                    an
                        electricity
            adding a charismatic joy
                        which

                    reverberates
                        across
        urban plantations   momentarily
            causing a transcendance
                        —Zen-like—
        interrupting the mundane schizophrenia
                            which
            normally smothers bluesy
                        shouters.
                            screamers.
            finga-poppin'
                on
            the urban
                killing ground.

Oyeah
Oyeah
Oyeah
Oyeah/   scarlet flametones highlight
            the
                satiny
                    skintight
                        elegant dress
of this gardinia-wearing goddess boppin
            to his
                complexities. (Sweaty
                        coon-toned
                            pianos
            smile their ivory teeth awaiting
                    his familiar
                        caress.)

Spotlight kissed,
   the
        bronze
            enchantress
                    enhances a language

rife
with
polished gestures
motion. silence.   dramatic pauses
round about midnight when the indigo sky
conjures
a mulatto moon/
spotlights pierce
the
purple haze
Dahomey profiles bedazzle
enchant

elements
of
Negritude
in patent leather conks
—marcels—
above Benin bronze. Atavistic
sweatstains. moans

embrace
the
harmony/joys
release the memories
of
Downsouth dues
(lynchrope screams amid
terror
tar
& kerosene).

But/
O the velvet-toned honey
ripe now
in his rippling fingers/
arpeggios
of
interwoven ecstasies
Flashpoint
of

profound perception/
vision
            highlighting
a new language. form. sound.
            highlighting
            a new
                humanity!

Rippling keys forsee
                a Revolution/
        a renaissance
            of
            sound/language: forms
                        heroic;
            at Minton's   a race of giants
            emerges.
"Salt Peanuts!
        Salt Peanuts!
                Salt Peanuts!"

Quincy Troupe

BORN and raised in St. Louis, Troupe (1943–)is the son of Quincy Troupe, Sr., the second greatest catcher of all time in the all Black baseball leagues. Troupe attended Grambling College with the help of a basketball and baseball scholarship and after graduating, played professional basketball in France. While living in Paris in 1963, Troupe met Jean-Paul Sartre. "He put ideas in my head," says Troupe in an interview with Christine Cassidy in *Poets and Writers* (January/February 1989). "He persisted. He kept saying that I was a Black American, that I had to fight for my rights and stand up for myself. I was a human being. I was intelligent and I couldn't be a coward and run away from it. Racism would be there when I got back. I could live in France, but France was racist, too. I would see that eventually, he said. He was a Marxist and blah, blah, blah, I had to get ideas in my head. The world's made up of ideas and I had to stand up for something. . . . Being a young man I wanted to shoot jumpshots."

Before leaving France for the United States in 1965, Troupe began to write and remembers asking Sartre, "How do you control a sentence? I seem to write too much and I can't control the form." Troupe recalls Satre suggesting "Why don't you write poetry to clean up your language and get a sharper focus or sharper grip. You might try walking around and keeping diary, a poetic diary, of what you see in Paris and what you see all over France as you play basketball."

His poetry, once influenced greatly by the poets he read, now has "moved out of some of the influences—Neruda, Cesaire, Jean-Joseph Rabearevello. I can see my own voice now. And getting older, I think my concerns are changing. The birth of my son has changed my work some, softened it a bit. I write more about domestic things than I ever did before. I write about connections between myself and other people more— the whole idea of constructing an interior life, my interior life."

Quincy Troupe has published four volumes of poetry, *Embryo* (1972), *Snake-Back Solos* (1979), *Skulls Along the River* (1984), and *Weather Reports* (1991); edited two anthologies, *Watts Poets and Writers* (1968) and *Giant Talk: An Anthology of Third World Writing* (1975); edited *James Baldwin: The Legacy* (1989), a project that grew out of an opportunity to conduct the last interview with Baldwin; co-authored with David L. Wolper *The Inside Story of TV's Roots* (1978); and wrote the definitive life story of Miles Davis, *Miles: The Autobiography* (1989). He is also the founding editor of *Confrontation: A Journal of Third World Literature* and *The American Rag* and is senior editor of the St. Louis-based literary journal, *River Styx*. He a professor of creative writing and American and third world literature at the University of California at San Diego.

—*S h a w n   W o n g*

From

SNAKE-BACK SOLOS: SELECTED POEMS, 1969–1977 (1979)

The Old People Speak of Death

For Leona Smith, my grandmother

the old people speak of death
frequently now
my grandmother speaks of those now
gone to spirit
now less than bone

they speak of shadows
that graced their days made lovelier
by their wings of light speak of years
& corpses of years of darkness
& of relationships buried
deeper even than residue of bone
gone now beyond hardness
gone now beyond form

they smile now from ingrown roots
of beginnings of those who have left us
& climbed back through the holes the old folks
left in their eyes
for them to enter through

eye walk back now with this poem
through the holes the old folks left in their eyes
for me to enter through walk back to where
eye see them there

the ones that have gone beyond hardness
the ones that have gone beyond form
see them there
darker than where roots began
& lighter than where they go
with their spirits
heavier than stone their memories
sometimes brighter than the flash
of sudden lightning

but green branches will grow
from these roots darker than time
& blacker than even the ashes of nations
sweet flowers will sprout
& wave their love-stroked language
in sun-tongued morning's shadow
the spirit in all our eyes

they have gone now back
to shadow as eye climb back out
from the holes of these old folks eyes
those spirits who sing through this poem
gone now back with their spirits
to fuse with greenness
enter stones & glue their invisible
faces upon the transmigration of earth
nailing winds singing guitar blues
voices through the ribcages
of these days
gone now to where the years run
darker than where roots begin
greener than what they bring

the old people speak of death
frequently now
my grandmother speaks of those now
gone to spirit
now less than bone

My Poems Have Holes Sewn into Them

my poems have holes sewn into them
& they run searching for light
at the end of tunnels they become trains
or at the bottom of pits they become blackness
or in the broad winging daylight
they are the words that fly

& the holes are these words
letters or syllables with feathered wings
that leave their marks on white pages
then fly off like footprints tracked in snow
& only God knows where they go

this poem has holes stitched into it
as our speech which created poetry in the first place
lacerated wounded words that strike out original
meaning bleeding into language
hemorrhaging out of thick or thin mouths
has empty spaces & silences sewn into it

so my poems have holes sewn into them
& their voices are like different keyholes
through which dumb men search for speech blind
men search for sight
words like drills penetrating sleep
keys turning in the keyholes of language
like knives of sunrays stabbing blind eyes

my poems have holes sewn into them
& they are the spaces between words
are the words themselves
falling off into one another/colliding

like people gone mad they space out
fall into bottomless pits
which are the words

like silent space between chords of a piano
or black eyes of a figure in any painting
they fall back into themselves
into time/sleep
bottom out on the far side of consciousness
where words of all the worlds poets go
& whisper in absolute silence

this poem has deep holes stitched into it
& their meanings have the deadly suck of quicksand
the irreversible pull of earth to any skydiver
the tortured pus-holes in arms of junkies

my poems have holes sewn into them
& they run searching for light at the end
of tunnels or at the bottom of yawning pits
or in the broad daylight where
the words flapping like wings of birds
fly whispering in absolute silence

Snake-Back Solo

*For Louis Armstrong, Steve Cannon, Miles
Davis & Eugene Redmond*

with the music up high
boogalooin bass down way way low
up & under eye come slidin on in mojoin
on in spacin on in on a riff
full of rain

riffin on in full of rain & pain
spacin on in on a sound like coltrane

my metaphor is a blues
hot pain dealin blues is a blues axin
guitar voices whiskey broken niggah deep
in the heart is a blues in a glass filled with rain
is a blues in the dark
slurred voices of straight bourbon
is a blues dagger stuck off in the heart
of night moanin like bessie smith
is a blues filling up the wings
of darkness is a blues

& looking through the heart
a dream can become a raindrop window to see through
can become a window to see through this moment
to see yourself hanging around the dark
to see through
can become a river catching rain
feeding time can become a window
to see through

while outside windows flames trigger
the deep explosion
time steals rivers that go on & stay where they are
inside yourself moving soon there will be daylight
breaking the darkness
to show the way soon there will be voices breaking music
to come on home by down & up river breaking darkness
swimming up river the sound of louie armstrong
carrying riverboats upstream on vibratos
climbing the rain filling the rain
swimming up river
up the river of rain satchmo breaking the darkness
his trumpet & grin polished overpain speaking
to the light flaming off the river's back
at sunset snake river's back
river mississippi big muddy up from new

orleans to alton & east st. louis illinois
cross the river from st. louis to come on home by
up river the music swims breaking silence of miles
flesh leaping off itself into space
creating music creating poems

now inside myself eye solo of rivers
catching rains & dreams & sunsets solo
of trane tracks screaming through night stark
a dagger in the heart solo
of the bird spreading wings for the wind
solo of miles pied piper prince of darkness
river rain voice now eye solo
at the root of the flower solo leaning voices
against promises of shadows soloing of bones
beneath the river's snake-back solo
of trees cut down by double-bladed axes
river rain voice now eye solo of the human condition
as blues solo of the matrix mojoin new blues solo
river rain voice now eye solo solo

& looking through the heart a dream
can become a raindrop window to see through
can become this moment this frame to see through
to see yourself hanging
around the dark to see through this pain
can become even more painful as the meaning of bones
crawling mississippi river bottoms snakepits beneath
the snake-back solo catching rain catching time
& dreams washed clean by ajax

but looking through the dream can be
like looking through a clean window crystal
prism the night where eye solo now too be-
come the wings of night
to see through this darkness
eye solo now to become wings & colors
to become a simple skybreak shattering darkness
to become lightning's jagged sword-like thunder

eye solo to become to become
eye solo now to become to become

with the music up high
up way way high boogalooin bass down
way way low
up & under eye come slidin on in mojoin on in
spacin on in on a riff full of rain
river riff full of rain & trains & dreams
come slidin on in another riff
full of flames
leanin & glidin eye solo solo
loopin & slidin eye solo now solo

Evangelina Vigil

IN 1983, Evangelina Vigil edited an anthology of Hispanic women writers entitled, *Woman of Her Word: Hispanic Women Write.* In her introduction she describes the Hispanic literary scene and the literary world of the Latina writer:

> As a persona in the literature, the Latina is a woman of her word—
> *mujer de su palabra.* In this role, the Latina is self-sacrificing to her
> family as a mother and wife. She conveys values to her family
> members by way of example, and through the oral tradition, and,
> as such, she represents a tie to the cultural past. The woman is
> portrayed as the sensitive one in the family who expresses love and
> teaches respect for self and others. And, most importantly, she is
> the giver of life.

Her poem " 'night vigil' " from *Thirty an' Seen a Lot* (1982) reinforces the notion of a woman's power as lifegiver as she implies above:

> I am back in this room
> I feel calm awareness of heart pumping lifeblood rhythmically
> my own body warmth sends chill through my bones
> warmth regenerates

Vigil's poetry also speaks of the continuation and transition of family myth, family culture, family history; for only out of the past can one define a future as in her poem, "warm heart contains life":

> pressed in-between the memories of your mind
> diary never written

but always remembered, felt
scripted en tu mente—
your daughters will never read it
but they'll inherit it
and they'll know it
when they look into your eyes
shining luz de amor, corazon
unspoken, untold

—*Shawn Wong*

"night vigil"

in the twilight hour all is still
all lights out
except for my nocturnal eyes, fluorescent
shining on oscuridades
spotlight rolling
exposing crevices on walls
shaded pastel surfaces
elongated door structures
furnishings converted into bultos by the darkness
como los que te espantaron cuando niña
"cúrala de susto"
dijo tu abuelita:
in your juvenile memory
four little broomstraws forming crosses
an egg, water

in night surroundings while others sleep
my heart thumps, off beat
absolutely refusing to align itself with time
ticking rhythmically
from faithful clock
marking time
advancing time
in night surroundings while others dream
I can taste my solitude

my imagination spins
images take form
I recall the splendor of beaches in the Caribbean
warmed by the sun
caressed by waters blue
I recall the powerful thrusts of the Atlantic
the Pacific
I envision beaches being swallowed up by night tide
the color of obsidian
moon illuminating rapture

I picture in my mind
receding waters
por la mañana
exposing sprinklings of starfish, urchins, seashell pedals pink
nocturnal creatures slithering, crawling, stretching
traces of last night's liquid passion
(what the stars will not tell)
realization anchored in this knowledge:

     the universe is immeasureable;
     the constellations shine so

thoughtglow spins into silvermist, then silverblack
then into live darkness
feelings, sensations have collected themselves back inward
to self-consuming origins
in depths of memories reconcealed

     images have disappeared before my very eyes
     like would they were the tails of comets
     or paths of falling stars

               images have vanished in colorful
               flashes dash by dash
               like silk scarf streamers would
               into elegant skillful, white-gloved
               hands of a magician

consciousness retreats into my breathing body
I am back in this room
I feel calm awareness of heart pumping lifeblood rhythmically
my own body warmth sends chill through my bones
warmth regenerates
I breathe in stillness
with ease

solitude, darkness, quiet
envelope my once more
feelings of loneliness, forlornness gather in my chest
they weigh my heart
sentimiento slowly transforms into a focused thought—
spotlight rolling again
mind fluorescent, sensors beaming
surveillant

sideglance:
the sky glows opaque
window frames silhouette of tree with winter limbs
the branches are brittle, made so by the frost
they are silver-lined with moonmist
they are beautiful, elegant
they express artistry, magic

closing my eyes, I turn inward
I feel fluid, serene, peaceful
my mind lies potent with imagination
all is silent around me
I am by myself
I am singular
the night's presence cushions me
its embrace is pillow soft

como un indio
who in stillness detects stampede
of approaching herd
I detect

far off in the distance
an approaching train
its heavy rhythmic speed transmits velocity through my bones
its iron clanking sounds are muffled, sifted
by the night air thick with mist and fog
I hear its familiar whistle
its distant call slowly permeates through nightspace
it rings solitude
immense sadness engulfs me
it is upon me
but it quickly begins to fade
like a tumbleweed of sound
rolling by:
I wonder who this nightrain traveler is
I wonder how he feels about this vast sea
of nocturnal singular existence

I pull multicolored quilt over my head
mind rests assured:
in the morning the sea will flow aquablue
sparkling and vibrant, activated by the sun
brilliance, inspiration
will explode from within the spirit, uncontained
but tonight
nocturnal naked eyes keep watch
beholding with awe
heart's inner vision:

moment's pause
del corazón
anchored in perennial motion
like cascades of the ocean waves
gushing
crowned with white lace liquid patterns
jeweled with watermist of pearls exquisite
crescents volatile, explosive
energía sculpted
by force of rolling tide

warm heart contains life

to our amás

warm heart contains life
heart's warmth
which penetrates through pen
lifeblood that reveals inner thoughts
subtly
like rustling leaves would secrets
to the winter wind

secrets collected
pressed between pages
to be kissed by lips red
protruding with warmth, desire
sometimes hurt, pain:

recuerdos
like that autumn leaf you singled out
and saved
pressed in-between the memories of your mind
diary never written
but always remembered, felt
scripted en tu mente—
your daughters will never read it
but they'll inherit it
and they'll know it
when they look into your eyes
shining luz de amor, corazón
unspoken, untold
keepsake for our treasure chests
que cargamos aquí adentro
radiant with jewels
sculpted by sentimientos y penas
y bastante amor:

intuition tells us
better having lived through pain
than never having felt
life's full intensity

to the personalities in the works by José Montoya and the chucos of the future

recall that memory
that keeps calling you back in time
but will not show itself:
invisible fiber connected to the past
needled through your ombligo
it pulls you onward
but at the same time
aback

aback
like a bato loco from the barrio
confident stacey adams steps
clicking rhythmically forward
but head swung back some
as if poised to say
"¿qué pajó, ese?"
"what's happenin' home!"

yes, head swung back some
because string of consciousness
pulls him back in time
although the dude
is really walking forward

was fun running 'round descalza

barefoot is how I always used to be
running barefoot
like on that hot summer
in the San Juan Projects
they spray-painted all the buildings
pastel pink, blue, green, pale yellow, gray
and in cauldrons tar bubbling, steaming
(time to repair the roofs)
its white smoke filling summer air with aromas of nostalgia
for the future
and you, barefoot,
tender feet jumping with precision
careful not to land on nest of burrs or stickers
careful not to tread too long on sidewalks
converted by the scorching sun into comales
"¡se puede freír hasta un huevo en esas banquetas!"
exclamaba la gente
ese verano tan caliente
no sooner than had the building wall/canvasses been painted
    clean
did barrio kids take to carving new inspirations
and chuco hieroglyphics
and new figure drawings of naked women
and their parts
and messages for all
"la Diana es puta"
"el Lalo es joto"
y que "la Chelo se deja"
decorated by hearts and crosses
and war communications
among rivaling gangs
El Circle
La India
pretty soon kids took to just plain peeling plastic pastel paint
to unveil historical murals

of immediate past well-remembered:
más monas encueradas
and "Lupe loves Tony"
"always and forever"
"Con Safos"
y "Sin Safos"
y que "El Chuy es relaje"
and other innocent desmadres de la juventud
secret fear in every child
que su nombre apareciera allí
y la música de los radios
animando

    "Do you wanna dance under the moonlight?
    Kiss me Baby, all through the night
    Oh, Baby, do you wanna dance?"

was fun running 'round descalza
playing hopscotch
correr sin pisar la líneas—
te vas con el diablo

was fun running 'round descalza
shiny brown legs leaping with precision
to avoid nido de cadillos crowned with tiny blossoms pink
to tread but ever so lightly on scorching cement
to cut across street glistening with freshly laid tar
its steam creating a horizon of mirages
rubber thongs sticking, smelting
to land on cool dark clover carpet green
in your child's joyful mind
"Got to get to la tiendita, buy us
some popsicles and Momma's Tuesday Light!"

was fun running 'round descalza

Julia Vinograd

JULIA VINOGRAD has been hanging out with the homeless since they were called street people. Known as "the Bubble Lady" and immortalized in a Berkeley mural of Telegraph Avenue, she roams the streets of Berkeley and San Francisco blowing soap bubbles and selling books of poetry. She was born in Berkeley; she has a B.A. from the University of California at Berkeley and an M.F.A. from the University of Iowa; and since 1969 she has published thirty slim volumes of street poems. Their quality is uneven, but each invariably contains several breathtaking poems of a kind you won't find anywhere else. The people Americans care about theoretically but don't like to meet on the street confront us here as unexpected friends. Vinograd does not set out to defend or justify street people; she merely dances through lives and moments with a poet's eye. She is part of the community she describes. She does not ask us to sympathize with people so much as she makes it impossible for us to dismiss them.

Vinograd is ever searching for that key which will unlock the secrets of humanity. Sometimes she searches overtly, as in "Don't Read This Poem":

> Pretend you've just arrived from Mars
> and for your world to survive
> it's vital that you understand people.
> So far you've met a landlord,
> a spare-changer, a student, a junkie,
> a musician, a wino, a waiter and a child. . . . And if you can
>   find the secret they share
> that makes them human
> your world will be saved. . . .

And you're scared
but this is important.
You sit down to start the report
and write this poem instead.

Other times Vinograd simply shares her own view of people
we might otherwise be tempted to dismiss. She tells us about
her "Conversation with a Deadhead" whose first pet rabbit
"came to all the shows" and "lived on junk food and rose pet-
als." She tells us about a veteran who can't sleep "because the
enemy is always there" and "it is suicidal to fall asleep, / it is
criminal, / it betrays his friends. . . ." She tells us about her
friend who is "Junksick." "I've no idea what it's like," she says.
"Junksick. Kicking. / I don't want to know." And she laments
the loss of the person he used to be. "Your fiery poems like red
exploding roses. / Your booming laugh . . . / The way you wag
your heart when you're glad to see someone. . . . / All these
shrunk, they're almost gone, / They're smaller than an itch."

Describing the incidental and the earth-shattering with the
same bemused affection for humanity and human foibles, she
offers up the ridiculous, the ambitious, the noble, the unful-
filled, and the minute. "It's Like This," she says, "Even the
samurai / have teddybears, / and even the teddybears / get
drunk."

In 1985 Vinograd won the American Book Award for *The
Book of Jerusalem,* a work quite unlike her street poems. In this
series of twenty-one poems about the ever-unconsummated
love affair between God and Jerusalem, Vinograd stepped out
of the world of her street poems and into a world that is over-
whelmingly mythic. The city of Jerusalem is a woman (almost),
and god is her lover (almost). *The Book of Jerusalem* captures
all the sweetness and longing of ill-fated love, and with this it
mixes the confusion of one who looks at the sufferings of the
world and cannot understand why they are necessary. Jerusa-
lem and God speak of human suffering as ornaments. We must
live in agony (says God) because we are poetry. The poet ac-
cuses God of being poetic when God should be in the compas-
sion business.

These poems reverberate with the drama of the world's most

profound love affair. And along the way the reader gets a chilling dose of a bitter but beautiful philosophy. The romantic notion that poetic agony is preferable to comfort and mediocrity is compelling. But since God inflicts poetry on the unwilling and unwitting, as well as on himself, that notion is undercut.

As different as these poems are from Vinograd's street poems, they too attempt to understand the world's mysteries. In Vinograd's street poems it is the mysteries of humanity that the poet seeks to understand; in *The Book of Jerusalem* it is the mysteries of God's universe.

—*Lorelei Bosserman*

Mourning

Jerusalem is weeping,
all temples shake in that sudden storm,
all faiths melt into wine and all who hear her
are suddenly young, innocent and furious again.
Jerusalem is never more beautiful
than when she mourns without hope, tears carving her face
like the last touches of a master sculptor.
No one is even sure why,
it doesn't seem to matter.

And though she infects all who hear her
with the same glittering improbable pain,
like the ache in the naked feet of a dancer
condemned to dance till she dies
by the whim of an idle forgotten king,
no one would comfort her
and change her beauty to safety.
And ease her beauty by kindness.
Jerusalem is weeping,
listen with your blood.

Costumes of Jerusalem

Time does not matter to Jerusalem.
The sleek modern treachery of a nation
or the out-of-date religious sacrilege?
She tries them on impartially like a professional model
showing how wedding dresses should be worn
without a wrinkle.
There are enough, too many, and the Lord removes them all
out of forgiveness, or desire, or simply a gentle reminder
that Jerusalem is still too young and may only play
at weddings or betrayals.
The skin of Jerusalem is always the same,
luminous and accusing,
a body made of eyes that never shut
except when the Lord caresses her
and at the same time creates new dangers
that require her blindness.

The wedding dresses fragment, nothing quite fits,
white lace decays over stone,
like the many versions of legends, no single one can be true
all by itself, it would not be enough all by itself.
So Jerusalem wears many costumes of faithfulness,
yes, and believes each one is the last while it lasts
and the same of the next.
She is always convincing on honeymoons
as a professional virgin who slips off her nightdress
to reach out trustfully for well earned trouble,
and finding it sensual and full of sorrow.
Time does not matter to the Lord.

Jerusalem's Jewel Box

Jerusalem going through her jewel-box of lives
finds an unset opal and shows it to God.
"You would have liked him," she explains,
"he was superstitious, he collected opals
because he thought they were unlucky,
then he saw me
and *knew* I was unlucky, and so he followed me.
Do you understand?"

"I'm afraid so," God tells her, waiting and watching
as she sifts diamond rings through her lazy fingers.
"There used to be so many," Jerusalem thinks out loud,
"there were those who died for me
and those who lived for me
and those who looked at me." She smiles lightly,
remembering. "I never gave them a moment's peace."
"Me neither," God reminds her
"Yes," Jerusalem strokes the opal as the colors pulse and coil,
"yes, I know.
But there used to be so many."

"All right," God tells her, "go ahead.
I know you. Your stones have been quiet too long.
Border skirmishes no longer satisfy you,
you want to run through the streets
arresting policemen and seducing lovers,
startling the flowers and starting another war.
Go right ahead, you need the exercise."

> "Do I look older?" Jerusalem asks God,
> overturning the jewel-box
> and ignoring the shining tangle.
> "No," God answers softly,
> "I will not let you look old. Ever."

"And you're sure you don't mind?" Jerusalem smiles, already
    planning armies.
"I mind very much," God sighs, watching her stride off
into restless brains and elegant favors.
The opal she spoke of breaks in a thousand pieces.
"You fool!" the fighting alchemist challenges God,
"Don't you know what she'll do?"
God looks at his fury,
already the warrior's hand is caressing the hilt of his sword.
"About the same as you will," God observes.
"Tell me," the man is urgent,
"I know she was talking about me,
did she mention my name, did she remember?"
"Go right ahead," God uses the same tone, "she went that
    way.
I'm sure she's expecting you." The man runs off.

        "Jerusalem," God mourns alone,
        "my blessing twists like a knife in your heart,
        war shall not ease you nor famine comfort you,
        all your sins shall not conceal you
        nor shall your murders hide you from my blessing.
        I have said it."

Tears from the face of God refill Jerusalem's empty jewel-box
in harmony with the approaching sounds of death.

The Calling of Jerusalem

"Jerusalem," the Lord called softly
and his voice reached all over the world
till drunkards shook their muddled heads
and the smiles of businessmen wavered briefly,

and lovers were suddenly jealous for a moment,
though not of each other.
But there was no answer.
"Jerusalem," the Lord commanded with all the authority of
    grief,
"Where are you hiding and why?"

There was no spoken answer
but the air between his hands shrugged of its own accord
and invisible hair, most sacred and desolate, fell against his
    face.
The Lord carried Jerusalem as a woman carries an unborn
    child.
"What are you doing here?" he asked her.
"I'm tired," Jerusalem drowsed, but forced herself back into
    words.
"They look, they pray, they dance, they're exalted,
and then they worry if their parking meters have expired.
I don't mind the wars, I never did, blood has a beautiful color
and my lips are even more beautiful.
But they fight out of habit now, the way they live,
and it's all small and unworthy
and most wearisome.
I'm tired of them, they're not real, they can't see me
and they make me lonely.
I want to stay with you."

"No," said the Lord, "not yet."
"Soon?" pleaded Jerusalem.
"And you promised you'd never ask that,"
the Lord reminded her gently.
"It hurts," she answered simply,
"to be always open in a hive of souls
shut in elegant boxes, but firmly shut.
They don't know how to touch or even how
to want such knowledge.
They don't want me, only my scalp.
They want to win their arguments,
not understand what they're arguing about,

they couldn't care less.
What have I to do with them?"

"You are them," the Lord told her,
"when you were passionate and fickle, so were they.
When you were restless and bitter, so were they.
Now that you want more, they may too.
Go back where you belong and make their parking meters
    explode;
you've been called a thief many times, pry open those boxes.
Do you think it will happen of itself?"

Jerusalem cast down her eyes,
shuddered as if with cold and nodded.
"But why did you call me then?"
she asked as she re-inhabited her stones.
The Lord caressed the air between his hands,
where she had been.

         "I was lonely," the Lord admitted to nobody,
         "but it's over now."

John Wieners

Born in Milton, Massachusetts in 1934, Wieners studied at
Black Mountain College under Charles Olson and Robert
Duncan from 1955 to 1956, returned to Boston where he ed-
ited the influential *Measure*, lived in San Francisco from 1958
to 1960, an active participant in the San Francisco Poetry Ren-
aissance. . . . I'm paraphrasing the back-page biography in Wi-
eners's *Selected Poems, 1958–1984*, published by Black Spar-
row Press in 1986. I knew John during the time he spent in the
Bay Area—in fact my wife and I used to hire John regularly as
our baby-sitter. One night, returning from a North Beach
event, we found John at the kitchen table, lit by a lone candle,
the record player playing an E P of Billie Holiday, his lit ciga-
rette in the ashtray, deep into the edge of "Strange Fruit,"
oblivious to our loud entrance.

We would betray the demands of his work to withdraw from
it and, instead, command the obliterating clang of critical dis-
tance and blur of vocabulary. The poems, with all their craft
and craftiness, do not accommodate the dispassionate reader.
Whether as hermetically enfolded as *Behind the State Capitol
or Cincinnati Pike*, (1975) or as direct in emotional richness
and dexterity as *The Hotel Wentley Poems* (1958), Wieners's
work is at once profoundly naked, fastidiously literary, and
bound to the poem and the life put into it and illuminating it.

Wieners spoke openly of the marginalized homosexual real-
ity of America and was one of the few gay poets to address his
sexuality directly, without veiling it in metaphor, euphemism,
code. *The Hotel Wentley Poems*—an ensemble of poems ex-
ploring the loss of a lover, night-life, jazz, the San Francisco of

the "Beat" fifties—elevates excluded and "underground" experiences to a new (and renewed) poetic legitimacy. Wieners literally gave voice to a set of realities that had remained mute or muted up until that moment. His work entered the avant-garde literary "mainstream" due, in no small part, to the shifting sense of subject brought about both by the Black Mountain school of poetry, the visibility of beat writers like Allen Ginsberg and Jack Kerouac, and the generational tribal wars between the old and new. (In this case, the old was represented by the New Criticism and what was seen as its academic chokehold on the equally valid American visionary poetics it repressed or ignored.)

His work of lost love, self-torment, romance tragedies, drug-fueled night flights, the pathos of postwar gay bars, the shell-shock of mental hospital "treatment," the utopian promises of prewar movies, and the glamorous allure of stars and their counter-lives, all inform the lyrical disordering of promises shattered, husked in debris of atomic light and holocaust dark. "Yes. Lyricism is still a quality of a political career," he stated in an interview in the *Chicago Review* (1974).

Wieners's work retains its elegiac tone during the decade following *The Hotel Wentley Poems*, turning more complex and playful, mixing popular cultural mythologies with metamorphosing realities, while also devoting his practice to more formal poetry with a decidedly subversive intent. *Behind the State Capitol or Cincinatti Pike* (1975) is another landmark of his achievement, a boldly inventive work thickly woven both with serious play and playful seriousness. It creates simultaneous texts of history as scenarios in which movie star voices become oracles recording and recombining the myths of camp and kitsch in wise, disjunctive loss and defiance.

Two major collections of Wieners' work—*Selected Poems, 1958–1984* and *Cultural Affairs in Boston: Poetry and Prose, 1956–1985*—thoroughly and thoughtfully assembled by editor Raymond Foye for Black Sparrow Press, are currently in print. They bring together works from his previously published books and also make available much unpublished poetry and prose. They are essential texts of modern American homoerotic writing and signal contributions to the constant lyric tradition each moment redefines.

—David Meltzer

A poem for the old man

God love you
   Dana my lover
lost in the horde
on this Friday night,
500 men are moving up
& down from the bath
room to the bar.
Remove this desire
from the man I love.
Who has opened
   the savagery
of the sea to me.

See to it that
his wants are filled
on California street
Bestow on him lar-
gesse that allows him
peace in his loins.

Leave him not
to the moths.
Make him out a lion
so that all who see him
hero worship his
thick chest as I did
moving my mouth

over his back bringing
our hearts to heights
I never hike over
    anymore.
Let blond hair burn
on the back of his
neck, let no ache
screw his face
up in pain, his soul
    is so hooked.
Not heroin.
Rather fix these
hundred men as his
lovers & lift him
with the enormous bale
of their desire.

The Eagle Bar

A lamp lit in the corner
the Chinese girl talks to her lover
At bar, saxophone blares—

blue music, while boy in white turtleneck sweater
seduces the polka player from Poland
left over from Union party.

Janet sits beside me,
Barbra Streisand signs on Juke box
James tends bar

It's the same old scene
in Buffalo or Boston
yen goes on, continues in the glare

of night, searching for its lover
oh will we go
where will we search

between potato chips and boys,
for impeccable one—
that impossible lover

who does not come in,
with fresh air and sea
off Lake Erie

but stays home, hidden in the sheets
with his wife and child, alone
ah, the awful ache

as cash register rings
and James the bartender sweeps
bottles off the bar.

Terence Winch

THE author of a volume of poetry, *Irish Musicians American Friends* (1985) and several chapbooks of poetry, poet Terence Winch (1945–   ) is also a musician and songwriter. He plays in a traditional Irish band called Celtic Thunder and his song, "When New York was Irish," has become very popular among Irish-Americans. He is currently at work on two projects: a volume of poetry entitled *The Great Indoors* and an anthology of Irish-American writing, *Ireland Over Here* (coedited with James Liddy).

His poetry speaks of his musical life, of his Irish-American roots, and of a first generation Irish-American culture becoming more distant. His collaborator, the poet James Liddy, said of Winch's poetry: "The poems completely move me as being Irish, they get the depth; the unspeaking of our very private people. The language is just right each time the way they pretend they are not poems. They rescue the lost emigrant culture, making real Ireland and real myth out of Irish America. I am convinced it is a pioneer effort."

"The Irish Riviera" captures the very essence of what Liddy wishes us to discover and preserve:

> I wish I could remember the names
> of these two old guys I used to see
> when I was a kid and spent my summers
> in Rockaway which was known as The Irish Riviera
> one of them played the fiddle   the other played
> the accordian   and I think one of them wore
> a top hat   they just wandered in and out of bars
> playing for drinks they were like bums
> but I still remember how fine they sounded

From

IRISH MUSICIANS AMERICAN FRIENDS (1985)

The Psychiatrist's Office Was Filled with Crazy People

I was scared shitless
when I got my One A
from local board number
twenty nine on Arthur Avenue
I had to be at Whitehall Street
at seven o'clock on a cold September
morning   I arrived on time
but went to the wrong room
and waited there alone till seven thirty
when I finally figured this must be the wrong room
so I went upstairs and found the right room
just as some dumb sergeant was finishing
his speech to the recruits   I spotted Brian Keenan
P.J.'s nephew in the crowd   my brother had started
him on the drums and now he was the drummer for
The Chambers Brothers   but I made believe I didn't
see him   since I wanted to be anonymous
the sergeant called out my name and gave me my folder
containing letters I had sent the draft board
proving that I had asthma and numerous psychological
    problems
then I went to another room and took the mental exam
it consisted of page after page of what looked to me
like unfolded boxes that you were supposed to fold
back up again mentally   and of other objects that looked

like electric train transformers   this was beyond me
so I just filled up the little boxes on the answer sheet
and was the first one to hand in my exam
after the test the soldier boys in charge
called me to the front of the room and told me I scored
in the bottom fifth percentile and asked me if I had ever
gone to school   I told them I had an M.A. from Fordham
from there I was sent with my folder to the office
of the psychiatrist   they told me I was not
going to take the physical exam like the rest of the guys
which I was very happy about since I had dreaded
being herded around naked by the U.S. Army
the psychiatrist's office was filled with crazy people
there were No Smoking signs on the walls but every single
person there was smoking   there were about forty other
        people
in the waiting room with me   "Fuck the War" was written
on the wall   one guy started marching up and down the room
stomping his boot every minute or so with great regularity
and letting out a holler that scared everybody   his entire body
except for his face was painted psychedelically   it was
nineteen sixty eight   a puerto rican guy next to me
told me he was an ex con   an arsonist   and illiterate
and claimed they would never take him   a few minutes later
he showed me where he had written on some form that he
        had been
convicted of arson   I pointed out that this proved
he wasn't illiterate   on the questionnaire I put down
that I had homosexual tendencies
that I used drugs and had thoughts of suicide
when I finally got to see the old psychiatrist
who had a little goatee and white smock and foreign accent
he asked me how long I had felt this way about girls
and I told him "always" and he stamped all my papers with
WAIVE PHYSICAL AND MENTAL REQUIREMENTS
        and I was out
of there by ten thirty and on my way home
on the uptown subway
I met the guy whose body was painted

psychedelically   he had convinced me
he was crazy   but I started talking to him
on the train   it turned out he was a high school
teacher from Long Island whose wife painted him
that morning   as a final desperate
attempt to avoid the draft
it worked
we were both Four F
and very happy

A Speech Former Mayor Bob Wagner Made

Head McKenna had a big head
and was very intelligent
I think he eventually got his Ph.D.
Hootchie Keenan like all of the Keenans
also had a big head   Mr. Keenan his father
was a kind of neighborhood legend
he got married when he was forty two
and became the father of ten children
before that he had been a boxer
and had also served in World War One
he was a bus driver for about forty years
and is now in his eighties   he works
part time driving the tour bus at the Bronx Zoo
Mrs. Keenan was at least twenty years younger
than her husband   she was a fine woman
who had asthma like me   we used to discuss
the new remedies for asthma   she died
a few years ago
most of the Keenan boys first became
bus drivers and then switched to the cops
I saw Jimmy Keenan not too long ago

at a speech former mayor Bob Wagner
made on the corner of Fordham Road
and Valentine Avenue   he was in the crowd
listening to his honor speak
just like everyone else
but I knew he was an undercover cop
guarding Mr. Wagner's life

The Meanest Gang in the Bronx

once when I was in the fifth grade
I heard a rumor that the Fordham Baldies
were going to invade my school during the lunch hour
I was terrified   everybody knew the Baldies
were the meanest gang in the Bronx
who not only killed people but were known
to carve tic tac toe with their knives
on the bellies of their girl victims
since my father was custodian of the school
I tried to warn him about the attack
so that he could shut the school down
but he didn't pay me any mind
and the Fordham Baldies never showed up
once they did come into our neighborhood
looking for the Elsmere Tims   our local gang
but the brave Tims were no where to be found

Six Families of Puerto Ricans

I guess it was the summer of nineteen
fifty five   I just got back from Rockaway

the first thing I heard when I got back
was the news that
six families of Puerto Ricans had moved
into nineteen fifteen Daly Avenue   the Mitchells'
building   as time went on
more and more pee ars moved into
the neighborhood   there was great hostility
on both sides   once on the fourth of July
Martin Conlon threw some cherry bombs
and ash cans through the windows of the Puerto
Ricans   they were just spics to us
I remember a Puerto Rican shooting
at me and some friends with a bee bee gun
from his roof   you could hear the bee bees
bouncing off the cars   bodegas opened
on Tremont Avenue   Spanish kids dropped
water balloons on Irish kids   there was
a Sunday mass in Spanish in the church basement
this was worse than a potato famine
and the Irish started moving out
Mr. Zayas moved in next door to us
where the Gormans had lived   Mr. Zayas
had a son named Efrain who married
a beautiful girl named Carmen   Puerto Rican men
played dominoes on the sidewalk
when me and my father left the block
in the fall of nineteen sixty eight
we were among a handful of Irish still
in the neighborhood   things were so bad
by then that even the respectable Puerto Ricans
like Mr. Zayas were long gone
we used to think Puerto Ricans
weren't too far from being animals
even if they were Catholics

Elizabeth Woody

We sit upon or near stone. I sit here mainly on granite; you, possibly, on great boulders rising from the Pacific.

We are thousands of miles apart. A beautiful land separates, and yet, in a more traditional sense, it includes us, is our bridge from one ocean to another, and mothers us, cradles our flesh and spirit on its board. Our feet are planted firmly on this earth, which would appear as though it does separate. But it doesn't at all. The great Mississippi is no wall. This earth enfolds us, gathers us together as if a great body of water, water which enables us to survive. And there are the mountains and the mysterious plains and what the Anglo invader suspected of being the dark and fearful woodlands. I am of the woodlands. You are of the vast waters, the ocean banking against your western valleys. And there is the drum . . . the water drum of the Iroquois, the drum of your people, the Warm Spring people and the tributaries which run through your veins . . . Wasco, Navajo. And the pow wow drum—drums pound the day, beat the night in ancient rhythms. We hear them. We dance to the rhythm . . . one-two, one-two—round and moccasin, salmon and snake, rabbit and quiver, and the women's dances—the drum of blood, of heart, and of our songs. A prayer feather sits beside my hand on this desk; an eagle wheels above your head. Trickster Crow pushes my fingers to mingle thoughts here on this page; ol' Trickster paws at you to tell stories of vast wanderings across mountains and through those wide valleys. There are the fish of your waters, . . . salmon, and the fish of my waters here in the Adirondacks, . . . mountain trout, lake bass. You have your camas, and I, trillium . . . beautiful, simple flowers.

We have the Great Spirit whom we share, and who gave us

winds, stars, and clouds, the varying seasons, Turtle itself on which we and all people live. We have the Great Spirit and the message given us through our leaders: Deganawidah, Seattle, and the many others. We share the Great Spirit who gave us breath through our mothers, survival through our fathers, continuum through our young. We feel the quiver of the wise and generous mind, and we are thankful that we have received such marvels as gifts.

I sit here in the Adirondack Mountains watching the December snow fall upon a tall white pine and the peaked range before me, hopeful that black bear, red fox, raccoon and the other animals and birds are warm, safe from the oncoming storms and snows of winter. I hope that all people are safe. Slowly those great mountains of the range in my view disappear in a thick shield of snow. The lake below vanishes. A man in a bright red coat walks breathlessly up the hill. An auto off in the distance beams light and illuminates a stand of cedar and white birch. I cannot help but think of you at this moment while snow falls ever so quietly on this village in the Adirondacks, and wonder exactly where you are in Oregon—Portland?—and how many years since we last met, and when and where we first met.

It seems now we last met in the fall of 1988 at the time of the publication of your first poetry collection, *Hand into Stone.* You were standing in the college lecture hall at North Country Community College reading poems from the new book. I pull out the tape recorder and play the cassette of your reading. Your lyrics, strong, tight, powerful, fill the room.

Your voice on the tape takes me back a few years to a reading I gave in the auditorium at the Institute of American Indian Art in Santa Fe, New Mexico. You sat among fellow students studying creative writing. You seemed not to pay any particular attention, your imagination out there someplace in the New Mexican mountains or at home at Warm Spring. I spotted you in the front row and was determined to gain your attention.

A year or more later, I returned to IAIA and gave a talk and short reading in a writing class instructed by Philip Foss. You were in attendance. If I remember correctly there were other young students who have since then published poetry—Phyllis

Wolf, Joe Dale, Tate Nevaquaya, Philip Minthorm—an amazing group. This day you sat up front smiling, serious, seemingly engrossed. After the class you asked if you might send me poems . . . as did the other student poets. You mailed a sheaf.

Perhaps a year later I returned again to the Institute and brought with me a copy of *Contact/11*, the poetry journal in which appeared your first published poem. I came to Santa Fe this trip with Diane Burns, the young Annishnabe poet who then lived in New York City. At the time, Phil Foss was editing the Native American anthology, *The Clouds Threw This Light*. It contained two of your poems and also poems of your classmates, Wolf, Minthorn, and Navaquaya. Mr. Foss showed us an early galley. Diane and I were tremendously impressed with your stunning poems and those of the other three. Your poems were pithy, with startling images . . .

> A barren thief scratches at the door
> and dims the moon as it reaches for the candle
> of familiar mentality . . .

>> *(from "Originating Fire")*

and

> The pain of empty flower
>   stems . . .

> *(from Of Steps to Drowning)*

That was in 1983.

Slowly your work began to appear in journals and other important anthologies: *Atlatl, Spawning The Medicine River, Calyx, Wooster Review, Songs from This Earth on Turtles Back*. And finally in 1988, five years after your first published poems, your premier collection was on the book shelves of America. *Hand Into Stone* received recognition and positive critical reviews and was eventually honored with the American Book Award. In seven or eight years of diligent work, sweat and tears, determination, resilient application, and, obviously, a depth of creativity, a work is born, not without joy, but also not without the pain of industry, the wounds and scars of life itself, the gnawing horrors of the wrongs of history, the chipping away of a culture of both magnitude and high sophistication. Consumed with the excitement of creativity, evoking ghosts and the past, with song in your throat and heart, your lyric voice insculpted language emerged. The storyteller in you sat side by side with the poet. Rich, dynamic words and images created a core of ancient and modern, death and re-birth, in an undeniable voice, self-assured and certainly magical.

Simon J. Ortiz of Acoma, New Mexico, a major poetic voice himself, wrote that your collected poems are "direct, deep and many dimensional . . . a major achievement." This is high, deserving praise for a voice so young, thirty-one now, which has worlds to conquer yet, horizons to discover and reach. I have no doubt that you will. Your song will move across the land, your painful, lyrical words resculpting history, reshaping thought, chipping off the lies and revealing the beauty of the Native American world for those sensitive to beauty. As in traditional storytelling, they will learn and be entertained by the lustre and magic of language.

I will stay in these Adirondack Mountains and observe not just the mystery around me and the change of seasons from winter to summer, but will also watch your movement, departure, growth, and development as an important voice for the People and for all people. It will be a happy watch; it will be a ceremony. As the great holy man of the Lakota people, Black Elk, has said: "It was a beautiful dream" in which the People lived. And though it was broken or bent, you with your creative tools and powers will help rebuild, repair the colorful images of that dream with strong, good words. The road is there. . . .

—*Maurice Kenny*

From
HAND INTO STONE (1988)

In Memory of Crossing the Columbia

For Charlotte Edwards Pitt and Charlotte Agnes Pitt

My board and blanket were Navajo,
but my bed is inside the River.
In the beads of remembrance,
I am her body in my father's hands.
She gave me her eyes
and the warmth of basalt.
The vertebrae of her back,
my breastplate, the sturdy
belly of mountainside.

"Pahtu," he whispered in her language.
She is the mountain of change.
She is the mountain of women
who have lain as volcanos
before men.

Red, as the woman much loved,
she twisted like silvery chinook
beyond his reach.

Dancing the Woman-Salmon dance,
there is not much time to waste.

She-Who-Watches...The Names
Are Prayer*

For David Sohappy

My humanness is an embellished tongue,
the bell, a yellow mouth of September's
moon beats outward. She speaks for all
the names that clang in memorial.

There is Celilo,
dispossessed, the village of neglect
and bad structure.
The Falls are faint rocks enrippled
in the placid lake of black waters.
With a sad, stone grief and wisdom
I overlook the railroad.
The tight bands rail along
the whirls of the Columbia.
Drowning is a sensation
Fishermen and their wives know of.
Men who fished son after father.
There are drownings in The Dalles,
hanging in jails and off-reservation-suicide-towns.

A Strange Land awaits
the Fishermen,
as it had for the Nez Perce, the Navajo, Cheyenne women,
those who wailed in the Long Walks,
keened open the graves of their families.
The dead children.
My Children,

---

*"She-Who-Watches," is a petroglyph on the Columbia River. Originally a
Woman Chief, the last, before Coyote changed her into rock to watch over her
people and the Men Chiefs who followed her. Celilo Falls was the longest site of
habitation for Indian people, an estimated 10,000 years. In 1956 it was sold to
accommodate The Dalles Dam on the Columbia River.

with names handed down and unused.
Nee Mee Poo, Diné, Tsistsista's.
THE PEOPLE pure in emergence.
The Immense Mother is crying.
"Human Beings,"
the word tremors in the rib cage
of hills.

The consumption of loneliness binds us.
Children lie on the railroad tracks
to die from the wall of night and spirits.
I watch for the rushing head of chaos
and flat hands grope from the cattle cars,
clamor in the swift, fresh air.
A sky is clicking through the regular slats.
The tail whips the dusty battles of the Indian Wars,
unsettling itself, nude and raw.
Celilo Falls sank unwillingly in the new trading
and everyone dissolved from the fall.

Birds in This Woman

For Lillian Pitt, maskmaker

The Eavesdropper

In her yard they feed
at the cylinder of seed
under her awning.
The birds sift
through the groves of junipers
that grasp and shudder
juices from their deep root.

They gossip, especially the black
and white magpie.

They steal words from people.
Raspy tales, choked
out without much attention
as to what is true
and what is lie.

They are mostly black
accentuated with white.
She is careful of her
words near this quick-tongued
gossip robber.

Feathers

In the clayish dirt she finds a feather,
then another, pockets them
with the bundle of wings,
bluejay tail, fluffs
she had found or children bring to her.
It is a marvel
birds can fly with a few scales
grown particular.

Lost in wind she collects feathers.
Later at distance,
they will be planted.
She does not hoard gifts.
They are experiences.

Ravens

She asked two Ravens
for feathers.
They winged over apple trees
and left two feathers
in the grass.

It is peculiar,
they do not shine.
They are not true black
but all blacks
fired into one another.
They dangle from the wall.
She visits Ravens, maybe once
every week. Cawing they are big
for birds, when one must eat
many times its own weight
to fly.

She saw a lifeless Raven
impaled on a branch, empty
eyed, ruffled.
He is a bird nested in ill wind.
Perhaps victim of the wind's secrets
that night hides. It was violence,
horribly corrupted magic
that killed that bird,
winged into crucifixion.

Hair raised on the nape
of her neck, she hurried to the river
to soak her face and cool the anger
and impulse of her hair.

The Gentle Bird

As a young girl, she had a small, black bird.
Unable to fly, she carried it on her shoulders.
At Pi-Ume-Sha, she talked with a woman called BIRD.
BIRD said, "Be careful with this bird.
They are delicate and hungry."
BIRD is a singer, she listened to her songs.
She stood there all day, shaded
the bird from June sun
and watched the feathers swing on the dancers.

She does not remember where her bird went,
only that it seemed gentle.
It scratched the dry grass
in its box, impatient for her.

How The Hawk Lives

There is a Hawk that lives
at our old ranch house
in Tenino Valley.
She kees, has a rough nest
that grows each year in the poplars.
It was here that she found a gray kitten.
Fighting with the Screech Hawk
she rescued her.
Her side had Hawk marks.
She fit in the hand
and became a strong cat,
one eyed and lithe,
protecting the house from spiders, snakes
and mice. No birds.
She allows the magpies to eat her food.
Only the dog chases them.
She is a bird dog.

Gifts

To rid themselves of ache,
mental and ones of the body,
she bathed in the Hot Springs with her Mother.
They inhaled the sulphurous smell
deep to keep as a remembrance,
for when it would become necessary to be healed again.

Feathers appear everywhere.
When she walks, feathers
are before her step.

She collects them all.
Even when she stops by the window
they fall past in spirals,
no bird in sight.
She lets them fall, it is enough
to remind her of birds.

There was that time she rode
from Wapnitia to Simnasho
with her Mother and Grandmother,
a brown, staring Eagle flew beside them,
looking at each one carefully.
Grandmother smiled, "This is a Blessing."

Whisper of Wings

Yellowhawk told of trees,
how they speak from their roots,
she hears it. It is undeniable.
Listen.
In her yard, birds chatter,
bustle together, consumed
in the old effort of gathering.
In a flight of circles, they migrate.

As witness, she makes birds,
makes animals and people who wear these feathers.
They have rushes and fibers sing from their mouths.
She pulls the feathers
from her bundle and places them,
liking the feel of wind
resisting the curving spines.

Winter boughs and needles
incant, "Birds. There are so many birds,"
as they whisper over wings.

Cyn. Zarco

CYN. ZARCO (1950–) describes a poetry seminar she took as an M.F.A. student at Columbia from Howard Moss, who was then the poetry editor of *The New Yorker*. "He assigned us a sonnet, and I couldn't get the hang of it, it was so forced. I felt like I was wearing lead shoes. . . . I find my rhythms elsewhere, and being trilingual and understanding American dialect, like Black English and other regionalisms, pop music, contemporary writing, magazine writing, television writing . . . if you take the much travelled path of academia, you will need to study history and write dissertations and ibid. and op. cit. your precious poet's life away. Get the *Cliff Notes;* then try hang gliding."

Born in Manila and raised in Miami from the age of nine, Zarco studied journalism at the University of California at Berkeley and has an M.F.A. degree from Columbia University. Writer Ishmael Reed was the first to publish Zarco in his landmark *Yardbird Reader* and later in an anthology entitled *Jambalaya: An Anthology of Four Poets* (1975). Of her background as Filipina-American poet she says, "When I left Manila in 1959 and again in 1965, I left the gene pool. Miami had no visible Asian American community. . . . I related best to mavericks, renegades of all tribes. Culturally, I was closest to Latinos, Blacks, and Chinese, but I also grew up with Jews, Italians, whites. It's important to learn your Asian American history, about Chinese exclusion laws, how they lynched Filipino migrant workers in California, how the Japanese were interned during World War II. It's important to know which Michener movie is rolling in the white mind; do they see you as Hop Sing in "Bonanza"? And why [is] that kid making funny kung-fu moves at you?"

Her volume of poetry, *Circumnavigation* (1986), is "about my life in Manila, Miami, and New York. It's about my discovery of the world." Of the sexuality in her poetry Zarco says, "I think that writers today should definitely not avoid the issues of sexuality in their work, just because this reactionary Jesse Helms is worried about obscenity. Today's writer, especially writers of color and un-Western culture, have the advantage of taking a more objective view on American culture. Sexuality, after all, was the first taboo imposed by Christians on their captives. There is a great fear of sexuality at the root of racism. Personal freedom must be protected at all costs. Know your enemy. Write every day."

—Shawn Wong

From

CIRCUMNAVIGATION (1986)

In Memory of Forgetting

SHE closed her eyes when she made love, that was how she escaped the longing, the embrace when he was gone. To her it was the man lapping between her legs, the strong stroke of loving, the kiss. She closed her eyes and did not suck in his tongue. This she might remember—the sight of him slipping into her, the look on his face, his heart opening in the small shape of his mouth. She closed her eyes and started to forget, forgetting as soon as he touched her that he touched her there and that way. She did not want to remember how he felt inside her as she moved to his slow motion, to his time. She covered her eyes with a raised arm to stop the light that edged its way around his waist, the firm curve of his backside, the length of his thigh. She saw nothing. Even when she gave him her cry her eyelids stayed shut.

AIR

IT wasn't that he loved her. No, that wasn't it at all. He was fascinated by her—the way she walked into the room, her off-stage manner, the faint gold chain she wore around her ankle. He had never seen a woman like her. He just wanted to find out who she was, smiling under that broad-brimmed summer hat she wore with MEXICO embroidered in bold red letters across the top like she had been there in the Twenties when things were hot. She was hot. Her brown skin wet as she stepped out of an antique porcelain bathtub with only that far-off look like Aphrodite out of a conch shell but with black hair flowing.

No, it wasn't that he loved her. That much she knew. Not that she didn't pretend that sometimes she saw love there in his eyes, dark and oval like the seeds of the sweet brown chico fruit she used to eat as a child. Something stirred there, but it was only his heartbeat she heard after making love, the rapid fanfare of a snare drum announcing someone new approaching.

When he had been with her a week or so, long enough to tell if something was going to happen, she asked him if they were falling in love now, asked him in that soft cello voice of hers across the table in a Japanese restaurant between bites of pink sushi and thin sake as she twirled a paper parasol counterclockwise.

He wasn't the kind of man who fell in love or longed to tell of it, but one who loved them all, loved to watch the unraveling of it, loved them like kites on long string when there was wind.

And there wasn't even a breeze that night. And it was hot as the clock ran and she wondered what he was up to this time when she felt like loving him.

And it wasn't that she loved him. At least, not yet, because she was the goldfish in this love story and the goldfish bowl was on top of the television where the late afternoon light hit it crisp as a cymbal would shoot prisms if it were sound.

And the only sound in the room was the sound of hand-clapping, clapping against an echo she remembered once in a dream. Or was it a telephone ringing in Chinatown, a love letter on the pavement, or her mother's voice telling her that when love comes, run from it. Run fast. If he loves you, he'll run after you. If he doesn't, you're gone.

Cocktails

"An event in the present can influence and/or cause an event in the future."

—from "Three Diamonds," Gerard Malanga

HE was wearing a pink T-shirt, ballerina pink, with a bright green alligator gaping over his left tit. She was wearing a low-cut V-neck sweater, black like her hair and the space cut around them, black as the shiny baby grand sitting at the edge of the room.

It was cocktails at Gracie Mansion. He was staring into the crowd as if he had something to look at. She gazed into his leather bag. He slung it low and open. There were a few good cameras in there. She looked up at his face. His eyes sat in his skull. Some kind of Siamese-cat blue.

"It was San Francisco, over ten years ago," she said. "You had a bottle of wine in one hand and an Italian in the other." Had they both been naked he would have grazed her with his cock when the half-filled silver tray of hors d'oeuvres pushed him closer to her.

Appendix: Winners of the Before Columbus Foundation's American Book Awards, 1980-1990

1990

Paula Gunn Allen, editor and author, *Spider Woman's Granddaughters: Traditional Tales and Contemporary Writing by Native American Women* (Beacon Press, 1989).

Martin Bernal, *Black Athena, Afroasiatic Roots of Classical Civilization*, Vol. 1, *The Fabrication of Ancient Greece, 1785–1985* (Rutgers University Press, 1987).

Michelle T. Clinton, Sesshu Foster, and Naomi Quiñonez, editors and authors, *Invocation L.A.: Urban Multicultural Poetry* (West End Press, 1989).

Miles Davis with Quincy Troupe, *Miles: The Autobiography* (Simon & Schuster, 1989).

James M. Freeman, *Hearts of Sorrow: Vietnamese-American Lives* (Stanford University Press, 1989).

Daniela Gioseffi, editor/author, *Women on War (Essential Voices for the Nuclear Age)* (Touchstone Books, 1989).

José Emilio Gonzalez, *Vivar a Hostos* (Comité Pro Celebración Sesquicentenario del Natalico de Eugenio Maria de Hostos, 1989).

Barbara Grizzuti Harrison *Italian Days* (Weidenfeld & Nicolson, 1989).

Sergei Kan *Symbolic Immortality: The Tlingit Potlatch of the Nineteenth Century* (Smithsonian Institution Press, 1989).

Adrienne Kennedy, *People Who Led to My Plays* (Alfred A. Knopf, 1987).

Shirley Geok-lin Lim, Mayumi Tsutakawa, and Margarita Donnelly, editors, *The Forbidden Stitch: An Asian American Women's Anthology* (Calyx Books, 1989).

Hualing Nieh, *Mulberry and Peach: Two Women of China* (Beacon Press, 1988).

Itabari Njeri, *Every Goodbye Ain't Gone: Family Portraits and Personal Escapades* (Times Books, 1990).

John Norton, *The Light at the End of the Bog* (Black Star Series, 1989).

Lloyd A. Thompson, *Romans and Blacks* (University of Oklahoma Press, 1989).

John C. Walter, *The Harlem Fox: J. Raymond Jones and Tammany, 1920–1970* (SUNY Press, 1989).

Elizabeth Woody, *Hand into Stone* (Contact II Publications, 1988).

WALTER & LILLIAN LOWENFELS
CRITICISM AWARD
Arnold Rampersad, *The Life of Langston Hughes*, Vol. I, *1902–1941: I, Too, Sing America* and Vol. II, *1941–1967: I Dream a World* (Oxford University Press, 1986).

EDUCATOR AWARD
James O. Freedman

EDITOR/PUBLISHER AWARD
John Crawford

LIFETIME ACHIEVEMENT AWARD
Allen Ginsberg
Sonia Sanchez

1989

Isabel Allende, trans. Margaret Sayers Peden, *Eva Luna* (Alfred A. Knopf, 1988).

Frank Chin, *The Chinaman Pacific & Frisco R.R. Co.* (Coffee House Press, 1988).

J. California Cooper, *Homemade Love* (St. Martin's Press, 1986).

Emory Elliott, ed. *Columbia Literary History of the United States,* (Columbia University Press, 1987).

Charles Fanning, *The Exiles of Erin: Nineteenth-Century Irish*

American Fiction, (University of Notre Dame Press, 1987).

Eduardo Galeano, trans. Cedric Belfrage, *Memory of Fire* (trilogy) (Pantheon, 1988).

Henry L. Gates, Jr., *The Signifying Monkey: A Theory of Afro-American Literary Criticism* (Oxford University Press, 1988).

Josephine Gattuso Hendin *The Right Thing to Do* (David R. Godine, 1988).

William Hohri *Repairing America* (Washington State University Press, 1988).

Carolyn Chong Lau, *Wode Shuofa (My Way of Speaking),* (Tooth of Time Books, 1988).

Audre Lorde, *A Burst of Light* (Firebrand Books, 1988).

Leslie Scalapino, *Way* (North Point Press, 1988).

Jennifer Stone, *Stone's Throw,* (North Atlantic Books, 1988).

Shuntaro Tanikawa, trans. William I. Elliott and Kazuo Kawamura (a bilingual edition), *Floating the River in Melancholy* (Prescott Street Press, 1988).

Askia Muhammed Touré, *From the Pyramids to the Projects: Poems of Genocide and Resistance!* (Africa World Press, 1988).

Alma Luz Villanueva, *The Ultraviolet Sky,* (Bilingual Review/Press, 1988).

LIFETIME ACHIEVEMENT AWARD
Amiri Baraka
Ed Dorn

EDITOR/PUBLISHER AWARD
Nicolás Kannellos

1988

Jimmy Santiago Baca, *Martín &
Meditations on the South Valley*
(New Directions, 1987).

Daisy Bates, *The Long Shadow of
Little Rock* (University of Arkansas
Press, 1987)

Allison Blakely, *Russia and the
Negro: Blacks in Russian History
and Thought* (Howard University
Press, 1986).

David Halberstam, *The Reckoning*
(William Morrow, 1986).

Marlon Hom, *Songs of Gold
Mountain* (University of California
Press, 1987).

Salvatore La Puma, *The Boys of
Bensonhurst: Stories* (University of
Georgia Press, 1987).

Wing Tek Lum, *Expounding the
Doubtful Points* (Bamboo Ridge
Press, 1987).

Toni Morrison, *Beloved* (Alfred A.
Knopf, 1987).

Charles Olson, George Butterick,
ed., *The Collected Poems of Charles
Olson,* (University of California
Press, 1987).

Edward Sanders, *Thirsting for
Peace in a Raging Century: Selected
Poems 1961–1985.* (Coffee House
Press, 1987).

Kesho Scott, Cherry Muhanji, and
Egyirba High *Tight Spaces*
(Spinsters/Aunt Lute, 1987).

Ronald Sukenick, *Down and In*
(Beech Tree Books/William
Morrow, 1987).

Gerald Vizenor, *Griever: An
American Monkey King in China*
(Fiction Collective, 1987).

Opal Whiteley, presented by
Benjamin Hoff, *The Singing Creek
Where the Willows Grow* (Warner
Books, 1987).

WALTER & LILLIAN LOWENFELS
CRITICISM AWARD
Thomas Parkinson, *Poets, Poems,
Movements* (UMI Research Press,
1987).

EDUCATIONAL MATERIAL AWARD
**Steve Allen, Jayne Meadows,
David Zaslow, Kathleen Bullock,
Lawson Inada**, and **Patti McCoy**,
Shakin' Loose with Mother Goose
(Kids Matter, 1987).

LIFETIME ACHIEVEMENT AWARD
James Spady

1987

Ai, *Sin* (Houghton Mifflin, 1986).

Lucia Chiavola Birnbaum,
*Liberazione Della Donna: Feminism
in Italy* (Wesleyan University Press,
1986).

Dorothy Bryant, *Confessions of
Madame Psyche* (Ata Press, 1986).

Ana Castillo, *The Mixquiahuala
Letters* (Bilingual Review/Press,
1986).

**Septima Clark, Cynthia Stokes
Brown**, ed. *Ready From Within*
(Wild Trees Press)

Gary Giddins, *Celebrating Bird: The Triumph of Charlie Parker* (Beech Tree Books/Morrow, 1987).

Juan Felipe Herrera, *Facegames* (As Is/So & So Press, 1987).

Etheridge Knight, *The Essential Etheridge Knight* (University of Pittsburgh Press, 1986).

Michael Mayo, ed., *Practising Angels, A Contemporary Anthology of San Francisco Bay Area Poetry* (Seismograph Publications, 1986).

Daniel McGuire, *Portrait of a Little Boy in Darkness* (Teal Press, 1986).

Terry McMillan, *Mama* (Houghton Mifflin, 1987).

Harvey Pekar, *American Splendor* (Doubleday, 1986).

John Wieners, *Selected Poems, 1958–1984* (Black Sparrow Press, 1986).

James Welch, *Fools Crow* (Viking, 1986).

Cyn. Zarco, *Circumnavigation* (Tooth of Time Press, 1986).

LIFETIME ACHIEVEMENT AWARD
Charles Blockson
Dennis Clark

1986

Miguel Algarin, *Time's Now* (Arte Publico Press, 1985).

Helen Barolini, editor, *The Dream Book: An Anthology of Writing by Italian American Women* (Schocken Books, 1985).

Natasha Borovsky, *A Daughter of the Nobility* (Holt, Rinehart, & Winston, 1985).

Raymond Federman, *Smiles on Washington Square (A Love Story of Sorts)* (Thunder's Mouth Press, 1985).

Jeff Hannusch (a.k.a. Almost Slim), *I Hear You Knockin'* (Swallow Publications, 1985).

Linda Hogan, *Seeing through the Sun* (University of Massachusetts Press, 1985).

Susan Howe, *My Emily Dickinson* (North Atlantic Books, 1985).

Cherrie Moraga and Gloria Anzaldua, editors, *This Bridge Called My Back: Writings by Radical Women of Color* (Kitchen Table: Women of Color Press, 1981).

Toshio Mori, *Yokohama, California* (University of Washington Press, 1985).

Anna Lee Walters, *The Sun Is Not Merciful* (Firebrand Books, 1985).

Terrence Winch, *Irish Musicians American Friends* (Coffee House Press, 1985).

WALTER AND LILLIAN LOWENFELS
CRITICISM AWARD
Michael Feingold, *Close Your Eyes and Think of England*, (Village Voice)

LIFETIME ACHIEVEMENT AWARD
Hisaye Yamamoto

1985

Sandra Cisneros, *The House on Mango Street* (Arte Publico Press, 1984).

Robert Duncan, *Ground Work: Before the War* (New Directions, 1984).

Louise Erdrich, *Love Medicine* (Holt, Rinehart & Winston, 1984).

Peter Irons, *Justice at War* (Oxford University Press, 1983).

Angela Jackson, *Solo in the Box Car, Third Floor E* (OBA House, 1984).

Ron Jones, *Say Ray* (Bantam, 1984).

Colleen J. McElroy, *Queen of the Ebony Isles* (Wesleyan University Press, 1984).

Jiro Nakano and Kay Nakano, editors and translators, *Poets Behind Barbed Wire* (Bamboo Ridge Press, 1984).

William Oandasan, *Round Valley Songs* (West End Press, 1984).

Maureen Owen, *Amelia Earhart (AE)* (Vortex Editions, 1984).

Sonia Sanchez, *Homegirls & Handgrenades* (Thunder's Mouth Press, 1984).

May Sarton, *At Seventy: A Journal* (W. W. Norton, 1984).

Gary Soto, *Living Up the Street* (Strawberry Hill Press, 1985).

John Kuo Wei Tchen, *Genthe's Photographs of San Francisco's Old Chinatown* (Dover)

Julia Vinograd, *The Book of Jerusalem* (Bench Press, 1984).

LIFETIME ACHIEVEMENT AWARDS
John Oliver Killens
Joe Flaherty

1984

Amiri Baraka and Amina Baraka, editors, *Confirmation: An Anthology of African-American Women* (William Morrow, 1983).

Mei-mei Berssenbrugge, *The Heat Bird* (Burning Deck Press, 1983).

Cecil Brown, *Days Without Weather* (Farrar, Straus & Giroux, 1983)

Joseph Bruchac, editor, *Breaking Silence: An Anthology of Contemporary Asian American Poets* (Greenfield Review Press, 1983).

Jesus Colon, *A Puerto Rican in New York and Other Sketches* (International Publishers, 1982).

William Kennedy, *O Albany!* (Viking Press and Washington Park Press, 1983).

Maurice Kenny, *The Mama Poems* (White Pine Press, 1984).

Venkatesh Kulkarni, *Naked in Deccan* (Stemmer House, 1983).

Paule Marshall, *Praisesong for the Widow* (Putnam, 1983).

Ruthanne Lum McCunn, You-shan Tang, illus., and Ellen Lai-shan Yeung, trans. *Pie-Biter* (Design Enterprises of San Francisco, 1983).

Thomas McGrath, *Echoes inside the Labyrinth* (Thunder's Mouth Press, 1983).

Miné Okubo, *Citizen 13660* (University of Washington Press, 1983).

Howard Schwartz, *The Captive Soul of the Messiah: New Tales*

About Reb Nachman (Schocken Books, 1983).

Gary Snyder, *Axe Handles* (North Point Press, 1983).

LIFETIME ACHIEVEMENT AWARD
Josephine Miles

1983

Nash Candelaria, *Not by the Sword* (Bilingual Press, 1982).

Barbara Christian, *Black Women Novelists* (Greenwood Press, 1980).

Judy Grahn, *The Queen of Wands* (The Crossing Press, 1982).

Peter Guralnick, *Lost Highway* (David R. Godine, 1979).

Jessica Tarahata Hagedorn, *Pet Food and Tropical Apparitions* (Momo's Press, 1981).

James D. Houston, *Californians* (Alfred A. Knopf, 1982).

Joy Kogawa, *Obasan* (David R. Godine, 1981).

Cecilia Liang, *Chinese Folk Poetry* (Beyond Baroque, 1982).

Sean O'Tuama and **Thomas Kinsella**, *An Duanaire* (University of Pennsylvania Press, 1982).

Harriet Rohmer, *The Legend of Food Mountain* (Childrens Book Press, 1982).

John A. Williams, *!Click Song* (Houghton Mifflin, 1982).

Evangelina Vigil, *Thirty an' Seen a Lot* (Arte Publico Press, 1982).

LIFETIME ACHIEVEMENT AWARD
Kay Boyle

1982

Russell Banks, *The Book of Jamaica* (Houghton Mifflin, 1980).

Lorna Dee Cervantes, *Emplumada* (University of Pittsburgh, 1981).

Frank Chin, *The Chickencoop Chinaman* and *The Year of the Dragon* (University of Washington Press, 1981).

Tato Laviera, *Enclave* (Arte Publico Press/Revista Chicano Riqueño, 1981).

E. L. Mayo, *Collected Poems* (New Letters/Swallow Press, 1981).

Duane Niatum, *Songs for the Harvester of Dreams* (University of Washington Press, 1981).

Hilton Obenzinger, *This Passover or the Next I Will Never Be in Jerusalem* (Momo's Press, 1980).

Leroy Quintana, *Sangre* (Prima Agua Press, 1981).

Jerome Rothenberg, *Pre-Faces & Other Writings* (New Directions, 1981).

Ronald Tanaka, *Shinto Suite* (Greenfield Review Press, 1981).

Joyce Carol Thomas, *Marked by Fire* (Avon, 1982).

Al Young, *Bodies & Soul* (Creative Arts Books, 1981).

Him Mark Lai, Genny Lim, and **Judy Yung**, editors, *Island: Poetry and History of Chinese Immigrants* *on Angel Island 1910–1949* (HOC DOI Project, 1980).

LIFETIME ACHIEVEMENT AWARD
Chester B. Himes

1981

Helen Adams, *Turn Again to Me & Other Poems,* (Kulchur Foundation, 1980).

Miguel Algarin, *On Call* (Arte Publico Press/Revista Chicano Riqueña, 1980).

alta, *The Shameless Hussy* (The Crossing Press, 1980).

Toni Cade Bambara, *The Salt Eaters* (Random House, 1980).

Peter Blue Cloud, *Back Then Tomorrow* (Blackberry Press, 1980).

Rose Drachler, *The Choice* (Tree Books, 1977).

Susan Howe, *The Liberties* (Loon Books, 1980).

Robert Kelly, *In Time* (Frontier Press, 1971).

Alan Chong Lau, *Songs for Jadina* (The Greenfield Review Press, 1980).

Lionel Mitchell, *Traveling Light* (Seaview Press, 1980).

Nicholasa Mohr, *Felita* (Dial Press, 1979).

Bienvenido N. Santos, *Scent of Apples: A Collection of Stories* (University of Washington Press, 1979).

LIFETIME ACHIEVEMENT AWARD:
Frank Stanford
Larry Neal

1980

Rudolfo Anaya, *Tortuga* (Editorial Justa Publications, 1979).

Mei-mei Berssenbrugge, *Random Possession* (I. Reed Books, 1979).

Jayne Cortez, *Mouth on Paper* (Bola Press, 1977).

Edward Dorn, *Hello, La Jolla* (Wingbow Press, 1979).

Milton Murayama, *All I Asking for Is My Body* (Supra Press, 1975).

Leslie Marmon Silko, *Ceremony* (Viking, 1977).

Quincy Troupe, *Snake-Back Solos: Selected Poems, 1969–1977* (I. Reed Books, 1979).

Douglas Woolf, *Future Preconditional* (Black Sparrow, 1979).

Permissions